BEST-EVER

500 SIMPLY DELICIOUS RECIPES

BEST-EVER

500 SIMPLY DELICIOUS RECIPES

bay books

CONTENTS

SOUPS

INGREDIENTS

80 g ($^1/_2$ cup) macaroni
1 tablespoon olive oil
1 leek, sliced
2 garlic cloves, crushed
1 carrot, sliced
1 waxy potato, chopped
1 zucchini (courgette), sliced
2 celery stalks, sliced
100 g ($3^1/_2$ oz) green beans, cut into short lengths
425 g (15 oz) tin chopped tomatoes
2 litres (8 cups) vegetable or beef stock
2 tablespoons tomato paste (purée)
425 g (15 oz) tin cannellini beans, rinsed and drained
2 tablespoons chopped flat-leaf (Italian) parsley
shaved Parmesan cheese, to serve

1 Bring a saucepan of water to the boil, add the macaroni and cook for 10–12 minutes, or until tender. Drain.

2 Meanwhile, heat the oil in a large heavy-based saucepan, add the leek and garlic and cook over medium heat for 3–4 minutes.

3 Add the carrot, potato, zucchini, celery, green beans, tomato, stock and tomato paste. Bring to the boil, then reduce the heat and simmer for 10 minutes, or until the vegetables are tender.

4 Stir in the cooked pasta and cannellini beans and heat through. Spoon into warmed serving bowls and garnish with parsley and shaved Parmesan.

SERVES 4

PRAWN GUMBO

2 tablespoons olive oil

1 large onion, finely chopped

3 garlic cloves, crushed

1 red capsicum (pepper), chopped

4 rashers bacon, chopped

1$\frac{1}{2}$ teaspoons dried thyme

2 teaspoons dried oregano

1 teaspoon paprika

$\frac{1}{2}$ teaspoon cayenne pepper

60 ml ($\frac{1}{4}$ cup) sherry

1 litre (4 cups) fish stock

100 g ($\frac{1}{2}$ cup) long-grain rice

2 bay leaves

400 g (14 oz) can chopped tomatoes

150 g (5$\frac{1}{2}$ oz) okra, thinly sliced

850 g (1 lb 14 oz) medium raw prawns (shrimp), peeled and deveined

3 tablespoons finely chopped flat-leaf (Italian) parsley

1 Heat the oil in a large saucepan over low heat. Cook the onion, garlic, capsicum and bacon for 5 minutes, or until soft. Stir in the herbs and spices. Season. Add the sherry and cook until evaporated, then add the stock and 500 ml (2 cups) water. Bring to the boil. Add the rice and bay leaves, reduce the heat and simmer, covered, for 20 minutes.

2 Add the tomato and okra. Simmer, covered, for 20–25 minutes. Stir in the prawns and parsley and simmer for 5 minutes, or until the prawns are cooked through.

SERVES 4

INGREDIENTS

2 tablespoons olive oil
1 large red onion, finely chopped
2 garlic cloves, crushed
2 tablespoons tomato paste (purée)
2 tomatoes, finely chopped
2 teaspoons paprika
1 teaspoon cayenne pepper
500 g (2 cups) red lentils
50 g ($^1/_4$ cup) long-grain rice
2.125 litres ($8^1/_2$ cups) chicken stock
45 g ($^1/_4$ cup) fine burghul (bulgar wheat)
2 tablespoons chopped mint
2 tablespoons chopped flat-leaf (Italian) parsley
90 g ($^1/_3$ cup) thick natural yoghurt
$^1/_4$ preserved lemon, pulp removed, zest washed and julienned

1 Heat the oil in a saucepan over medium heat. Add the onion and garlic and cook for 2–3 minutes, or until soft. Stir in the tomato paste, tomato and spices and cook for 1 minute.

2 Add the lentils, rice and chicken stock, then cover and bring to the boil over high heat. Reduce the heat and simmer for 30–35 minutes, or until the rice is cooked.

3 Stir in the burghul and herbs, then season to taste. Divide the soup among serving bowls, garnish with yoghurt and preserved lemon and serve immediately.

NOTE This soup will thicken on standing, so if reheating you may need to add more liquid.

RED LENTIL, BURGHUL AND MINT SOUP

SERVES 6-8

INGREDIENTS

8 raw prawns (shrimp)
1 carrot, chopped
1 onion, chopped
1 celery stick, chopped
3 spring onions, thinly sliced
6 cm (2$\frac{1}{2}$ inch) piece fresh ginger, thinly shredded
1 tablespoon mirin
1 teaspoon kecap manis
1 tablespoon soy sauce
4 large scallops
100 g (3$\frac{1}{2}$ oz) boneless white fish fillet
1 egg white
200 g (6$\frac{1}{2}$ oz) round gow gee wrappers
$\frac{1}{3}$ cup (10 g/$\frac{1}{4}$ oz) fresh coriander (cilantro) leaves

1 To make the soup, peel the prawns, reserve 4 for the ravioli filling and chop the rest into small pieces and reserve. Put the prawn heads and shells in a large pan, cook over high heat until starting to brown, then cover with 1 litre water. Add the carrot, onion and celery, bring to the boil, reduce the heat and simmer for 10 minutes. Strain and discard the prawn heads, shells and vegetables. Return the stock to a clean pan and add the spring onion, ginger, mirin, kecap manis and soy sauce. Set aside.

2 To make the ravioli, chop the whole reserved prawns with the scallops and fish in a food processor until smooth. Add enough egg white to bind. Lay half the gow gee wrappers on a work surface and place a rounded teaspoon of filling in the centre of each. Brush the edges with water. Top each with another wrapper and press the edges to seal, eliminating air bubbles as you go. Trim with a fluted cutter. Cover with plastic wrap.

3 Bring a large pan of water to the boil. Meanwhile, heat the stock and leave simmering. Just prior to serving, drop a few ravioli at a time into the boiling water. Cook for 2 minutes, remove with a slotted spoon and divide among heated bowls. Cook the chopped reserved prawns in the same water for 2 minutes; drain. Pour the hot stock over the ravioli and serve, sprinkled with the chopped cooked prawns and coriander leaves.

SERVES 4

INGREDIENTS

2 tablespoons butter
100 g (about 4) French shallots, roughly chopped
3 garlic cloves, crushed
30 g (1 cup) firmly packed flat-leaf (Italian) parsley
315 ml (1^1/$_4$ cups) vegetable or chicken stock
315 ml (1^1/$_4$ cups) milk
600 g (1 lb 5 oz) button mushrooms
^{1}/$_4$ teaspoon ground nutmeg
^{1}/$_4$ teaspoon cayenne pepper
150 g (5^1/$_2$ oz) light sour cream
cayenne pepper, to garnish

1 Melt the butter in a large heavy-based saucepan and add the shallots, garlic and parsley. Cook over medium heat for 2–3 minutes. Put the stock and milk in a separate saucepan and bring to the boil.

2 Gently wipe the mushrooms, then chop and add to the shallot mixture. Season with salt and pepper, and stir in the nutmeg and cayenne pepper. Cook, stirring, for 1 minute. Add the stock and milk, bring to the boil, then reduce the heat and simmer for 5 minutes. Transfer the soup to a blender or food processor and blend until smooth. Return to the pan.

3 Stir in the sour cream, adjust the seasoning and reheat gently. Serve sprinkled with cayenne pepper.

FRESH MUSHROOM, SHALLOT AND SOUR CREAM SOUP

SERVES 4

INGREDIENTS

2 corn cobs (700 g/1 lb 9 oz)

1 tablespoon olive oil

1 red onion, finely chopped

1 small red chilli, finely chopped

$^1/_2$ teaspoon ground allspice

4 vine-ripened tomatoes, peeled and finely diced

1.5 litres (6 cups) fish stock or light chicken stock

300 g (10$^1/_2$ oz) boneless firm white fish fillets (ling or perch), diced

200 g (7 oz) fresh crab meat

200 g (7 oz) peeled raw prawns (shrimp), roughly chopped

1 tablespoon lime juice

Quesadillas

4 flour tortillas (19 cm/7$^1/_2$ in)

85 g ($^2/_3$ cup) grated Cheddar cheese

4 tablespoons coriander (cilantro) leaves

2 tablespoons olive oil

1 Preheat the oven to 200°C (400°F/Gas 6). Peel back the husks on the corn cobs (making sure they stay intact at the base) and remove the silks. Fold the husks back over the corn, place in a baking dish and bake for 1 hour, or until the corn is tender.

2 Heat the oil in a large saucepan over medium heat. Add the onion and cook until soft. Add the chilli and allspice and cook for 1 minute, then add the tomato and stock and bring to the boil. Reduce the heat and simmer, covered, for 45 minutes.

3 Slice off the kernels from the corn cobs with a sharp knife, add to the soup and simmer, uncovered, for 15 minutes. Add the fish, crab and prawn meat to the soup and simmer for 5 minutes, or until the seafood is cooked. Stir in the lime juice and serve with the quesadillas, if desired.

4 To make the quesadillas, top one tortilla with half the cheese and half the coriander. Season, then top with another tortilla. Heat 1 tablespoon of the oil in a frying pan and cook the quesadilla for 30 seconds on each side, or until the cheese just begins to melt. Repeat to make the other quesadilla. Cut into wedges.

SERVES 4

500 g (1 lb) raw prawns (shrimp)
1 tablespoon oil
2 tablespoons tom yam curry paste
2 tablespoons tamarind purée
2 teaspoons ground turmeric
1 teaspoon chopped small red chillies
4 kaffir lime (makrut) leaves, shredded
2 tablespoons fish sauce
2 tablespoons lime juice
2 teaspoons grated palm sugar or soft brown sugar
kaffir lime (makrut) leaves, shredded, extra, to garnish

TOM YAM GOONG

1 Peel the prawns, leaving the tails intact. Devein the prawns, starting at the head end. Reserve the shells and heads. Cover and refrigerate the prawn meat. Heat the oil in a wok or large saucepan and cook the shells and heads over medium heat, stirring frequently, for 10 minutes, or until the shells turn orange.

2 Add 1 cup (250 ml/8 fl oz) water and the tom yam paste to the pan. Bring to the boil and cook for 5 minutes, or until reduced slightly. Add another 2 litres water, bring to the boil, reduce the heat and simmer for 20 minutes. Strain, discarding the shells and heads, and return the stock to the pan.

3 Add the tamarind, turmeric, chilli and lime leaves to the pan, bring to the boil and cook for 2 minutes. Add the prawns and cook for 5 minutes, or until pink. Stir in the fish sauce, lime juice and sugar. Garnish with shredded kaffir lime leaves.

ASIAN NOODLE SOUP

8 dried Chinese mushrooms
100 g (3^1/$_2$ oz) dried rice vermicelli
800 g (1 lb 12 oz) Chinese broccoli, cut into 5 cm (2 inch) lengths
8 fried tofu puffs, cut into strips
125 g (4^1/$_2$ oz) bean sprouts
1 litre (4 cups) vegetable stock
2 tablespoons light soy sauce
1^1/$_2$ tablespoons Chinese rice wine
3 spring onions (scallions), finely chopped
coriander (cilantro) leaves, to serve

1 Place the dried mushrooms in a bowl, cover with boiling water and soak for 15 minutes. Drain, reserving 125 ml (^{1}/$_2$ cup) of the liquid. Squeeze the mushrooms to remove any excess liquid. Discard the stems and thinly slice the caps.

2 Soak the vermicelli in boiling water for 5 minutes. Drain. Divide the vermicelli, broccoli, tofu puffs and bean sprouts among the four serving bowls.

3 Place the reserved mushroom liquid, stock, soy sauce, rice wine, spring onion and mushrooms in a saucepan and bring to the boil. Cook, covered, for 10 minutes.

4 Ladle the soup into the serving bowls and garnish with the coriander leaves.

SERVES 4

175 g (6 oz) dried thin egg noodles
2 tablespoons peanut oil
2 chicken breasts (about 250 g/9 oz each)
1 onion, sliced
1 small fresh red chilli, seeded and finely chopped
1 tablespoon finely chopped fresh ginger
2 tablespoons Indian curry powder
3 cups (750 ml/25 fl oz) chicken stock
800 ml (27 fl oz) coconut milk
300 g (10$^{1}/_{2}$ oz) baby bok choy, cut into long strips
$^{1}/_{3}$ cup (20 g/$^{3}/_{4}$ oz) fresh basil, torn

1   Cook the noodles in a large saucepan of boiling water for 3–4 minutes, or until cooked. Drain well and set aside. Wipe the saucepan clean and dry.

2   Heat the oil in the dry pan and add the chicken. Cook on each side for 5 minutes, or until cooked through. Remove the chicken and keep warm.

3   Place the onion in the pan and cook over low heat for 8 minutes, or until softened but not browned. Add the chilli, ginger and curry powder and cook for a further 2 minutes. Add the chicken stock and bring to the boil. Reduce the heat and simmer for 20 minutes. Thinly slice the chicken on the diagonal.

4   Add the coconut milk to the saucepan and simmer for 10 minutes. Add the bok choy and cook for 3 minutes, then stir in the basil.

5   To serve, divide the noodles among four deep serving bowls. Top with slices of chicken and ladle in the soup. Serve immediately.

CURRIED CHICKEN NOODLE SOUP

SERVES 4

INGREDIENTS

100 g (¹/₂ cup) dried haricot beans
125 g (4¹/₂ oz) bacon, cubed
40 g (1¹/₂ oz) butter
1 carrot, sliced
1 onion, chopped
1 leek, white part only, roughly chopped
1 turnip, peeled and chopped
bouquet garni
1.25 litres (5 cups) chicken stock
400 g (14 oz) white cabbage, finely shredded

1   Soak the beans overnight in cold water. Drain, put in a saucepan and cover with cold
water. Bring to the boil and simmer for 5 minutes, then drain. Put the bacon in the same
saucepan, cover with water and simmer for 5 minutes. Drain and pat dry with paper towels.

2   Melt the butter in a large heavy-based saucepan, add the bacon and cook for 5 minutes,
without browning. Add the beans, carrot, onion, leek and turnip and cook for 5 minutes.
Add the bouquet garni and chicken stock and bring to the boil. Cover and simmer for
30 minutes. Add the cabbage, uncover and simmer for 30 minutes, or until the beans are
tender. Remove the bouquet garni before serving and season to taste.

SERVES 4

CAPSICUM, SPINACH AND CHICKPEA SOUP

1 tablespoon olive oil
8 spring onions (scallions), finely sliced
1 red capsicum (pepper)
1 garlic clove, crushed
1 teaspoon cumin seeds
375 ml (1^1/$_2$ cups) Italian tomato passata
750 ml (3 cups) vegetable or beef stock
300 g (10^1/$_2$ oz) tin chickpeas, rinsed and drained
2 teaspoons red wine vinegar
1–2 teaspoons sugar
100 g (3^1/$_2$ oz) baby English spinach leaves

1 Heat the oil in a large heavy-based saucepan and stir in the spring onion. Reduce the heat and cook, covered, for 2–3 minutes, or until softened. Meanwhile, remove the seeds and membrane from the capsicum and finely dice. Add the capsicum, garlic and cumin seeds to the pan and cook for 1 minute.

2 Add the passata and stock and bring the mixture to the boil. Reduce the heat and simmer for 10 minutes. Add the chickpeas, vinegar and sugar to the soup and simmer for a further 5 minutes.

3 Stir in the baby spinach and season to taste with salt and ground black pepper. Cook until the spinach begins to wilt, then serve immediately.

SERVES 4

INGREDIENTS

750 ml (3 cups) vegetable stock
1 tablespoon oil
1 onion, chopped
1 tablespoon grated fresh ginger
1 kg (2 lb 4 oz) carrots, chopped
2 tablespoons chopped coriander (cilantro) leaves

1   Place the stock in a pan and bring to the boil. Heat the oil in a large heavy-based pan, add the onion and ginger and cook for 2 minutes, or until the onion has softened.

2   Add the stock and carrots. Bring to the boil, then reduce the heat and simmer for 10–15 minutes, or until the carrot is cooked and tender.

3   Place in a blender or food processor and process in batches until smooth. Return to the pan and add a little more stock or water to thin the soup to your preferred consistency.

4   Stir in the coriander and season to taste. Heat gently before serving.

CARROT AND GINGER SOUP

SERVES 4

GAZPACHO

750 g (1¹/₂ lb) ripe tomatoes

1 Lebanese cucumber, chopped

1 green capsicum (pepper), chopped

2-3 cloves garlic, crushed

1-2 tablespoons finely chopped black olives (optional)

¹/₃ cup (80 ml/2³/₄ fl oz) red or white wine vinegar

¹/₄ cup (60 ml/2 fl oz) olive oil

1 tablespoon tomato paste (purée)

Accompaniments

1 onion, finely chopped

1 red capsicum (pepper), finely chopped

2 spring onions, finely chopped

1 Lebanese cucumber, finely chopped

2 hard-boiled eggs, chopped

chopped mint or parsley

Garlic and herb croutons

1 Score a cross in the base of each tomato. Cover with boiling water for 1 minute, plunge into cold water, drain and peel away the skins. Chop the flesh so finely that it is almost a purée.

2 Mix together the tomato, cucumber, capsicum, garlic, olives, vinegar, oil, and tomato paste, and season to taste. Cover and refrigerate for 2-3 hours.

3 Use 2-3 cups (750 ml/24 fl oz) of chilled water to thin the soup to your taste. Serve chilled, with the chopped onion, capsicum, spring onion, cucumber, boiled egg, herbs and croutons served separately for diners to add to their own bowls.

INGREDIENTS

30 g (1 oz) butter
2 large fennel bulbs, thinly sliced
2 leeks, thinly sliced
1 litre (4 cups) hot vegetable or chicken stock
2 rosemary sprigs
$1/_8$ teaspoon ground nutmeg
80 g ($1/_3$ cup) sour cream
25 g ($1/_4$ cup) finely grated Parmesan cheese
1 tablespoon oil
1 leek, extra, cut in half lengthways, and cut into 4 cm ($1^1/_2$ inch) lengths
grated Parmesan cheese, extra, to garnish
sour cream, extra, to garnish

1   Heat the butter in a large heavy-based saucepan, add the sliced fennel and leek, and
cook, covered, over medium heat for 2–3 minutes, stirring occasionally.

2   Put the hot stock, rosemary sprigs and nutmeg in a saucepan and bring to the boil.
Simmer over low heat for about 15 minutes, then remove the rosemary sprigs and add the
fennel and leek mixture to the pan.

3   Transfer the soup to a blender or food processor and blend in batches until smooth. Return
to the pan, and stir in the sour cream and Parmesan. Reheat over medium heat until hot.
Season to taste with salt and cracked black pepper and keep warm.

4   Heat the oil in a frying pan and cook the extra leek for 2–3 minutes, or until soft but
not browned.

5   Spoon the soup into six warm soup bowls and top with the fried leek. Garnish with the
extra Parmesan and sour cream and serve immediately.

SERVES 6

CREAM OF TOMATO SOUP

1.25 kg (2¹/₂ lb) tomatoes
1 tablespoon oil
1 onion, chopped
1 clove garlic, chopped
1¹/₂ cups (375 ml/12 fl oz) chicken stock
2 tablespoons tomato paste (purée)
1 teaspoon sugar
1 cup (250 ml/8 fl oz) cream

1 Cut a cross in the base of each tomato. Cover with boiling water for 1 minute, plunge in iced water, drain and peel away the skins. Scoop out the seeds and discard, then roughly chop the flesh.

2 Heat the oil in a large pan and cook the onion for 3 minutes, or until soft. Add the garlic and cook for 1 minute longer. Add the tomato and cook for 5 minutes, stirring occasionally, until very soft. Stir in the stock, bring to the boil, reduce the heat and simmer for 10 minutes.

3 Cool slightly, then transfer to a food processor. Process in batches until smooth, and return to the pan. Add the tomato paste and sugar and bring to the boil, stirring continuously. Reduce the heat and stir in the cream but do not allow the soup to boil. Season to taste before serving. Serve with an extra spoonful of cream and chopped parsley, if you want.

SERVES 4

INGREDIENTS

1 tablespoon oil
1 onion, chopped
2 garlic cloves, finely chopped
1–2 small red chillies, finely chopped
$1/4$ teaspoon paprika
750 g (1 lb 10 oz) orange sweet potato (kumera), chopped into small pieces
1 litre (4 cups) vegetable or beef stock
chopped dried chilli, to garnish

1 Heat the oil in a large heavy-based saucepan, add the onion and cook for 1–2 minutes, or until soft. Add the garlic, chilli and paprika and cook for a further 2 minutes, or until aromatic. Add the sweet potato to the pan and toss to coat with the spices.

2 Pour in the stock, bring to the boil, then reduce the heat and simmer for 15 minutes, or until the vegetables are tender. Cool slightly, then transfer to a blender or food processor and blend in batches until smooth, adding extra water if needed to reach the desired consistency. Do not overblend or the mixture may become gluey.

3 Season to taste with salt and black pepper. Ladle the soup into bowls, sprinkle with dried chilli and serve.

SWEET POTATO AND CHILLI SOUP

SERVES 4

INGREDIENTS

25 g (1 oz) butter
1 small white onion, finely chopped
750 g (1 lb 10 oz) orange sweet potato, peeled and cut into 2 cm ($^3/_4$ inch) dice
2 firm pears (500 g/1 lb 2 oz), peeled, cored and cut into 2 cm ($^3/_4$ inch) dice
750 ml (3 cups) vegetable or chicken stock
250 ml (1 cup) cream
mint leaves, to garnish

1   Melt the butter in a saucepan over medium heat, add the onion and cook for 2–3 minutes, or until softened but not brown. Add the sweet potato and pear, and cook, stirring, for 1–2 minutes. Add the stock to the pan, bring to the boil and cook for 20 minutes, or until the sweet potato and pear are soft.

2   Cool slightly, then place the mixture in a blender or food processor and blend in batches until smooth. Return to the pan, stir in the cream and gently reheat without boiling. Season with salt and ground black pepper. Garnish with the mint.

SERVES 4

INGREDIENTS

750 g (1 lb 10 oz) vine-ripened tomatoes
1 loaf (450 g/1 lb) day-old crusty Italian bread
1 tablespoon olive oil
3 garlic cloves, crushed
1 tablespoon tomato paste (purée)
1.25 litres (5 cups) hot vegetable stock
4 tablespoons torn basil leaves
2–3 tablespoons extra virgin olive oil, plus extra, to serve

1 Score a cross in the base of each tomato. Place in a bowl of boiling water for 1 minute, then plunge into cold water and peel the skin away from the cross. Cut the tomatoes in half and scoop out the seeds with a teaspoon. Chop the tomato flesh.

2 Remove most of the crust from the bread and discard. Cut the bread into 3 cm (1¼ in) pieces.

3 Heat the oil in a large saucepan. Add the garlic, tomato and tomato paste, then reduce the heat and simmer, stirring occasionally, for 15 minutes until thickened. Add the stock and bring to the boil, stirring for 2 minutes. Reduce the heat to medium, add the bread pieces and cook, stirring, for 5 minutes, or until the bread softens and absorbs most of the liquid. Add more stock or water if necessary.

4 Stir in the torn basil leaves and extra virgin olive oil, and leave for 5 minutes so the flavours have time to develop. Drizzle with a little of the extra oil.

NOTE This soup is popular in Italy in the summer months when tomatoes are at their tastiest, and as a way of using up leftover bread. In Italy, the soup is called Pappa al pomodoro.

SERVES 4

TOMATO AND CAPSICUM SOUP WITH POLENTA AND OLIVE STICKS

INGREDIENTS

2 tablespoons vegetable oil
2 tablespoons olive oil
2 red onions, finely chopped
2 garlic cloves, crushed
1 tablespoon ground cumin
$\frac{1}{4}$ teaspoon ground cayenne pepper
2 teaspoons paprika
2 red capsicums (peppers), diced
90 g ($\frac{1}{3}$ cup) tomato paste (purée)
250 ml (1 cup) dry white wine
2 x 400 g (14 oz) cans chopped tomatoes
2 long red chillies, seeded and chopped
500 ml (2 cups) chicken or vegetable stock
3 tablespoons chopped flat-leaf (Italian) parsley
4 tablespoons chopped coriander (cilantro) leaves

Polenta and olive sticks
500 ml (2 cups) chicken or vegetable stock
185 g ($1\frac{1}{4}$ cups) coarse polenta (cornmeal)
100 g ($3\frac{1}{2}$ oz) pitted Kalamata olives, chopped
125 ml ($\frac{1}{2}$ cup) olive oil, to deep-fry

1 Heat the oils in a large saucepan over medium heat and cook the onion and garlic for 2–3 minutes, or until soft.

2 Reduce the heat to low, add the spices and cook for 1–2 minutes. Add the capsicum and cook for 5 minutes. Stir in the tomato paste and wine, simmer for 2 minutes, or until reduced slightly. Add the tomato, chilli, stock and 500 ml (2 cups) water. Season. Simmer for 20 minutes. Purée the soup with the herbs.

3 To make the polenta and olive sticks, grease a 20 cm x 30 cm (8 inch x 12 inch) baking tray. Bring the stock and 500 ml (2 cups) water to the boil in a saucepan. Slowly add the polenta in a fine stream, whisking until smooth. Reduce the heat to low. Cook, stirring constantly, for 15–20 minutes, or until it starts to come away from the side. Stir in the olives, then spoon into the tray, smoothing the surface. Cover and chill for 30 minutes, or until firm. Cut into sticks.

4 Heat the oil in a large deep frying pan to 190°C (375°F), or until a cube of bread browns in 10 seconds. Cook the sticks in batches on each side for 1–2 minutes, or until crisp. Drain well, and serve with the soup.

SERVES 4-6

INGREDIENTS

2 tablespoons olive oil
1 small leek, white part only, chopped
2 garlic cloves, crushed
2 teaspoons curry powder
1 teaspoon ground cumin
1 teaspoon garam masala
1 litre (4 cups) vegetable stock
1 bay leaf
185 g (1 cup) brown lentils
450 g (1 lb) butternut pumpkin (squash), peeled and cut into
    1 cm ($\frac{1}{2}$ inch) cubes
2 zucchini (courgettes), cut in half lengthways and sliced
400 g (14 oz) tin chopped tomatoes
200 g (7 oz) broccoli, cut into small florets
1 small carrot, diced
80 g ($\frac{1}{2}$ cup) peas
1 tablespoon chopped mint

Spiced yoghurt
250 g (1 cup) thick plain yoghurt
1 tablespoon chopped coriander (cilantro) leaves
1 garlic clove, crushed
3 dashes Tabasco sauce

1   Heat the oil in a saucepan over medium heat. Add the leek and garlic and cook for
    4–5 minutes, or until soft and lightly golden. Add the curry powder, cumin and garam
    masala and cook for 1 minute, or until fragrant.

2   Add the stock, bay leaf, lentils and pumpkin. Bring to the boil, then reduce the heat to low
    and simmer for 10–15 minutes, or until the lentils are tender. Season well.

3   Add the zucchini, tomatoes, broccoli, carrot and 500 ml (2 cups) water and simmer for
    10 minutes, or until the vegetables are tender. Add the peas and simmer for 2–3 minutes.

4   To make the spiced yoghurt, place the yoghurt, coriander, garlic and Tabasco in a small
    bowl and stir until combined.

5   Dollop a spoonful of the yoghurt on each serving of soup and garnish with the
    chopped mint.

SERVES 6

INGREDIENTS

10 g ($^1/_4$ oz) dried porcini mushrooms
25 g (1 oz) butter
1 leek (white part only), thinly sliced
250 g (9 oz) pancetta or bacon, chopped
200 g (7 oz) Swiss brown mushrooms, roughly chopped
300 g (10$^1/_2$ oz) large field mushrooms, roughly chopped
2 tablespoons plain (all-purpose) flour
125 ml ($^1/_2$ cup) Madeira
1.25 litres (5 cups) chicken stock
1 tablespoon olive oil
2 chicken breast fillets (about 200 g/7 oz each)
80 g ($^1/_3$ cup) light sour cream
2 teaspoons chopped marjoram, plus whole leaves, to garnish

1   Soak the porcini in 250 ml (1 cup) boiling water for 20 minutes.

2   Melt the butter in a large saucepan over medium heat and cook the leek and pancetta for
    5 minutes, or until the leek is softened. Add all the mushrooms and the porcini soaking
    liquid and cook for 10 minutes.

3   Stir in the flour and cook for 1 minute. Add the Madeira and cook, stirring, for 10 minutes.
    Stir in the stock, bring to the boil, then reduce the heat and simmer for 45 minutes.
    Cool slightly.

4   Heat the oil in a frying pan and cook the chicken fillets for 4–5 minutes each side, or until
    cooked through. Remove from the pan and thinly slice.

5   Blend the soup until smooth. Return to the cleaned saucepan, add the sour cream and
    chopped marjoram and stir over medium heat for about 1–2 minutes to warm through.
    Season. Top with the chicken and garnish with marjoram.

SERVES 4

INGREDIENTS

1 tablespoon olive oil
1 large onion, finely chopped
2 garlic cloves, crushed
750 ml (3 cups) vegetable or chicken stock
750 g (1 lb 10 oz) zucchini (courgettes), thinly sliced
60 ml ($^1/_4$ cup) cream
toasted ciabatta bread, to serve

Pesto
50 g (1 cup) basil
25 g ($^1/_4$ cup) finely grated Parmesan cheese
2 tablespoons pine nuts, toasted
2 tablespoons extra virgin olive oil

1   Heat the oil in a large heavy-based saucepan. Add the onion and garlic and cook over medium heat for 5 minutes, or until the onion is soft.

2   Bring the stock to the boil in a separate saucepan. Add the zucchini and hot stock to the onion mixture. Bring to the boil, then reduce the heat, cover and simmer for about 10 minutes, or until the zucchini is very soft.

3   To make the pesto, process the basil, Parmesan and pine nuts in a food processor for 20 seconds, or until finely chopped. Gradually add the olive oil and process until smooth. Spoon into a small bowl.

4   Transfer the zucchini mixture to a blender or food processor and blend in batches until smooth. Return the mixture to the pan, stir in the cream and 2 tablespoons of the pesto, and reheat over medium heat until hot. Season with salt and black pepper and serve with toasted ciabatta bread. Serve the remaining pesto in a bowl for diners to help themselves, or cover with olive oil and store in the refrigerator for up to 1 week.

ZUCCHINI PESTO SOUP

SERVES 4

INGREDIENTS

2 kg (4 lb 8 oz) oxtails, trimmed
2 tablespoons vegetable oil
2 onions, finely chopped
1 leek, finely chopped
2 carrots, diced
1 celery stalk, diced
2 garlic cloves, crushed
2 bay leaves
2 tablespoons tomato paste (purée)
1 thyme sprig
2 flat-leaf (Italian) parsley sprigs
3.5 litres (14 cups) chicken stock
375 ml (1¹/₂ cups) stout
2 tomatoes, seeded and diced
100 g (3¹/₂ oz) cauliflower florets
100 g (3¹/₂ oz) green beans
100 g (3¹/₂ oz) broccoli florets
100 g (3¹/₂ oz) asparagus, cut into 3 cm (1¹/₄ inch) lengths

1 Preheat the oven to 200°C (400°F/Gas 6). Place the oxtails in a baking dish and bake for 1 hour, turning occasionally, or until dark golden. Leave to cool.

2 Heat the oil in a large saucepan over medium heat and cook the onion, leek, carrot and celery for 3–4 minutes, or until soft. Stir in the garlic, bay leaves and tomato paste, then add the oxtails, thyme and parsley.

3 Add the stock and bring to the boil over high heat. Reduce the heat and simmer for 3 hours, or until the oxtails are tender and the meat falls off the bone. Skim off any scum that rises to the surface. Remove the oxtails and cool slightly.

4 Take the meat off the bones and discard any fat or sinew. Roughly chop and add to the soup with the stout, tomato and 500 ml (2 cups) water. Add the vegetables and simmer for 5 minutes, or until the vegetables are tender. Season.

SERVES 4

INGREDIENTS

200 g (7 oz) rice noodle sticks
1.5 litres (6 cups) beef stock
1 star anise
4 cm (1$^1/_2$ in) piece fresh ginger, sliced
2 pigs trotters (ask your butcher to cut them in half)
$^1/_2$ onion, studded with 2 cloves
2 stems lemon grass, pounded
2 garlic cloves, pounded
$^1/_4$ teaspoon white pepper
1 tablespoon fish sauce
400 g (14 oz) beef fillet, partially frozen, and thinly sliced
90 g (1 cup) bean sprouts
2 spring onions (scallions), thinly sliced on the diagonal
25 g ($^1/_2$ cup) fresh coriander (cilantro) leaves, chopped
25 g ($^1/_2$ cup) fresh Vietnamese mint, chopped
1 fresh red chilli, thinly sliced
fresh red chillies, extra, to serve
fresh Vietnamese mint, extra, to serve
fresh coriander (cilantro) leaves, extra, to serve
2 limes, cut into quarters
fish sauce, extra, to serve

1 Soak the noodles in boiling water for 15–20 minutes. Drain.

2 Bring the stock, star anise, ginger, trotters, onion, lemon grass, garlic and white pepper to the boil in a large saucepan. Reduce the heat and simmer for 30 minutes. Strain, return to the same pan and stir in the fish sauce.

3 Divide the noodles among bowls, then top with beef strips, sprouts, spring onion, coriander, mint and chilli. Ladle on the broth.

4 Place the extra chilli, mint, coriander, lime quarters and fish sauce in small bowls on a platter, serve with the soup and allow your guests to help themselves.

SERVES 4

INGREDIENTS

5 x 2 cm (2 x $^3/_4$ in) piece fresh galangal, peeled and cut into thin slices
500 ml (2 cups) coconut milk
250 ml (1 cup) chicken stock
4 fresh kaffir lime (makrut) leaves, torn
1 tablespoon finely chopped fresh coriander (cilantro) roots
500 g (1 lb 2 oz) chicken breast fillets, cut into thin strips
1–2 teaspoons finely chopped fresh red chillies
2 tablespoons fish sauce
1$^1/_2$ tablespoons lime juice
3 teaspoons palm sugar or soft brown sugar
4 tablespoons fresh coriander (cilantro) leaves

1   Place the galangal in a saucepan with the coconut milk, stock, lime leaves and coriander roots. Bring to the boil, reduce the heat to low and simmer for 10 minutes, stirring occasionally.

2   Add the chicken and chilli to the pan and simmer for 8 minutes.

3   Stir in the fish sauce, lime juice and palm sugar and cook for 1 minute. Stir in the coriander leaves. Serve immediately garnished with extra coriander, if desired.

SERVES 4

1.5 kg (2$^1/_2$ lb) chicken
2 carrots, roughly chopped
2 sticks celery, roughly chopped
1 onion, quartered
4 parsley sprigs
2 bay leaves
4 black peppercorns
50 g (1$^3/_4$ oz) butter
2 tablespoons plain (all-purpose) flour
2 potatoes, chopped
250 g (8 oz) butternut pumpkin (squash), chopped into bite-sized pieces
2 carrots, extra, cut into matchsticks
1 leek, cut into matchsticks
3 sticks celery, extra, cut into matchsticks
100 g (3$^1/_2$ oz) green beans, cut into short lengths or baby green beans, halved
200 g (6$^1/_2$ oz) broccoli, cut into small florets
100 g (3$^1/_2$ oz) sugar snap peas, trimmed
50 g (1$^3/_4$ oz) English spinach leaves, shredded
$^1/_2$ cup (125 ml/4 fl oz) cream
$^1/_4$ cup (15 g/$^1/_2$ oz) chopped parsley

1 To make the chicken stock, place the chicken in a large pan with the carrot, celery, onion, parsley, bay leaves, 2 teaspoons of salt and the peppercorns. Add 3 litres of water. Bring to the boil, reduce the heat and simmer for 1 hour, skimming the surface as required. Allow to cool for at least 30 minutes. Strain and reserve the liquid.

2 Remove the chicken and allow to cool enough to handle. Discard the skin, then cut or pull the flesh from the bones and shred into small pieces. Set the chicken meat aside.

3 Heat the butter in a large pan over medium heat and, when foaming, add the flour. Cook, stirring, for 1 minute. Remove from the heat and gradually stir in the stock. Return to the heat and bring to the boil, stirring continuously. Add the potato, pumpkin and extra carrot and simmer for 7 minutes. Add the leek, extra celery and beans and simmer for a further 5 minutes. Finally, add the broccoli and sugar snap peas and cook for a further 3 minutes.

4 Just before serving, add the chicken meat, spinach, cream and chopped parsley. Reheat gently but do not allow the soup to boil. Keep stirring until the spinach has wilted. Season to taste with plenty of salt and freshly ground black pepper. Serve immediately.

SERVES 6-8

CHICKEN AND VEGETABLE SOUP

CREAMY CHICKEN AND CORN SOUP

INGREDIENTS

20 g (³/₄ oz) butter
1 tablespoon olive oil
500 g (1 lb 2 oz) chicken thigh fillets, trimmed and thinly sliced
2 garlic cloves, chopped
1 leek, chopped
1 large celery stalk, chopped
1 bay leaf
¹/₂ teaspoon thyme
1 litre (4 cups) chicken stock
60 ml (¹/₄ cup) sherry
550 g (1 lb 4 oz) corn kernels (fresh, canned or frozen)
1 large floury potato (russet), cut into 1 cm (¹/₂ in) cubes
185 ml (³/₄ cup) cream, plus extra, to drizzle
chives, to garnish

1   Melt the butter and oil in a large saucepan over high heat. Cook the chicken in batches for 3 minutes, or until lightly golden and just cooked through. Place in a bowl, cover and refrigerate until needed.

2   Reduce the heat to medium and stir in the garlic, leek, celery, bay leaf and thyme. Cook for 2 minutes, or until the leek softens — do not allow the garlic to burn. Add the stock, sherry and 500 ml (2 cups) water and stir, scraping up any sediment stuck to the bottom of the pan. Add the corn and potato and bring to the boil. Reduce the heat and simmer for 1 hour, skimming any scum off the surface. Cool slightly.

3   Remove the bay leaf and purée the soup. Return to the cleaned pan, add the cream and chicken and stir over medium–low heat for 2–3 minutes, or until heated through — do not boil. Season. Drizzle with extra cream and garnish with chives. If desired, serve with crusty bread.

SERVES 4-6

3 dried shiitake mushrooms
1 Chinese roast duck (1.5 kg/3 lb 5 oz)
500 ml (2 cups) chicken stock
2 tablespoons light soy sauce
1 tablespoon Chinese rice wine
2 teaspoons sugar
400 g (14 oz) fresh flat rice noodles
2 tablespoons oil
3 spring onions (scallions), thinly sliced
1 teaspoon finely chopped ginger
400 g (14 oz) bok choy (pak choi), trimmed and leaves separated
$1/4$ teaspoon sesame oil

1 Place the shiitake mushrooms in a heatproof bowl, cover with 250 ml (1 cup) boiling water and soak for 20 minutes. Drain, reserving the liquid and squeezing the excess liquid from the mushrooms. Discard the woody stems and thinly slice the caps.

2 Remove the skin and flesh from the roast duck. Discard the fat and carcass. Finely slice the duck meat and the skin.

3 Place the chicken stock, soy sauce, rice wine, sugar and the reserved mushroom liquid in a saucepan over medium heat. Bring to a simmer and cook for 5 minutes. Meanwhile, place the rice noodles in a heatproof bowl, cover with boiling water and soak briefly. Gently separate the noodles with your hands and drain well. Divide evenly among large soup bowls.

4 Heat the oil in a wok over high heat. Add the spring onion, ginger and shiitake mushrooms and cook for several seconds. Transfer to the broth with the bok choy and duck meat and simmer for 1 minute, or until the duck has warmed through and the bok choy has wilted. Ladle the soup over the noodles and drizzle sesame oil on each serving. Serve immediately.

DUCK, SHIITAKE MUSHROOMS AND RICE NOODLE BROTH

SERVES 4-6

FIVE-SPICE DUCK AND SOMEN NOODLE SOUP

4 duck breasts, skin on
1 teaspoon five-spice powder
1 teaspoon peanut oil
200 g (7 oz) dried somen noodles

Star anise broth
1 litre (4 cups) chicken stock
3 whole star anise
5 spring onions (scallions), chopped
15 g (1/4 cup) chopped fresh coriander (cilantro) leaves

1 Preheat the oven to moderately hot 200°C (400°F/Gas 6). Trim the duck breast of excess fat, then lightly sprinkle both sides with the five-spice powder.

2 Heat the oil in a large frying pan. Add the duck skin-side down and cook over medium heat for 2–3 minutes, or until brown and crisp. Turn and cook the other side for 3 minutes. Transfer to a baking tray and cook, skin-side up, for another 8–10 minutes, or until cooked to your liking.

3 Meanwhile, place the chicken stock and star anise in a small saucepan. Bring to the boil, then reduce the heat and simmer for 5 minutes. Add the spring onion and coriander and simmer for 5 minutes.

4 Cook the noodles in a saucepan of boiling water for 2 minutes, or until soft. Drain and divide among four bowls. Ladle the broth on the noodles and top each bowl with one sliced duck breast.

SERVES 4

INGREDIENTS

500 g (1 lb 2 oz) Italian pork sausages
200 g (7 oz) piece speck (see note)
1 tablespoon olive oil
1 large onion, chopped
3 garlic cloves, crushed
1 celery stalk, cut in half and sliced
1 large carrot, cut into 1 cm ($^1/_2$ in) cubes
bouquet garni (1 parsley sprig, 1 oregano sprig, 2 bay leaves)
1 small red chilli, halved lengthways
400 g (14 oz) can chopped tomatoes
1.75 litres (7 cups) chicken stock
300 g (10$^1/_2$ oz) Brussels sprouts, cut in half from top to base
300 g (10$^1/_2$ oz) green beans, cut into 3 cm (1$^1/_4$ inch) lengths
300 g (10$^1/_2$ oz) shelled broad beans, fresh or frozen
2 tablespoons chopped flat-leaf (Italian) parsley

1 Grill (broil) the sausages under a hot grill (broiler) for 8–10 minutes, turning occasionally, or until brown. Remove and cut into 3 cm (1$^1/_4$ in) lengths. Trim and reserve the fat from the speck, then dice the speck.

2 Heat the oil in a large saucepan over medium heat. Add the speck and reserved speck fat and cook for 2–3 minutes, or until golden. Add the onion, garlic, celery and carrot, reduce the heat to low and cook for 6–8 minutes, or until softened. Discard the remains of the speck fat.

3 Stir in the sausages, bouquet garni, chilli and chopped tomato and cook for 5 minutes. Add the stock, bring to the boil, then reduce the heat and simmer for 1 hour. Add the Brussels sprouts, green beans and broad beans and simmer for 30 minutes. Discard the bouquet garni, then stir in the parsley. Season to taste. Divide among four bowls and serve.

NOTE Speck is cured smoked ham or pork belly. It has a strong taste and is usually cut into small pieces and used as a flavour base.

GRILLED ITALIAN SAUSAGE AND VEGETABLE SOUP

SERVES 4

HOT AND SOUR LIME SOUP WITH BEEF

1 litre (4 cups) beef stock
2 stems lemon grass, white part only, halved
3 garlic cloves, halved
2.5 x 2.5 cm (1 x 1 in) piece ginger, sliced
90 g (1 bunch) coriander (cilantro), leaves and stalks separated, leaves chopped
4 spring onions (scallions), thinly sliced on the diagonal
2 strips of 1.5 x 4 cm ($^5/_8$ x 1$^1/_2$ in) lime zest
2 star anise
3 small red chillies, seeded and finely chopped
500 g (1 lb 2 oz) fillet steak, trimmed
2 tablespoons fish sauce
1 tablespoon grated palm sugar or soft brown sugar
2 tablespoons lime juice
coriander (cilantro) leaves, extra, to garnish

1 Place the stock, lemon grass, garlic, ginger, coriander stalks, 2 spring onions, the lime zest, star anise, 1 teaspoon of the chopped chilli and 1 litre (4 cups) water in a saucepan. Bring to the boil and simmer, covered, for 25 minutes. Strain and return the liquid to the pan.

2 Heat a chargrill pan (griddle) until very hot. Brush lightly with olive oil and sear the steak on both sides until browned on the outside, but very rare in the centre.

3 Reheat the soup, adding the fish sauce and palm sugar. Season with salt and black pepper. Add the lime juice to taste (you may want more than 2 tablespoons) — you should achieve a hot and sour flavour.

4 Add the remaining spring onion and the chopped coriander leaves to the soup. Slice the beef across the grain into thin strips. Curl the strips into a decorative pattern, then place in the centre of four deep serving bowls. Pour the soup over the beef and garnish with the remaining chilli and a few extra coriander leaves.

SERVES 4

INGREDIENTS

2 stems lemon grass, white part finely chopped, stem ends reserved and halved

6 cloves garlic, chopped

3 red Asian shallots, chopped

8 black peppercorns

1 teaspoon ready-made red curry paste

1 cup (250 ml/8 fl oz) coconut cream

400 ml (13^1/$_2$ fl oz) coconut milk

400 ml (13^1/$_2$ fl oz) chicken stock

2^1/$_2$ tablespoons thinly sliced fresh galangal

7 kaffir lime (makrut) leaves, shredded

400 g (14 oz) chicken breast fillets or thigh fillets, thinly sliced

2 tablespoons lime juice

2 tablespoons fish sauce

1 teaspoon grated palm sugar or soft brown sugar

3 tablespoons fresh coriander (cilantro) leaves

1 small fresh red chilli, thinly sliced

1   Process the chopped lemon grass, garlic, shallots, peppercorns and curry paste in a food processor to form a paste.

2   Heat a wok over low heat, add the coconut cream, increase the heat to high and bring to the boil. Add the paste and cook, stirring, for 5 minutes. Add the coconut milk and stock, return to the boil and add the sliced galangal, the kaffir lime leaves and reserved lemon grass stems. Reduce the heat and simmer for 5 minutes.

3   Add the chicken and simmer for 8 minutes, or until cooked. Stir in the lime juice, fish sauce, palm sugar, coriander leaves and chilli. Serve immediately.

THAI-STYLE CHICKEN AND COCONUT SOUP

MOROCCAN LAMB, CHICKPEA AND CORIANDER SOUP

INGREDIENTS

165 g (³/₄ cup) dried chickpeas
1 tablespoon olive oil
850 g (1 lb 14 oz) boned lamb leg, cut into 1 cm (¹/₂ in) cubes
1 onion, chopped
2 garlic cloves, crushed
¹/₂ teaspoon ground cinnamon
¹/₂ teaspoon ground turmeric
¹/₂ teaspoon ground ginger
4 tablespoons chopped coriander (cilantro) leaves
2 x 400 g (14 oz) cans chopped tomatoes
1 litre (4 cups) chicken stock
160 g (²/₃ cup) dried red lentils, rinsed
coriander (cilantro) leaves, to garnish

1 Soak the chickpeas in cold water overnight. Drain and rinse well.

2 Heat the oil in a large saucepan over high heat and brown the lamb in batches for 2–3 minutes. Reduce the heat to medium, return the lamb to the pan with the onion and garlic and cook for 5 minutes. Add the spices, season and cook for 2 minutes. Add the coriander, tomato, stock and 500 ml (2 cups) water and bring to the boil over high heat.

3 Add the lentils and chickpeas and simmer, covered, over low heat for 1¹/₂ hours. Uncover and cook for 30 minutes, or until the lamb is tender and the soup is thick. Season. Garnish with coriander.

SERVES 4-6

300 g (10¹/₂ oz) minced (ground) pork
4 spring onions (scallions), sliced
3 garlic cloves, roughly chopped
2 teaspoons grated ginger
2 teaspoons cornflour (cornstarch)
125 ml (¹/₂ cup) light soy sauce
3 tablespoons Chinese rice wine
30 won ton wrappers
3 litres (12 cups) ready-made Chinese chicken broth, or home-made or ready-made chicken stock
200 g (7 oz) dried flat egg noodles
2 spring onions (scallions), extra, sliced on the diagonal

1 Put the minced pork, spring onion, garlic, grated ginger, cornflour, 1¹/₂ tablespoons of the soy sauce and 1 tablespoon of the rice wine in a food processor and process until well combined. Place 2 teaspoons of the mixture in the centre of a won ton wrapper and lightly brush the edges with water. Lift the sides up tightly and pinch around the filling to form a pouch. Repeat this process to make 30 won tons.

2 Place the chicken broth in a large saucepan and bring to a simmer over medium–high heat. Stir in the remaining soy sauce and rice wine.

3 Meanwhile, bring a large pan of water to the boil. Reduce the heat, add the won tons and simmer for 1 minute, or until they float to the surface and are cooked through, then remove with a slotted spoon. Return the water to the boil, add the egg noodles and cook for 3 minutes, or until tender. Drain and add to the chicken broth along with the cooked won tons. Simmer for 2 minutes, or until heated through.

4 Divide the broth, noodles and won tons among six large serving bowls, sprinkle with extra spring onion and drizzle each with a little sesame oil.

LONG AND SHORT NOODLE SOUP

SERVES 6

INGREDIENTS

200 g (7 oz) Chinese barbecued pork (char sui) fillet in one piece
2 small fresh corn cobs (550 g/1 lb 4 oz)
200 g (7 oz) dried ramen noodles
2 teaspoons peanut oil
1 teaspoon grated ginger
1.5 litres (6 cups) chicken stock
2 tablespoons mirin
2 spring onions (scallions), sliced on the diagonal
20 g ($^3/_4$ oz) unsalted butter
1 spring onion, extra, sliced on the diagonal
Cut the pork into thin slices and remove the corn kernels from the cob using a sharp knife.

1   Bring a large saucepan of water to the boil, add the ramen noodles and cook for
    4 minutes, or until tender. Drain, then rinse in cold water.

2   Heat the oil in a large saucepan over high heat. Stir-fry the grated ginger for 1 minute. Add
    the chicken stock and mirin and bring to the boil. Reduce the heat and simmer for
    8 minutes.

3   Add the pork slices to the liquid and cook for 5 minutes, then add the corn kernels and
    spring onion and cook for a further 4–5 minutes, or until the kernels are tender.

4   Separate the noodles by running them under hot water, then divide among four deep
    bowls. Ladle on the soup, then place 1 teaspoon butter on each serving. Garnish with the
    extra spring onion and serve at once.

NOTE This soup is traditionally served with the butter on top. However, for a healthier option, it is
    also quite delicious without the butter.

SERVES 4

300 g (1^1/$_2$ cups) long-grain rice, thoroughly rinsed
^{1}/$_2$ star anise
2 spring onions (scallions), white part only
4 x 4 cm (1^1/$_2$ x 1^1/$_2$ inch) piece ginger, cut into slices
3.5 litres (14 cups) chicken stock
1 tablespoon peanut oil
2 garlic cloves, crushed
1 teaspoon grated ginger, extra
400 g (14 oz) minced (ground) pork
ground white pepper
60 ml (^{1}/$_4$ cup) light soy sauce
sesame oil, to drizzle
6 fried dough sticks (see note)

1 Put the rice in a large saucepan with the star anise, spring onions, sliced ginger and chicken stock. Bring to the boil, then reduce the heat to low and simmer for 1^1/$_2$ hours, stirring occasionally.

2 Heat the oil in a frying pan over high heat. Cook the garlic and grated ginger for 30 seconds. Add the mince and cook for 5 minutes, or until browned, breaking up any lumps with the back of a spoon.

3 Remove the star anise, spring onions and ginger from the soup and discard them. Add the mince mixture and simmer for 10 minutes. Season with white pepper and stir in the soy sauce. Serve with a drizzle of sesame oil and the dough sticks.

NOTE Fried dough sticks are available at Chinese bakeries and speciality shops and are best eaten soon after purchasing. If not, reheat in a 200°C (400°F/Gas 6) oven for 5 minutes, then serve.

PORK CONGEE

SERVES 4-6

SPAGHETTI AND MEATBALL SOUP

150 g (5¹/₂ oz) spaghetti, broken into 8 cm (3 in) lengths
1.5 litres (6 cups) beef stock
3 teaspoons tomato paste (purée)
400 g (14 oz) can chopped tomatoes
3 tablespoons basil leaves, torn
shaved Parmesan cheese, to garnish

Meatballs
1 tablespoon oil
1 onion, finely chopped
2 garlic cloves, crushed
500 g (1 lb 2 oz) lean minced (ground) beef
3 tablespoons finely chopped flat-leaf (Italian) parsley
3 tablespoons fresh breadcrumbs
2 tablespoons finely grated Parmesan cheese
1 egg, lightly beaten

1 Cook the spaghetti in a large saucepan of boiling water according to packet instructions until al dente. Drain. Put the stock and 500 ml (2 cups) water in a large saucepan and slowly bring to a simmer.

2 Meanwhile, to make the meatballs, heat the oil in a small frying pan over medium heat and cook the onion for 2–3 minutes, or until soft. Add the garlic and cook for 30 seconds. Allow to cool.

3 Combine the mince, parsley, breadcrumbs, Parmesan, egg, the onion mixture, and salt and pepper. Roll a heaped teaspoon of mixture into a ball, making 40 balls in total.

4 Stir the tomato paste and tomato into the beef stock and simmer for 2–3 minutes. Drop in the meatballs, return to a simmer and cook for 10 minutes, or until cooked through. Stir in the spaghetti and basil to warm through. Season, garnish with shaved Parmesan and serve.

SERVES 4

INGREDIENTS

2 dried Chinese mushrooms
15 raw prawns (shrimp)
100 g (3$^{1}/_{2}$ oz) minced (ground) pork
2 spring onions, chopped
1 teaspoon grated ginger
2 tablespoons canned water chestnuts, chopped
2 teaspoons chopped lemon grass, white part only
1 clove garlic, finely chopped
3 tablespoons soy sauce
225 g (7 oz) won ton wrappers
coriander (cilantro) leaves
6 cups (1.5 litres) beef stock
3 baby carrots, cut diagonally
3 spring onions, cut diagonally

1 Soak the mushrooms in hot water for 30 minutes. Peel and devein the prawns, then cut in half lengthways. Drain the mushrooms, remove the stems and chop the caps.

2 Mix the chopped mushroom with the pork, spring onion, ginger, water chestnut, lemon grass, garlic and 1 tablespoon of the soy sauce. Work with 1 won ton wrapper at a time, keeping the rest covered. Put 2–3 coriander leaves, half a prawn and a heaped teaspoon of the pork mixture in the centre of a wrapper. Brush the edges with water and lay another wrapper on top. Press to seal. Repeat with the remaining wrappers.

3 Bring the stock, remaining soy sauce, carrot and spring onion to the boil. Bring another large pan of water to the boil and cook the won tons in batches for 4–5 minutes; drain. Pour the hot soup over the won tons.

SERVES 4

VIETNAMESE BEEF SOUP

INGREDIENTS

400 g (14 oz) rump steak, trimmed
$^1/_2$ onion
$1^1/_2$ tablespoons fish sauce
1 star anise
1 cinnamon stick
pinch ground white pepper
1.5 litres (6 cups) beef stock
300 g (10$^1/_2$ oz) fresh thin rice noodles
3 spring onions (scallions), thinly sliced
15 g ($^3/_4$ cup) Vietnamese mint leaves
90 g (1 cup) bean sprouts
1 small white onion, cut in half and thinly sliced
1 small red chilli, thinly sliced on the diagonal
lemon wedges, to serve

1   Wrap the rump steak in plastic wrap and freeze for 40 minutes.

2   Meanwhile, put the onion, fish sauce, star anise, cinnamon stick, pepper, stock and 500 ml (2 cups) water in a large saucepan. Bring to the boil, then reduce the heat, cover and simmer for 20 minutes. Discard the onion, star anise and cinnamon stick.

3   Cover the noodles with boiling water and gently separate the strands. Drain and refresh under cold water.

4   Remove the meat from the freezer and thinly slice it across the grain.

5   Divide the noodles and spring onion among four deep bowls. Top with the beef, mint, bean sprouts, onion and chilli. Ladle the hot broth over the top and serve with the lemon wedges.

SERVES 4

INGREDIENTS

1 small fresh red chilli, seeded and chopped
1 stem lemon grass, white part only, sliced
1 teaspoon ground coriander
1 tablespoon chopped fresh ginger
2 cups (500 ml) vegetable stock
2 tablespoons oil
1 onion, finely chopped
800 g pumpkin flesh, cubed
1$^1/_2$ cups (375 ml) coconut milk
3 tablespoons chopped fresh coriander (cilantro) leaves
2 teaspoons shaved palm sugar or soft brown sugar
extra coriander (cilantro) leaves, to garnish

1 Place the chilli, lemon grass, ground coriander, ginger and 2 tablespoons vegetable stock in a food processor, and process until smooth.

2 Heat the oil in a large saucepan, add the onion and cook over medium heat for 5 minutes. Add the spice paste and cook, stirring, for 1 minute.

3 Add the pumpkin and remaining vegetable stock. Bring to the boil, then reduce the heat and simmer, covered, for 15–20 minutes, or until the pumpkin is tender. Cool slightly then process in a food processor or blender until smooth. Return to the cleaned pan, stir in the coconut milk, coriander and palm sugar, and simmer until hot. Garnish with the extra coriander leaves.

SERVES 4

INGREDIENTS

2 tablespoons olive oil
1 onion, chopped
2 cloves garlic, crushed
500 g (17$^1/_2$ oz) beef chuck steak, cut into 2 cm (1 inch) cubes
1 litre (34 fl oz) beef stock
2 small beetroot (250 g/9 oz)
200 g (7 oz) canned crushed tomatoes
1 carrot, diced
2 potatoes (280 g/10 oz), diced
2$^1/_2$ cups (190 g/6$^3/_4$ oz) finely shredded cabbage
2 teaspoons lemon juice
2 teaspoons sugar
2 tablespoons chopped fresh flat-leaf parsley
2 tablespoons chopped fresh dill
$^1/_3$ cup (90 g) sour cream

1 Preheat the oven to moderately hot 200°C (400°F/Gas 6). Heat the oil in a large saucepan, and cook the onion and garlic over medium heat for 3–5 minutes. Add the beef, stock and 1 litre water, and bring to the boil. Reduce the heat and simmer, covered, for 1 hour 15 minutes, or until the meat is tender. Remove the meat.

2 Trim the beetroot just above the end of the leaf stalks. Wrap in foil and bake for 30–40 minutes, or until tender. Unwrap and leave to cool.

3 Return the stock to the boil and add the tomato, carrot and potato, and season with salt. Cook over medium heat for 10 minutes. Add the cabbage and cook for 5 minutes. Peel and dice the beetroot. Return the meat to the pan and add the beetroot, lemon juice, sugar and 1$^1/_2$ tablespoons each of parsley and dill. Cook for 2 minutes, or until heated through. Season to taste.

4 Remove from the heat and leave for 10 minutes. Serve with a dollop of sour cream and garnish with the remaining dill and parsley.

BEEF AND BEET BORSCHT

FINGERFOOD

ROLLED OMELETTE WITH OCEAN TROUT CAVIAR

4 eggs
$^1/_3$ cup (80 ml) thick (double) cream
4 tablespoons finely chopped fresh chives
1 tablespoon olive oil
40 g butter, melted
3 slices white bread
$^1/_4$ cup (60 g) sour cream
100 g ocean trout caviar or salmon roe
chopped fresh chives, to garnish

1 Whisk together one egg, 1 tablespoon of the cream and 1 tablespoon of the chopped chives, and season with salt and cracked black pepper. Pour into a 25 cm (10 inch) lightly greased non-stick frying pan and cook over medium heat on one side for 3 minutes, or until just set; the omelettes will be difficult to roll if cooked for too long. Turn out onto a sheet of baking paper. Repeat with the remaining eggs and cream until you have four omelettes.

2 Tightly roll one omelette into a neat roll, then take another omelette and wrap it around the first. Repeat with the remaining omelettes so that you have two rolls. Wrap separately in plastic wrap and refrigerate for 1 hour.

3 Meanwhile preheat the oven to moderate 180°C (350°F/Gas 4). Combine the oil and butter. Using a 3 cm ($1^1/_4$ inch) cutter, cut 24 rounds from the bread and brush with the butter and oil mixture. Place on a baking tray and bake for 20–30 minutes, or until crisp and golden. Allow to cool.

4 Cut each of the cooled omelette rolls into 12 rounds. Spread $^1/_2$ teaspoon of the sour cream onto each croûton, and sit a round of omelette on top. Top with a teaspoon of salmon roe and garnish with chopped chives.

MAKES 24

INGREDIENTS

125 g (1 cup) plain (all-purpose) flour
$^1/_2$ teaspoon baking powder
$^1/_2$ teaspoon sugar
2 tablespoons linseeds
60 ml ($^1/_4$ cup) milk
2 tablespoons olive oil

1   Preheat the oven to 200°C (400°F/Gas 6). Process the flour, baking powder, sugar and
    $^1/_2$ teaspoon salt. Add pepper to taste, and stir in the linseeds. Add the milk and oil and
    mix to form a wet crumbly mixture, adding extra milk if the mixture is too dry.

2   Turn the mixture out onto a flat, lightly floured surface and bring the mixture together into
    a ball.

3   Divide the mixture in half, place one half between two sheets of baking paper and roll out
    to a thickness of 2–3 mm ($^1/_8$ inch). Prick liberally with a fork. Cut the dough into 12
    irregular triangles and arrange in a single layer on a lightly greased baking tray. Repeat
    with the remaining dough.

4   Bake for 15–20 minutes, or until the bases are lightly golden. Turn over and bake for a
    further 4–5 minutes, or until the other side is also lightly golden. Transfer to a wire rack to
    cool completely.

LINSEED CRACKERS

MAKES 24

141

FALAFEL

2 cups (440 g) dried chickpeas
1 onion, finely chopped
2 cloves garlic, crushed
2 tablespoons chopped fresh parsley
1 tablespoon chopped fresh coriander (cilantro)
2 teaspoons ground cumin
$1/2$ teaspoon baking powder
oil, for deep-frying

1 Soak the chickpeas in 3 cups (750 ml/24 fl oz) of water for 4 hours or overnight. Drain and place in a food processor, and process for 30 seconds, or until finely ground.

2 Add the onion, garlic, parsley, coriander, cumin, baking powder, 1 tablespoon of water, salt and pepper and process for 10 seconds, or until the mixture forms a rough paste. Cover and leave for 30 minutes.

3 Using your hands, shape heaped tablespoons of the falafel mixture into balls and squeeze out any excess liquid. Fill a deep heavy-based pan one-third full of oil to 180°C (350°F) and heat until a cube of bread browns in 15 seconds. Gently lower the falafel balls into the oil. Cook in batches of five at a time, for 3–4 minutes each batch. When the balls are browned, remove with a large slotted spoon. Drain well. Serve with Lebanese bread, tabbouleh and hummus.

MAKES 30

INGREDIENTS

1 kg (2 lb) orange sweet potato (kumera)
1 tablespoon oil
30 g (1 oz) butter
4 leeks, white part only, finely sliced
2 cloves garlic, crushed
250 g (8 oz) feta cheese, crumbled
8 eggs
$^1/_2$ cup (125 ml/4 fl oz) cream

1 Preheat the oven to moderate 180°C (350°F/Gas 4). Grease or brush twelve 1 cup (250 ml/8 fl oz) muffin holes with oil or melted butter. Cut small rounds of baking paper and place into the base of each hole. Cut the sweet potato into small cubes and boil, steam or microwave until tender. Drain well and set aside.

2 Heat the oil and butter in a frying pan and cook the leek for 10 minutes, stirring occasionally, or until very soft and lightly golden. Add the garlic and cook for a further 1 minute. Cool, then stir in the feta and sweet potato. Divide among the muffin holes.

3 Whisk the eggs and cream together and season with salt and cracked black pepper. Pour the egg mixture into each hole until three-quarters filled, then press the vegetables down gently. Bake for 25–30 minutes, or until golden and set. Leave in the tins for 5 minutes, then ease out with a knife. Delicious either served hot or at room temperature.

MAKES 12

INGREDIENTS

Pesto
1 cup (50 g/1³/₄ oz) fresh basil leaves
¹/₂ cup (50 g/1³/₄ oz) pecan nuts
¹/₄ cup (60 ml/2 fl oz) olive oil
3 cloves garlic

1 French bread stick, thinly sliced
10 large sun-dried (sun-blushed) tomatoes, cut into thin
   strips
150 g (5 oz) Parmesan, thinly shaved

1 To make the pesto, mix the basil leaves, pecans, oil and garlic in a food processor until the mixture is smooth.

2 Toast the bread slices under a grill until brown on both sides.

3 Spread the pesto evenly over the pieces of toast. Top each slice with sun-dried tomatoes and some of the Parmesan.

2 cloves garlic, chopped
$\frac{1}{2}$ cup (125 ml/4 fl oz) olive oil
2 tablespoons finely chopped fresh dill
15 g ($\frac{1}{2}$ oz) finely chopped fresh parsley
2 tablespoons finely chopped fresh basil
2 tablespoons lemon juice
2 x 400 g (13 oz) cans artichoke hearts
3 tablespoons finely diced red capsicum (pepper)

1   To make the marinade, combine the garlic, oil, herbs and lemon juice in a bowl and whisk
     until well combined. Season with salt and cracked black pepper.

2   Drain the artichoke hearts and add to the marinade with the red pepper. Mix well to coat.
     Cover and marinate in the refrigerator overnight. Serve as part of an antipasto platter or
     use in salads. Return the artichokes to room temperature before serving.

GARLIC AND HERB MARINATED ARTICHOKES

MAKES 6

CRUNCHY WEDGES

6 floury or all-purpose potatoes
1 tablespoon oil
25 g ($^{1}/_{4}$ cup) dry breadcrumbs
2 teaspoons chopped chives
1 teaspoon celery salt
$^{1}/_{4}$ teaspoon garlic powder
$^{1}/_{2}$ teaspoon chopped rosemary

1 Preheat the oven to 200°C (400°F/Gas 6). Cut the potatoes into eight wedges each and toss in the oil.

2 Combine the breadcrumbs, chives, celery salt, garlic powder and rosemary in a bowl. Add the wedges and coat well. Place on greased baking trays and bake for 40 minutes, or until crisp and golden.

MAKES 48

INGREDIENTS

Classic Tuscan

6 ripe Roma (plum) tomatoes

15 g ($^{1}/_{2}$ cup) basil, shredded

1 garlic clove, finely chopped

2 tablespoons extra virgin olive oil

16 slices crusty white Italian-style bread, cut into 1 cm
  ($^{1}/_{2}$ inch) slices

4 garlic cloves, halved

60 ml ($^{1}/_{4}$ cup) olive oil

Mushroom and parsley

2 tablespoons olive oil

200 g (7 oz) small button mushrooms, quartered

1 tablespoon lemon juice

50 g ($1^{3}/_{4}$ oz) goat's cheese, crumbled

1 tablespoon finely chopped flat-leaf (Italian) parsley

1 teaspoon chopped thyme

1 To make the classic Tuscan topping, score a cross in the base of each tomato and place in a bowl of boiling water for 10 seconds, then plunge into cold water. Peel the skin away from the cross. Cut in half and scoop out the seeds with a teaspoon. Finely dice the flesh, then combine with the basil, garlic and oil.

2 To make the mushroom and parsley topping, heat the oil in a frying pan and cook the mushrooms over medium heat for 5 minutes, or until just tender. Remove from the heat and transfer to a small bowl. Stir in the lemon juice, goat's cheese, parsley and thyme.

3 Toast the bread and, while still hot, rub with the cut side of a garlic clove. Drizzle oil over each slice of bread, then season with salt and freshly ground black pepper. Divide the toppings among the bread slices.

NOTE Each topping makes enough for eight slices of bruschetta. You will only need eight slices of bread if you only want to make one topping.

PUMPKIN AND PESTO CHICKEN IN FILO PASTRY

4 chicken breast fillets
1 tablespoon oil
250 g (8 oz) pumpkin
1 bunch English spinach
12 sheets filo pastry
100 g (3^1/$_2$ oz) butter, melted
^{1}/$_4$ cup (25 g/^{3}/$_4$ oz) dry breadcrumbs
100 g (3^1/$_2$ oz) ricotta
^{1}/$_3$ cup (90 g/3 oz) pesto
1 tablespoon pine nuts, chopped

1 Preheat the oven to moderately hot 200°C (400°F/Gas 6). Season the chicken fillets with salt and pepper. Heat half the oil in a frying pan and fry the chicken until browned on both sides, then remove from the pan.

2 Cut the peeled pumpkin into 5 mm (¼ inch) slices. Heat the remaining oil in the same pan and fry the pumpkin until lightly browned on both sides. Allow to cool.

3 Put the spinach leaves into a bowl of boiling water and stir until just wilted. Drain well and pat dry with paper towels. Layer 3 sheets of filo pastry, brushing each with some of the melted butter, sprinkling between layers with some of the breadcrumbs.

4 Wrap each chicken breast in a quarter of the spinach and place on one short side of the filo, leaving a 2 cm (¾ inch) gap. Top the chicken with a quarter of the pumpkin slices, then spread a quarter of the ricotta down the centre of the pumpkin. Top with a table-spoon of the pesto.

5 Fold the sides of the pastry over the filling, then roll the parcel up until it sits on the unsecured end. Repeat with the remaining ingredients. Place the parcels on a lightly greased baking tray, brush with any remaining butter and sprinkle with the pine nuts. Bake for 15 minutes, then cover loosely with foil and bake for a further 20 minutes, or until the pastry is golden brown.

MAKES 4

INGREDIENTS

500 g (1 lb) mixed nuts (almonds, brazil nuts, pecans, macadamias, cashew nuts)
1 egg white
2 tablespoons curry powder
1 teaspoon ground cumin

1 Preheat the oven to slow 150°C (300°F/Gas 2). Spread the nuts in a single layer on a baking tray and roast for 10 minutes.

2 Whisk the egg white until frothy, then add the nuts, curry powder, cumin and 1 teaspoon salt. Toss together and return to the oven for a further 10–15 minutes, then allow to cool.

CURRIED NUTS

MAKES 4¹/₂ cups

INGREDIENTS

1 tablespoon oil
2 cloves garlic, crushed
1 tablespoon grated fresh ginger
2 spring onions, chopped
500 g (1 lb) raw prawns (shrimp), peeled and chopped
$\frac{1}{2}$ teaspoon fish sauce
$\frac{1}{2}$ teaspoon sugar
1 tablespoon lemon juice
2 tablespoons chopped fresh coriander (cilantro)
6 large spring roll wrappers, cut into quarters
oil, for deep-frying
fresh chives, for serving
sweet chilli sauce, for serving

1 Heat the oil in a frying pan, add the garlic and ginger and cook over low heat for 2 minutes. Add the spring onion and cook for 2 minutes. Increase the heat to high, add the prawns and stir-fry for 2 minutes, or until the colour just changes. Be careful not to overcook the prawns or they will become tough once deep-fried.

2 Add the fish sauce, sugar, lemon juice and coriander to the pan. Toss with the prawns for 1 minute. Remove from the heat; cool slightly.

3 Divide the cooled mixture into 24 portions. Place one portion in the centre of each piece of spring roll wrapper. Brush the edges with water and fold to form a parcel.

4 Fill a deep heavy-based pan one third full of oil. Heat the oil to 180°C (350°F). The oil is hot enough when a cube of bread dropped into the oil turns golden brown in 15 seconds. Deep-fry the parcels one at a time, holding them with tongs for the first few seconds to keep them intact. Cook until golden brown. Drain on crumpled paper towels. Tie with lengths of chives. Serve with sweet chilli sauce.

NOTE If the spring roll wrappers are very thin, you may need to use two together.

PORK SAN CHOY BAU

1 tablespoon oil

400 g (13 oz) minced (ground) pork

230 g (7¹/₂ oz) can water chestnuts, drained and chopped
finely

125 g (4 oz) canned bamboo shoots, drained and chopped
finely

6 spring onions, finely chopped

2 tablespoons dry sherry

1 tablespoon soy sauce

2 teaspoons sesame oil

2 teaspoons oyster sauce

tiny lettuce leaves (cos, iceberg or witlof)

chopped fresh mint, for serving

Sauce

2 tablespoons plum sauce

1 tablepoon hoisin sauce

1 teaspoon soy sauce

1 Heat the oil in a pan or wok, add the pork and cook, stirring, over high heat until brown all over. Break up any lumps of mince with the back of a fork. Add the water chestnuts, bamboo shoots and spring onion, toss well and cook for 1 minute.

2 Combine the sherry, soy sauce, sesame oil and oyster sauce, add to the wok, toss well and cook for 2 minutes. Remove from the heat.

3 To make the dipping sauce, stir all the ingredients in a bowl with 2 tablespoons water.

4 To serve, put about 1 tablespoon of warm pork mixture on each lettuce leaf. Sprinkle with the chopped mint. Serve with the sauce, for drizzling over the top.

INGREDIENTS

3 cups (450 g/14 oz) char sui pork bun flour
1 cup (250 ml/8 fl oz) milk
$^1/_2$ cup (125 g/4 oz) caster sugar
1 tablespoon oil

Filling

2 teaspoons oil
1 clove garlic, crushed
2 spring onions, finely chopped
3 teaspoons cornflour (cornstarch)
2 teaspoons hoisin sauce
$1^1/_2$ teaspoons soy sauce
$^1/_2$ teaspoon caster sugar
150 g (5 oz) Chinese barbecued pork, finely chopped

1   Set aside two tablespoons of flour. In a small pan, combine the milk and sugar and stir over low heat until dissolved. Sift the remaining flour into a large bowl and make a well in the centre. Gradually add the milk, stirring until it just comes together. Lightly dust a work surface with some of the reserved flour. Turn out the dough and knead for 10 minutes, or until smooth and elastic. Gradually incorporate the tablespoon of oil by kneading it into the dough a little at a time, kneading for about 10 minutes. Cover with plastic wrap and refrigerate for 30 minutes.

2   For the filling, heat the oil in a pan, add the garlic and spring onion and stir over medium heat until just soft. Blend the cornflour with $^1/_3$ cup (80 ml/2$^3/_4$ fl oz) water, the sauces and sugar and add to the pan. Stir over medium heat until the mixture boils and thickens, remove from the heat and stir in the pork. Allow to cool.

3   Divide the dough into 24 portions and flatten slightly, making the edges slightly thinner than the centre. Place teaspoons of filling in the centre of each and pull up the edges around the filling to enclose, pinching firmly to seal. Place each bun on a small square of greaseproof paper and place 3 cm (1$^1/_4$ inches) apart on a bamboo or metal steamer. Place over a large pan of simmering water and steam in batches for 15 minutes, or until the buns have risen and are cooked through.

NOTE   Char sui pork bun flour is available at Asian food stores.

STEAMED PORK BUNS

MAKES 24

193

INGREDIENTS

$^1/_2$ cup (90 g/3 oz) roasted peanuts

$^1/_4$ cup (60 ml/2 fl oz) coconut milk

2 tablespoons lime juice

$^1/_2$ teaspoon ground turmeric

$^1/_4$ cup (60 ml/2 fl oz) oil

3 eggs, lightly beaten

125 g (4 oz) dried rice vermicelli

3 cloves garlic, crushed

1 tablespoon finely chopped fresh ginger

2 teaspoons shrimp paste (blachan)

6 spring onions, thinly sliced

400 g (13 oz) can baby corn, drained, quartered lengthways

150 g (5 oz) bean shoots

500 g (1 lb) Chinese cabbage, hard stems removed, thinly sliced

$^1/_2$ small red capsicum (pepper), thinly sliced

10 g ($^1/_4$ oz) fresh coriander (cilantro) leaves

$1^1/_2$ tablespoons fish sauce

2–3 large banana leaves, for serving

$^1/_2$ cup (90 g/3 oz) roasted peanuts, extra, chopped, to garnish

lime wedges, for serving

1 Mix the peanuts, coconut milk, lime juice and turmeric in a food processor until combined, but so the peanuts are only roughly chopped.

2 Heat 1 tablespoon of the oil in a large wok. Add the eggs and tilt the uncooked egg to the outside edge of the wok. Cook until firm, then remove from the wok and roll up firmly. Cut into thin slices.

3 Place the vermicelli in a bowl, cover with boiling water and soak for 5 minutes. Drain and cut into short lengths with scissors.

4 Heat the remaining oil in the wok. Add the garlic, ginger and shrimp paste and stir-fry for 30 seconds, or until aromatic. Add the vegetables and stir-fry until tender. Add the vermicelli and stir-fry until heated through. Stir in the peanut mixture and stir-fry until well combined and heated through. Turn off the heat and gently stir in the omelette and coriander leaves and fish sauce.

5 Cut the banana leaves into 11 cm ($4^1/_2$ inch) squares and blanch them in hot water for 10–15 seconds. Hold one corner of a square down on a flat surface with your finger, then fold one side of the banana leaf across, overlapping it into a cone shape. Secure down the side through to the base with a toothpick. Repeat to make 35 cones.

6 Spoon the filling into the cones, sprinkle with the extra peanuts and serve with lime wedges.

NOTE Banana leaves are available in the fruit and vegetable section of most supermarkets or in Asian or Pacific Island stores.

MAKES 35

ARANCINI

440 g (2 cups) risotto rice (arborio, vialone nano or carnaroli)
1 egg, lightly beaten
1 egg yolk
50 g (¹/₂ cup) grated Parmesan cheese
plain (all-purpose) flour
2 eggs, lightly beaten
dry breadcrumbs, to coat
oil, for deep-frying

Meat sauce

1 dried porcini mushroom
1 tablespoon olive oil
1 onion, chopped
125 g (4¹/₂ oz) minced (ground) beef or veal
2 slices prosciutto, finely chopped
2 tablespoons tomato paste (purée)
80 ml (¹/₃ cup) white wine
¹/₂ teaspoon dried thyme leaves
3 tablespoons finely chopped parsley

1 Cook the rice in boiling water for 20 minutes, or until just soft. Drain, without rinsing and cool. Put in a large bowl and add the egg, egg yolk and Parmesan. Stir until the rice sticks together. Cover and set aside.

2 To make the meat sauce, soak the porcini in hot water for 10 minutes, then squeeze dry and chop finely. Heat the oil in a frying pan. Add the mushroom and onion and cook for 3 minutes, or until soft. Add the mince and cook, stirring, until browned. Add the prosciutto, tomato paste, wine, thyme and pepper to taste. Cook, stirring, for 5 minutes, or until all the liquid is absorbed. Stir in the parsley and set aside to cool. With wet hands, form the rice mixture into 10 balls. Wet your hands again and gently pull the balls apart. Place 3 teaspoons of the meat sauce in the centre of each. Reshape to enclose the filling. Roll in the flour, beaten egg and breadcrumbs and chill for 1 hour.

3 Fill a deep heavy-based pan one-third full of oil and heat to 180°C (350°F), or until a cube of bread browns in 15 seconds. Deep-fry the croquettes, two at a time, for 3–4 minutes, or until golden. Drain on paper towels and keep warm while cooking the rest.

INGREDIENTS

¹/₂ cup (125 ml/4 fl oz) olive oil
6 spring onions, chopped
³/₄ cup (150 g/5 oz) long-grain rice
¹/₄ cup (15 g/¹/₂ oz) chopped fresh mint
2 tablespoons chopped fresh dill
²/₃ cup (170 ml/5¹/₂ fl oz) lemon juice
¹/₄ cup (35 g/1¹/₄ oz) currants
¹/₄ cup (40 g/1¹/₄ oz) pine nuts
240 g (7¹/₂ oz) packaged vine leaves (about 50)
2 tablespoons olive oil, extra

1 Heat the oil in a medium pan. Add the spring onion and cook over medium heat for 1 minute. Stir in the rice, mint, dill, half the lemon juice, and season, to taste. Add 1 cup (250 ml/8 fl oz) water and bring to the boil, then reduce the heat, cover and simmer for 20 minutes. Remove the lid, fork through the currants and pine nuts, cover with a paper towel, then the lid and leave to cool.

2 Rinse the vine leaves and gently separate. Drain, then dry on paper towels. Trim any thick stems with scissors. Line the base of a 20 cm (8 inch) pan with any torn or misshapen leaves. Choose the larger leaves for filling and use the smaller leaves to patch up any gaps.

3 Place a leaf shiny-side-down. Spoon a tablespoon of filling into the centre, bring in the sides and roll up tightly from the stem end. Place seam-side-down, with the stem end closest to you, in the base of the pan, arranging them close together in a single layer.

4 Pour in the rest of the lemon juice, the extra oil and about ³/₄ cup (185 ml/6 fl oz) water to just cover the dolmades. Cover with an inverted plate and place a tin on the plate to firmly compress the dolmades and keep them in place while they are cooking. Cover with the lid.

5 Bring to the boil, then reduce the heat and simmer for 45 minutes. Cool in the pan. Serve at room temperature.

NOTE Store, covered with the cooking liquid, in the refrigerator for up to 2 weeks.

HERBED GRIDDLE CAKES WITH PEAR AND BLUE CHEESE TOPPING

INGREDIENTS

1 cup (125 g/4$\frac{1}{2}$ oz) self-raising flour
2 eggs, lightly beaten
$\frac{1}{2}$ cup (125 ml/4$\frac{1}{4}$ fl oz) milk
2 tablespoons finely chopped fresh parsley
2 teaspoons finely chopped fresh sage

Pear and blue cheese topping

100 g (3$\frac{1}{2}$ oz) Blue Castello or other creamy blue cheese
75 g (2$\frac{1}{2}$ oz) cream cheese
2 teaspoons brandy
1 large ripe green-skinned pear
$\frac{1}{4}$ cup (30 g/1 oz) toasted walnuts, finely chopped
$\frac{1}{2}$ lemon
30 g (1 oz) chives, cut into 3–4 cm (1–2 inch) lengths

1. Sift the flour into a bowl and make a well in the centre. Gradually add the combined eggs and milk, mixing the flour in slowly. When the flour is incorporated, add the parsley and sage and season well. Whisk until a smooth batter forms.

2. Heat a large non-stick frying pan over medium heat and spray with cooking oil spray. Drop heaped teaspoons of batter into the pan and flatten them to give 5 cm (2 inch) circles. Cook until bubbles appear in the surface of the pikelet, then turn and brown the other side. Lift out to cool on a wire rack.

3. To make the topping, beat the cheeses and brandy together until smooth. Season with pepper. Cut the pear in half and peel and core one half, then dice it into 5 mm ($\frac{1}{4}$ inch) pieces, leaving the other half untouched. Stir the diced pear and walnuts into the cheese mixture. Core the other half of the pear but do not peel it. Thinly slice the pear lengthways. Cut each slice into 2 cm (1 inch) triangles with green skin on one side. Squeeze some lemon juice over the cut surfaces to prevent discoloration.

4. Spread 1 teaspoon of topping on each pikelet. Arrange three pear triangles on top and garnish with chives.

MAKES 36

LENTIL PATTIES WITH CUMIN SKORDALIA

INGREDIENTS

1 cup (185 g/6¹/₂ oz) brown lentils
1 teaspoon cumin seeds
¹/₂ cup (90 g/3¹/₄ oz) burghul (bulgur wheat)
1 tablespoon olive oil
3 cloves garlic, crushed
4 spring onions, thinly sliced
1 teaspoon ground coriander (cilantro)
3 tablespoons chopped fresh parsley
3 tablespoons chopped fresh mint
2 eggs, lightly beaten
oil, for deep-frying

Skordalia
500 g (1 lb) floury potatoes, cut into 2 cm (1 inch) cubes
3 cloves garlic, crushed
¹/₂ teaspoon ground cumin
pinch of ground white pepper
³/₄ cup (185 ml) olive oil
2 tablespoons white vinegar

1 Place the lentils in a saucepan, add 2¹/₂ cups (625 ml/1 pint) water and bring to the boil. Reduce the heat to low and cook, covered, for 30 minutes, or until soft. Meanwhile, toast the cumin in a dry frying pan over low heat for 1–2 minutes, or until fragrant. Grind.

2 Remove the lentils from the heat and stir in the burghul. Set aside to cool.

3 Heat the oil in a frying pan and cook the garlic and spring onion for 1 minute. Add the coriander and cumin and cook for 30 seconds. Add to the lentil mixture with the parsley, mint and egg. Mix well. Chill for 30 minutes.

4 To make the skordalia, cook the potato in a saucepan of boiling water for 10 minutes, or until very soft. Drain and mash until smooth. Add the garlic, cumin, white pepper and 1 teaspoon salt. Gradually add the oil, mixing with a wooden spoon. Add the vinegar.

5 Roll tablespoons of the lentil mixture into balls, then flatten slightly. Fill a deep heavy-based saucepan or deep-fryer one-third full of oil and heat to 180°C (350°F), or until a cube of bread browns in 15 seconds. Cook the patties in batches for 1–2 minutes, or until crisp and browned. Drain on paper towels. Serve with the skordalia.

MAKES 32

SESAME BEEF SKEWERS

$^1/_2$ cup (125 ml/4$^1/_4$ oz) soy sauce
$^1/_3$ cup (80 ml/2$^3/_4$ oz) Chinese rice wine
2 cloves garlic, crushed
1 teaspoon finely grated fresh ginger
1 teaspoon sesame oil
225 g (8 oz) beef fillet, cut into 2 cm (1 inch) cubes
8 spring onions
2 tablespoons toasted sesame seeds

1 Combine the soy sauce, wine, garlic, ginger and oil, and pour over the beef. Marinate for 20 minutes. Drain, reserving the marinade.

2 Cut six of the spring onions into 24 x 3 cm (1 inch) pieces and thread a piece plus two meat cubes onto 24 skewers. Cook on a hot barbecue hotplate or chargrill pan for 5 minutes, or until cooked. Remove, sprinkle with sesame seeds and keep warm.

3 Put the reserved marinade in a saucepan and bring to the boil for 1 minute, then add 2 thinly sliced spring onions. Pour into a bowl and serve with the skewers.

MAKES 24

CHIPOLATA SAUSAGES WITH HORSERADISH CREAM

INGREDIENTS

2 tablespoons virgin olive oil
2 red onions, cut into thin wedges
2 tablespoons dark brown sugar
3 teaspoons balsamic vinegar
100 g (3$^1/_2$ oz) spreadable cream cheese
1 tablespoon horseradish cream
12 chipolata sausages
12 par-baked mini bread rolls
100 g (3$^1/_2$ oz) rocket leaves, stalks removed

1 Preheat the oven to hot 220°C (425°F/Gas 7). Heat 1$^1/_2$ tablespoons olive oil in a small pan. Add the onion and 11/2 tablespoons water, cover, and cook over medium heat for about 10 minutes, stirring occasionally, until the onion is soft and starting to brown. Stir in the sugar and vinegar and cook, uncovered, for 3 minutes, or until thick. Season and keep warm.

2 Meanwhile, in a small bowl, mix the cream cheese and horseradish cream until smooth.

3 Heat the remaining oil in a large frying pan and cook the sausages in batches over medium-low heat for 6–8 minutes, or until brown and cooked. Remove; drain on crumpled paper towels.

4 Meanwhile, heat the bread rolls according to the manufacturer's instructions. When hot, slice vertically, three-quarters of the way through, and spread with the horseradish mixture. Fill the rolls with rocket and a sausage, then onion. Serve.

NOTE If you can't get chipolatas, you can use thin sausages and twist them through the centre.

MAKES 12

STIR-FRIES

INGREDIENTS

250 g (8 oz) instant noodles
500 g (1 lb) beef, thinly sliced
2 teaspoons sesame oil
2 cloves garlic, crushed
1 tablespoon grated fresh ginger
oil, for cooking
6 spring onions, sliced on the diagonal
1 small red capsicum (pepper), thinly sliced
125 g (4 oz) snow peas (mangetout), halved on the diagonal
4 tablespoons black bean and garlic sauce (see note)
2 tablespoons hoisin sauce
$^{1}/_{2}$ cup (60 g/2 oz) bean sprouts

1   Cook the noodles according to the manufacturer's directions, then drain and keep warm.

2   Place the beef, sesame oil, garlic and ginger in a bowl and mix together well. Heat the wok until very hot, add 1 tablespoon of the oil and swirl it around to coat the side. Add half the beef and stir-fry for 2–3 minutes, or until the beef is just cooked. Remove from the wok, add a little more oil and cook the rest of the beef. Remove all the beef from the wok.

3   Heat 1 tablespoon oil in the wok. Add the spring onion, capsicum and snow peas and stir-fry for 2 minutes. Return the beef to the wok and stir in the black bean and garlic sauce, hoisin sauce and 1 tablespoon water.

4   Add the noodles to the wok and toss to heat through. Serve immediately, topped with bean sprouts.

NOTE Black bean and garlic sauce is available at Asian grocery stores or good supermarkets.

BLACK BEAN BEEF WITH NOODLES

SERVES 4

ASIAN PEPPERED BEEF

600 g (1¼ lb) skirt steak, thinly sliced
2 cloves garlic, finely chopped
2 teaspoons finely chopped fresh ginger
2 onions, thinly sliced
2 tablespoons Chinese rice wine
1 teaspoon sesame oil
1 tablespoon soy sauce
1 tablespoon oyster sauce
2 teaspoons sugar
1 teaspoon Sichuan peppercorns, crushed
1 tablespoon black peppercorns, crushed
2 spring onions, chopped into 2.5 cm (1 inch) lengths
oil, for cooking

1 Place the beef strips in a large bowl. Add the garlic, ginger, onion, rice wine, sesame oil, soy sauce, oyster sauce, sugar and peppercorns, and mix together well. Cover and marinate in the refrigerator for at least 2 hours.

2 Drain, discarding any excess liquid, and stir in the spring onion.

3 Heat the wok until very hot, add 1 tablespoon of the oil and swirl it around to coat the side. Add half the beef and stir-fry for 6 minutes, or until seared and cooked to your liking. Repeat with the rest of the beef. Serve immediately.

NOTE The wok needs to be searing hot for this recipe. The beef is easier to thinly slice if you put it in the freezer for half an hour beforehand.

SERVES 4

INGREDIENTS

oil, for cooking
500 g (1 lb) beef fillet or lean rump, thinly sliced
2 cloves garlic, crushed
¼ cup finely chopped coriander (cilantro) roots and stems
1 tablespoon grated palm sugar
⅓ cup (80 ml/2¾ fl oz) lime juice
2 tablespoons fish sauce
2 small red chillies, seeded, finely sliced
2 red Asian shallots, finely sliced
2 telegraph cucumbers, sliced into thin ribbons
1 cup (30 g/1 oz) mint leaves
1 cup (90 g/3 oz) bean sprouts
¼ cup (30 g/1 oz) chopped roasted peanuts

1   Heat the wok until very hot, add 1 tablespoon of the oil and swirl it around to coat the side. Add half the beef and cook for 1–2 minutes, or until medium rare. Remove from the wok and set aside. Repeat with the rest of the beef.

2   Place the garlic, coriander, palm sugar, lime juice, fish sauce, ¼ teaspoon ground white pepper and ¼ teaspoon salt in a bowl, and stir until all the sugar has dissolved. Add the chilli and shallots and mix well.

3   Pour the sauce over the beef while still hot, mix well, then cool to room temperature.

4   In a separate bowl, toss together the cucumber and mint leaves, and refrigerate until required.

5   Place the cucumber and mint on a serving platter, and top with the beef, bean sprouts and roasted peanuts. Serve immediately.

THAI BEEF SALAD

SERVES 6

PORK AND GREEN BEANS WITH GINGER SAUCE

³/₄ cup (185 ml/6 fl oz) soy sauce
4 tablespoons white or rice wine vinegar
1 teaspoon sugar
pinch of dried chilli flakes
3 teaspoons cornflour (cornstarch)
600 g (1¹/₄ lb) pork fillet, trimmed and cut into thin slices
2 tablespoons peanut oil
350 g (11 oz) green beans, cut into short lengths
2 cloves garlic, chopped
2 tablespoons grated fresh ginger

1 Place the soy sauce, vinegar, sugar, chilli flakes, cornflour and ¹/₃ cup (80 ml/2³/₄ fl oz) water in a bowl and mix well. Add the pork and toss to coat well.

2 Heat a wok over high heat, add half the oil and swirl to coat the side. Drain the pork, reserving the liquid, and add to the wok. Stir-fry over high heat for 1–2 minutes, or until brown. Remove the pork from the wok.

3 Heat the remaining oil, add the beans and stir-fry for 3–4 minutes. Add the garlic and ginger and stir-fry for 1 minute, or until fragrant. Return the pork and any juices to the pan and add the reserved marinade. Bring to the boil and cook, stirring, for 1–2 minutes, or until slightly thickened. Serve with steamed rice.

NOTE   Rice wine vinegar is made by oxidising beer or wine made from fermented rice starch.

INGREDIENTS

2 tablespoons oil
375 g (12 oz) pork fillet, thinly sliced
2 small red chillies, seeded and finely chopped
6 spring onions, chopped
1 tablespoon mild curry paste
2 tablespoons fish sauce
1–2 tablespoons lime juice
2 teaspoons crushed palm sugar
2 teaspoons cornflour (cornstarch)
½–1 teaspoon seasoning sauce
⅓ cup (50 g/1¾ oz) roasted unsalted cashews
shredded lime rind, to garnish

1 Heat the wok until very hot, add the oil and swirl it around to coat the side. Stir-fry the pork slices, chilli and spring onion in batches over high heat for 2 minutes, or until the pork just changes colour. Stir in the curry paste and stir-fry for 1 minute. Remove from the wok and set aside.

2 Combine the fish sauce, lime juice, sugar and cornflour with ½ cup (125 ml/4 fl oz) water. Pour into the wok and stir for 1 minute, or until heated through and slightly thickened. Return the meat to the wok and toss until heated through.

3 Stir in the seasoning sauce, to taste, and cashews. Top with the lime rind.

INGREDIENTS

2 tablespoons ghee (see note) or oil
1 onion, finely chopped
½ red capsicum (pepper), finely chopped
10 spring onions, thinly sliced
2–3 small red chillies, seeded and finely chopped
2–3 cloves garlic, finely chopped
1 tablespoon grated fresh ginger
125 g (4 oz) Chinese barbecued pork, finely chopped
6 eggs, lightly beaten
4 cups (740 g/1½ lb) cold cooked jasmine rice
1–2 teaspoons seasoning sauce
⅓ cup (20 g/¾ oz) chopped coriander (cilantro)
onion flakes, to garnish

1   Heat the wok until very hot, add the ghee and swirl it around to coat the side. Stir-fry the onion, capsicum, spring onion, chilli, garlic and ginger over medium-high heat for 2–3 minutes, or until the vegetables are cooked but not brown. Add the barbecued pork and toss to combine.

2   Reduce the heat, then pour in the beaten eggs. Season well with salt and pepper. Gently stir the egg mixture until it is creamy and almost set. Add the rice and gently stir-fry to incorporate all the ingredients and heat the mixture through.

3   Sprinkle with the seasoning sauce and stir in the coriander. Serve the savoury rice immediately, sprinkled with onion flakes.

NOTE   Ghee is a form of clarified butter. It is the main type of fat used in Indian cooking and is available in most supermarkets.

SERVES 4

SINGAPORE NOODLES

INGREDIENTS

150 g (5 oz) dried rice vermicelli
oil, for cooking
250 g (8 oz) Chinese barbecued pork, cut into small pieces
250 g (8 oz) peeled raw prawns (shrimp), cut into small pieces
2 tablespoons Madras curry powder
2 cloves garlic, crushed
100 g (3½ oz) shiitake mushrooms, thinly sliced
1 onion, thinly sliced
100 g (3½ oz) green beans, thinly sliced on the diagonal
1 tablespoon soy sauce
4 spring onions, thinly sliced on the diagonal

1 Place the vermicelli in a large bowl, cover with boiling water and soak for 5 minutes. Drain well and spread out on a clean tea towel to dry.

2 Heat the wok until very hot, add 1 tablespoon of the oil and swirl it around to coat the side. Stir-fry the barbecued pork and the prawn pieces in batches over high heat. Remove from the wok and set aside.

3 Reheat the wok, add 2 tablespoons of the oil and stir-fry the curry powder and garlic for 1–2 minutes, or until fragrant. Add the mushrooms and onion and stir-fry over medium heat for 2–3 minutes, or until the onion and mushrooms are soft.

4 Return the pork and prawns to the wok, add the beans and 2 teaspoons water, and toss to combine. Add the drained noodles, soy sauce and spring onion. Toss well and serve.

SERVES 4-6

INGREDIENTS

1.6 kg (3¹/₄ lb) Chinese broccoli, cut into short lengths
1 tablespoon peanut oil
2.5 cm (1 inch) piece fresh ginger, julienned
2 cloves garlic, crushed
500 g (1 lb) Chinese barbecue pork, thinly sliced
¹/₄ cup (60 ml/2 fl oz) chicken or vegetable stock
¹/₄ cup (60 ml/2 fl oz) oyster sauce
1 tablespoon kecap manis

1 Place the broccoli in a steamer over a wok of simmering water and cook for 5 minutes, or until just tender but still crisp.

2 Drain the wok, dry thoroughly and heat until very hot. Add the oil and swirl to coat. Add the ginger and garlic and stir-fry for 30 seconds, or until fragrant. Add the broccoli and pork and toss to coat.

3 Mix together the stock, oyster sauce and kecap manis and add to the wok. Toss thoroughly until heated through and then serve immediately.

SERVES 4

INGREDIENTS

2 cloves garlic, finely chopped
1 tablespoon finely chopped fresh ginger
$^1/_2$ teaspoon salt
1 tablespoon ground cumin
1 tablespoon ground coriander (cilantro)
1 teaspoon ground cinnamon
$^1/_2$ teaspoon ground allspice
$^1/_4$ cup (60 ml/2 fl oz) oil
600 g (1$^1/_4$ lb) lamb fillet, sliced diagonally
oil, for cooking
2 onions, thinly sliced
500 g (1 lb) English spinach, shredded
1 tablespoon lime juice
2 tablespoons toasted pine nuts

1   Combine the garlic, ginger, salt, spices and oil in a shallow glass or ceramic bowl. Add the sliced lamb and mix until well combined. Cover and refrigerate for at least 2 hours.

2   Heat the wok until very hot, and stir-fry the lamb in three batches over high heat for 2–3 minutes, or until the lamb is golden brown and just cooked. Remove the lamb from the wok and cover to keep warm.

3   Reheat the wok and add 1 tablespoon of the oil. Stir-fry the sliced onion over medium-high heat for 2–3 minutes, or until slightly softened. Add the spinach, cover and steam for 1–2 minutes, or until the spinach has just wilted. Return all the lamb and juices to the wok along with the lime juice and toasted pine nuts. Toss until thoroughly combined and season well with salt and pepper. Serve immediately.

SERVES 4

INGREDIENTS

3 teaspoons Sichuan pepper
500 g (1 lb) chicken thigh fillets, cut into strips
2 tablespoons soy sauce
1 clove garlic, crushed
1 teaspoon grated fresh ginger
3 teaspoons cornflour (cornstarch)
100 g (3½ oz) dried thin egg noodles
oil, for cooking
1 onion, sliced
1 yellow capsicum (pepper), cut into thin strips
1 red capsicum (pepper), cut into thin strips
100 g (3½ oz) sugar snap peas
¼ cup (60 ml/2 fl oz) chicken stock

1 Heat the wok until very hot and dry-fry the Sichuan pepper for 30 seconds. Remove from the wok and crush with a mortar and pestle or in a spice mill or small food processor.

2 Combine the chicken pieces with the soy sauce, garlic, ginger, cornflour and Sichuan pepper in a bowl. Cover and refrigerate for 2 hours.

3 Cook the egg noodles in boiling water for 5 minutes, or until tender. Drain, then drizzle with a little oil and toss it through the noodles to prevent them from sticking together. Set aside.

4 Heat the wok until very hot, add 1 tablespoon of the oil and swirl it around to coat the side. Stir-fry the chicken in batches over medium-high heat for 5 minutes, or until golden brown and cooked. Add more oil when necessary. Remove from the wok and set aside.

5 Reheat the wok, add 1 tablespoon of the oil and stir-fry the onion, capsicum and sugar snap peas over high heat for 2–3 minutes, or until the vegetables are tender. Add the chicken stock and bring to the boil.

6 Return the chicken and egg noodles to the wok and toss over high heat. Serve immediately.

SERVES 4

SICHUAN PEPPER CHICKEN

CHICKEN WITH WALNUTS AND STRAW MUSHROOMS

INGREDIENTS

375 g (12 oz) chicken breast fillets or tenderloins, cut into thin strips
$^{1}/_{2}$ teaspoon five-spice powder
2 teaspoons cornflour (cornstarch)
2 tablespoons soy sauce
2 tablespoons oyster sauce
2 teaspoons soft brown sugar
1 teaspoon sesame oil
oil, for cooking
75 g (2$^{1}/_{2}$ oz) walnuts
150 g (5 oz) snake beans or green beans, chopped
6 spring onions, sliced
425 g (14 oz) can straw mushrooms, rinsed
230 g (7$^{1}/_{2}$ oz) can sliced bamboo shoots, rinsed

1   Dry the chicken strips with paper towels and sprinkle with the five-spice powder. Mix the cornflour with the soy sauce in a bowl until smooth. Add $^{1}/_{2}$ cup (125 ml/4 fl oz) water along with the oyster sauce, brown sugar and sesame oil.

2   Heat the wok until very hot, add 1 tablespoon of the oil and swirl it around to coat the side. Stir-fry the walnuts for 30 seconds, or until lightly browned. Drain on paper towels.

3   Reheat the wok over high heat. Add 1 tablespoon of the oil and stir-fry the chicken in batches for 2–3 minutes, or until just cooked through. Remove all of the chicken from the wok and set aside.

4   Add the snake beans, spring onion, straw mushrooms and bamboo shoots to the wok, and stir-fry for 2 minutes. Remove from the wok. Add the soy sauce mixture and heat for 1 minute, or until slightly thickened. Return the chicken and vegetables to the wok, and toss to coat with the sauce. Season well. Serve at once, sprinkled with the stir-fried walnuts.

SERVES 4

Chilli jam

10 dried long red chillies

4 tablespoons peanut oil

1 red capsicum (pepper), chopped

1 head (50 g/1³/₄ oz) garlic, peeled and roughly chopped

200 g (7 oz) red Asian shallots, chopped

100 g (3¹/₂ oz) palm sugar, grated, or soft brown sugar

2 tablespoons tamarind purée (see note)

1 tablespoon peanut oil

6 spring onions (scallions), cut into 3 cm (1¹/₄ inch) lengths

500 g (1 lb 2 oz) chicken breast fillet, cut into slices

50 g (¹/₃ cup) roasted unsalted cashews

1 tablespoon fish sauce

15 g (¹/₂ cup) Thai basil

1   To make the chilli jam, soak the chillies in a bowl of boiling water for 15 minutes. Drain, remove the seeds and chop. Put in a food processor, then add the oil, capsicum, garlic and shallots and blend until smooth.

2   Heat a wok over medium heat and add the chilli mixture. Cook, stirring occasionally, for 15 minutes. Add the sugar and tamarind and simmer for 10 minutes, or until it darkens and reaches a jam-like consistency. Remove from the wok.

3   Clean and reheat the wok over high heat, add the oil and swirl to coat. Stir-fry the spring onion for 1 minute, then add the chicken and stir-fry for 3–5 minutes, or until golden brown and tender. Stir in the cashews, fish sauce and 4 tablespoons of the chilli jam. Stir-fry for a further 2 minutes, then stir in the basil and serve.

NOTE   Use a non-stick or stainless steel wok to cook this recipe because the tamarind purée will react with the metal in a regular wok and will taint the dish.

SERVES 4

CHICKEN WITH CHILLI JAM AND CASHEWS

INGREDIENTS

500 g (1 lb) chicken thigh fillets, cut into strips
5 cm (2 inch) piece ginger, cut into paper-thin slices
4 spring onions, thinly sliced
oil, for cooking
1 red capsicum (pepper), thinly sliced
1 tablespoon mirin
1 tablespoon lime marmalade
2 teaspoons grated lime rind
2 tablespoons lime juice

1 Put the chicken, ginger, spring onion and some ground black pepper in a dish. Toss well to combine.

2 Heat a wok until very hot, add 1 tablespoon of the oil and swirl it around to coat the side. Stir-fry the chicken mixture in three batches over high heat for about 3 minutes, or until it is golden brown and cooked through. Reheat the wok in between each batch, adding more oil when necessary. Remove all the chicken from the wok and set aside.

3 Reheat the wok, add the capsicum and stir-fry for 30 seconds. Add the mirin, marmalade, lime rind and juice, and season with salt and freshly ground black pepper. Cover and steam for 1 minute. Add the chicken and cook, uncovered, for 2 minutes, or until heated through.

SERVES 4

1 tablespoon oil
750 g lamb fillet, thinly sliced (see note)
4 cloves garlic, finely chopped
2 small fresh red chillies, thinly sliced
$^1/_3$ cup (80 ml) oyster sauce
$2^1/_2$ tablespoons fish sauce
$1^1/_2$ teaspoons sugar
$^1/_2$ cup (25 g) chopped fresh mint
$^1/_4$ cup (5 g) whole fresh mint leaves

1 Heat a wok over high heat, add the oil and swirl to coat. Add the lamb and garlic in batches and stir-fry for 1–2 minutes, or until the lamb is almost cooked. Return all the lamb to the wok. Stir in the chilli, oyster sauce, fish sauce, sugar and the chopped mint leaves, and cook for another 1–2 minutes.

2 Remove from the heat, fold in the whole mint leaves and serve immediately with rice.

NOTE Make sure you slice the lamb across the grain—this will minimise the meat breaking up and shrinking when cooking.

STIR-FRIED LAMB WITH MINT AND CHILLI

SERVES 4

NASI GORENG

INGREDIENTS

5–8 long red chillies, seeded and chopped
2 teaspoons shrimp paste
8 cloves garlic, finely chopped
oil, for cooking
2 eggs, lightly beaten
350 g (12 oz) chicken thigh fillets, cut into thin strips
200 g (6½ oz) peeled raw prawns (shrimp), deveined
8 cups (1.5 kg/3 lb) cold cooked rice (see note)
⅓ cup (80 ml/2¾ fl oz) kecap manis
⅓ cup (80 ml/2¾ fl oz) soy sauce
2 small Lebanese cucumbers, finely chopped
1 large tomato, finely chopped
lime wedges, to serve

1 Mix the chilli, shrimp paste and garlic to a paste in a food processor.

2 Heat the wok until very hot, add 1 tablespoon of the oil and swirl it around to coat the side. Add the beaten eggs and push the egg up the edges of the wok to form a large omelette. Cook for 1 minute over medium heat, or until the egg is set, then flip it over and cook the other side for 1 minute. Remove from the wok and cool before slicing into strips.

3 Reheat the wok, add 1 tablespoon of the oil and stir-fry the chicken and half the chilli paste over high heat until the chicken is just cooked. Remove the chicken from the wok.

4 Reheat the wok, add 1 tablespoon of the oil and stir-fry the prawns and the remaining chilli paste until cooked. Remove from the wok and set aside.

5 Reheat the wok, add 1 tablespoon of the oil and the rice, and toss over medium heat for 4–5 minutes to heat through. Add the kecap manis and soy sauce and toss constantly until all of the rice is coated in the sauces. Return the chicken and prawns to the wok, and toss to heat through. Season well. Transfer to a serving bowl and top with the omelette strips, cucumber and tomato. Serve with the lime wedges.

NOTE Rice should be refrigerated overnight before making fried rice to let the grains dry out and separate.

SERVES 4-6

INGREDIENTS

100 g (3¹/₂ oz) dried rice vermicelli
oil, for cooking
500 g (1 lb) chicken breast fillets, cut into thin strips
2 cloves garlic, crushed
1 teaspoon grated fresh ginger
2 teaspoons Asian-style curry powder
1 red onion, sliced
1 red capsicum (pepper), cut into short strips
2 carrots, cut into matchsticks
2 zucchini (courgette), cut into matchsticks
1 tablespoon soy sauce

1   Place the vermicelli in a large bowl, cover with boiling water and soak for 5 minutes. Drain well and place on a tea towel to dry.

2   Heat the wok until very hot, add 1 tablespoon of the oil and swirl it around to coat the side. Stir-fry the chicken in batches over high heat until browned and tender. Remove all the chicken and drain on paper towels.

3   Reheat the wok, add 1 tablespoon of the oil and stir-fry the garlic, ginger, curry powder and onion for 1–2 minutes, or until fragrant. Add the capsicum, carrot and zucchini to the wok, and stir-fry until well coated in the spices. Add 1 tablespoon water and stir-fry for 1 minute.

4   Add the drained noodles and chicken to the wok. Add the soy sauce and toss using two wooden spoons until well combined. Season well with salt and serve.

CURRY CHICKEN NOODLE STIR-FRY

SERVES 4

CHILLI PLUM BEEF

INGREDIENTS

2 tablespoons vegetable oil
600 g (1 lb 5 oz) lean beef fillet, thinly sliced across the grain
1 large red onion, cut into wedges
1 red capsicum (pepper), thinly sliced
1¹/₂ tablespoons chilli garlic sauce
125 ml (¹/₂ cup) good-quality plum sauce
1 tablespoon light soy sauce
2 teaspoons rice vinegar
good pinch of finely ground white pepper
4 spring onions (scallions), sliced on the diagonal

1   Heat a wok over high heat, then add 1 tablespoon of the oil and swirl to coat the side of
    the wok. Stir-fry the beef in two batches for 2–3 minutes each batch, or until browned and
    just cooked. Remove from the wok.

2   Heat the remaining oil in the wok, add the onion and stir-fry for 1 minute before adding
    the capsicum and continuing to stir-fry for 2–3 minutes, or until just tender. Add the chilli
    garlic sauce and stir for 1 minute, then return the meat to the wok and add the plum
    sauce, soy sauce, rice vinegar, white pepper and most of the spring onion.

3   Toss everything together for 1 minute, or until the meat is reheated. Sprinkle with the
    remaining spring onion, then serve with steamed rice or noodles.

SERVES 4

NOODLES WITH CHICKEN AND FRESH BLACK BEANS

2 teaspoons salted black beans
oil, for cooking
2 teaspoons sesame oil
500 g (1 lb) chicken thigh fillets, cut into thin strips
3 cloves garlic, very thinly sliced
4 spring onions, chopped
1 teaspoon sugar
1 red capsicum (pepper), sliced
100 g (3½ oz) green beans, cut into short pieces
300 g (10 oz) Hokkien noodles
2 tablespoons oyster sauce
1 tablespoon soy sauce

1 Rinse the black beans in running water. Drain and roughly chop.

2 Heat a wok until very hot, add 1 tablespoon of oil and the sesame oil and swirl it around to coat the side. Stir-fry the chicken in three batches, until well browned, tossing regularly. Remove from the wok and set aside.

3 Reheat the wok, add 1 tablespoon of the oil and stir-fry the garlic and spring onion for 1 minute. Add the black beans, sugar, capsicum and green beans, and cook for 1 minute. Sprinkle with 2 tablespoons of water, cover and steam for 2 minutes.

4 Gently separate the noodles and add to the wok with the chicken, oyster sauce and soy sauce, and toss well to combine. Cook, covered, for about 2 minutes, or until the noodles are just softened.

SERVES 2-3

INGREDIENTS

$^1/_2$ Chinese barbecued duck (about 500 g/1 lb), boned
1 tablespoon oil
12 spring onions, cut into short lengths
1 large carrot, cut into batons
1 tablespoon cornflour (cornstarch)
1 tablespoon honey
1 tablespoon sherry
1 tablespoon vinegar
$^1/_4$ cup (60 ml/2 fl oz) plum sauce
1 tablespoon soy sauce
12 Chinese barbecued duck pancakes, to serve

1 Remove and discard any excess fat and some of the skin from the duck. Cut the duck into bite-sized pieces. Heat the wok until very hot, add the duck pieces and cook over high heat for 3–4 minutes, or until the skin starts to become crispy. Remove the duck from the wok.

2 Reheat the wok, add the oil and swirl it around to coat the side. Stir-fry the spring onion and the carrot over medium heat for 3–4 minutes, or until the carrot has softened slightly. Combine the cornflour with the honey, sherry, vinegar, plum sauce and soy sauce. Increase the heat to high, return the duck to the wok and toss well. When the wok is very hot, add the sauce mixture and toss constantly for 2–3 minutes to coat the duck and vegetables. The sauce will begin to caramelize and reduce to form a glaze.

3 Remove the wok from the heat. Serve the stir-fried duck mixture with the pancakes, which have been steamed for 3–4 minutes or warmed in the microwave. Place a small portion of duck in the middle of each pancake, fold in the edges and roll up.

PEKING DUCK PANCAKES WITH PLUM SAUCE

SERVES 2-3

SINGAPORE PEPPER CRAB

INGREDIENTS

Stir-fry sauce
2 tablespoons dark soy sauce
2 tablespoons oyster sauce
1 tablespoon grated palm sugar or soft brown sugar

2 kg (4 lb 8 oz) blue swimmer crabs
1–2 tablespoons peanut oil
150 g (5$^1/_2$ oz) butter
2 tablespoons finely chopped garlic
1 tablespoon finely chopped ginger
1 small red chilli, seeded and finely chopped
1$^1/_2$ tablespoons ground black pepper
1 spring onion, green part only, thinly sliced on the diagonal

1 Mix the ingredients for the sauce in a small bowl or jug and set aside.

2 Wash the crabs well with a stiff brush. Pull back the apron and remove the top shell from each crab (it should come off easily). Remove the intestine and the grey feathery gills. Using a large sharp knife, cut the crab lengthways through the centre of the body to form two halves with the legs attached. Cut each half in half again, crossways. Crack the thicker part of the legs with the back of a heavy knife or crab crackers.

3 Heat a wok over high heat, add a little oil and swirl to coat. Add the crab in a few batches, stir-frying over very high heat for 4 minutes each batch, or until the shells turn bright orange, adding more oil if needed. Remove from the wok. Reduce the heat to medium-high, add the butter, garlic, ginger, chilli and pepper and stir-fry for 30 seconds, then add the stir-fry sauce and simmer for 1 minute, or until glossy.

4 Return the crab to the wok, cover, stirring every minute for 4 minutes, or until cooked. Sprinkle with the spring onion and serve with rice. Provide bowls of warm water with lemon slices for rinsing sticky fingers.

SERVES 4

INGREDIENTS

1 Chinese barbecued duck (about 1 kg/2 lb), boned
1 tablespoon oil
1 onion, sliced
2 cloves garlic, crushed
2 teaspoons grated fresh ginger
1 tablespoon orange rind
$^2/_3$ cup (170 ml/5$^1/_2$ fl oz) orange juice
$^1/_4$ cup (60 ml/2 fl oz) chicken stock
2 teaspoons soft brown sugar
2 teaspoons cornflour (cornstarch)
1.5 kg (3 lb) baby bok choy, leaves separated
1 orange, segmented

1 Cut the duck meat into pieces. Reserve and thinly slice some crispy skin for garnish. Heat the wok until very hot, add the oil and swirl it around to coat the side. Stir-fry the onion for 3 minutes, or until tender. Stir in the garlic and ginger for 1–2 minutes. Pour in the combined orange rind, juice, stock and sugar. Bring to the boil.

2 Mix the cornflour with a little water to form a paste. Pour into the wok, stirring until the mixture boils and thickens. Place the duck pieces in the sauce and simmer for 1–2 minutes, or until heated through. Remove from the wok and keep warm.

3 Place the bok choy in the wok with 2 tablespoons water. Cover and steam until just wilted. Arrange on a serving plate, spoon the duck mixture over the top and garnish with the orange segments and the crispy duck skin.

DUCK AND ORANGE STIR-FRY

SERVES 4

INGREDIENTS

60 ml ($^1/_4$ cup) kecap manis
2$^1/_2$ teaspoons sambal oelek
2 garlic cloves, crushed
$^1/_2$ teaspoon ground coriander (cilantro)
1 tablespoon grated palm sugar or soft brown sugar
1 teaspoon sesame oil
400 g (14 oz) beef fillet, partially frozen, thinly sliced
1 tablespoon peanut oil
2 tablespoons chopped roasted peanuts
3 tablespoons chopped coriander (cilantro) leaves

1   Combine the kecap manis, sambal oelek, garlic, ground coriander, palm sugar, sesame oil and 2 tablespoons water in a large bowl. Add the beef slices and coat well. Cover with plastic wrap and refrigerate for 20 minutes.

2   Heat a wok over high heat, add the peanut oil and swirl to coat. Add the meat in batches and cook each batch for 2–3 minutes, or until browned.

3   Arrange the beef on a serving platter, sprinkle with the chopped peanuts and coriander and serve with steamed rice.

SERVES 4

GARLIC AND GINGER PRAWNS

INGREDIENTS

2 tablespoons oil
1 kg (2 lb) raw king prawns (shrimp), peeled, deveined and butterflied, tails left intact
3-4 cloves garlic, finely chopped
5 cm (2 inch) piece fresh ginger, cut into matchsticks
2-3 small red chillies, seeded and finely chopped
6 coriander (cilantro) roots, finely chopped, plus a few leaves to garnish
8 spring onions, cut into short lengths
½ red capsicum (pepper), thinly sliced
2 tablespoons lemon juice
½ cup (125 ml/4 fl oz) white wine
2 teaspoons crushed palm sugar
2 teaspoons fish sauce

1 Heat the wok until very hot, add the oil and swirl to coat. Stir-fry the prawns, garlic, ginger, chilli and coriander root in two batches for 1–2 minutes over high heat, or until the prawns turn pink. Remove all the prawns from the wok and set aside.

2 Add the spring onion and capsicum to the wok. Cook over high heat for 2–3 minutes. Add the lemon juice, wine and palm sugar. Cook until the liquid has reduced by two thirds.

3 Add the prawns and sprinkle with fish sauce. Toss to heat through. Garnish with coriander to serve.

SERVES 4

QUICK THAI CHICKEN

1 tablespoon red curry paste

2 tablespoons oil

2 tablespoons fish sauce

2 tablespoons lime juice

$^1/_4$ cup (15 g/$^1/_2$ oz) chopped coriander (cilantro) leaves

1 tablespoon grated fresh ginger

1 teaspoon caster sugar

1 teaspoon sesame oil

750 g (1$^1/_2$ lb) chicken thigh fillets, cut into strips

1 tablespoon oil, extra

10 spring onions, cut into short lengths

100 g (3$^1/_2$ oz) snow peas (mangetout), trimmed

1 Whisk together the curry paste, oil, fish sauce, lime juice, coriander, ginger, sugar and sesame oil in a large non-metallic bowl. Add the chicken strips and toss to coat thoroughly.

2 Heat the extra oil in a wok. Add the chicken in batches and stir-fry for 3–5 minutes, or until browned all over, then remove from the wok and set aside. Add the spring onion and snow peas and stir-fry for 2 minutes. Return the chicken and any juices to the wok and stir-fry for 2–3 minutes, or until the chicken is heated through. Season with salt and pepper and serve.

SPICY CELLOPHANE NOODLES WITH MINCED PORK

200 g (7 oz) minced (ground) pork
1 teaspoon cornflour (cornstarch)
1¹/₂ tablespoons light soy sauce
2 tablespoons Chinese rice wine
1 teaspoon sesame oil
150 g (5¹/₂ oz) cellophane noodles (mung bean vermicelli)
2 tablespoons oil
4 spring onions (scallions), finely chopped
1 garlic clove, crushed
1 tablespoon finely chopped ginger
2 teaspoons chilli bean sauce
185 ml (³/₄ cup) chicken stock
¹/₂ teaspoon sugar
2 spring onions (scallions), green part only, extra, thinly sliced on the diagonal

1 Combine the mince, cornflour, 1 tablespoon of the soy sauce, 1 tablespoon of the rice wine and ¹/₂ teaspoon of the sesame oil in a bowl, using a fork or your fingers. Cover with plastic wrap and marinate for 10–15 minutes.

2 Meanwhile, place the noodles in a heatproof bowl, cover with boiling water and soak for 3–4 minutes, or until softened. Drain well.

3 Heat a wok over high heat, add the oil and swirl to coat. Cook the spring onion, garlic, ginger and chilli bean sauce for 10 seconds, then add the mince mixture and cook for 2 minutes, stirring to break up any lumps. Stir in the stock, sugar, ¹/₂ teaspoon salt, and the remaining soy sauce, rice wine and sesame oil.

4 Add the noodles to the wok and toss to combine. Bring to the boil, then reduce the heat to low and simmer, stirring occasionally, for 7–8 minutes, or until the liquid is almost completely absorbed. Garnish with the extra spring onion and serve.

SERVES 4

INGREDIENTS

500 g (1 lb) squid tubes
1 tablespoon finely chopped fresh ginger
2–3 teaspoons finely chopped red chilli
3 cloves garlic, finely chopped
¼ cup (60 ml/2 fl oz) oil
2 onions, thinly sliced
500 g (1 lb) baby bok choy, roughly chopped

1　Wash the squid well and dry with paper towels. Cut into 1 cm (½ inch) rings and place in a bowl with the ginger, chilli, garlic and oil. Toss well. Cover and refrigerate for 2–3 hours.

2　Heat the wok until very hot and stir-fry the squid rings over high heat in three batches for 1–2 minutes, reserving the marinade. Remove from the wok as soon as the squid turns white. Keep the wok very hot and don't cook the squid for too long or it will toughen. Remove all the squid from the wok.

3　Pour the reserved marinade into the wok and bring to the boil. Add the onion and cook over medium heat for 3–4 minutes, or until slightly softened. Add the bok choy, cover and steam for 2 minutes, or until wilted. Add the squid and toss. Serve immediately.

MARINATED CHILLI SQUID

SERVES 4

INGREDIENTS

2 garlic cloves, crushed

2 teaspoons grated ginger

1 teaspoon five-spice powder

1/4 teaspoon ground white pepper

2 tablespoons Chinese rice wine

1 teaspoon sugar

1 kg (2 lb 4 oz) boneless lamb shoulder, trimmed and cut
   into 3 cm (1 1/4 inch) pieces

30 g (1 oz) whole dried Chinese mushrooms

1 tablespoon peanut oil

1 large onion, cut into wedges

2 cm (3/4 inch) piece ginger, julienned

1 teaspoon Sichuan peppercorns, crushed or ground

2 tablespoons sweet bean paste

1 teaspoon black peppercorns, ground and toasted

500 ml (2 cups) chicken stock

60 ml (1/4 cup) oyster sauce

2 star anise

60 ml (1/4 cup) Chinese rice wine, extra

80 g (2 3/4 oz) can sliced bamboo shoots, drained

100 g (3 1/2 oz) can water chestnuts, drained and sliced

400 g (14 oz) fresh rice noodles, cut into 2 cm (3/4 inch)
   wide strips

1 spring onion (scallion), sliced on the diagonal

1   Combine the garlic, grated ginger, five-spice powder, white pepper, rice wine, sugar and 1 teaspoon salt in a large bowl. Add the lamb and toss to coat. Cover and marinate for 2 hours.

2   Meanwhile, soak the mushrooms in boiling water for 20 minutes. Drain. Discard the stems and slice the caps.

3   Heat a wok over high heat, add the oil and swirl to coat. Stir-fry the onion, julienned ginger and Sichuan pepper for 2 minutes. Cook the lamb in three batches, stir-frying for 2–3 minutes each batch, or until starting to brown. Stir in the bean paste and ground peppercorns and cook for 3 minutes, or until the lamb is brown. Add the stock and transfer to a 2 litre (8 cup) flameproof clay pot or casserole dish. Stir in the oyster sauce, star anise and extra rice wine and simmer, covered, over low heat for 1 hours, or until the lamb is tender. Stir in the bamboo shoots and water chestnuts and cook for 20 minutes. Add the mushrooms.

4   Cover the noodles with boiling water and gently separate. Drain and rinse, then add to the hotpot, stirring for 1–2 minutes, or until heated through. Sprinkle with the spring onion.

SERVES 4

1$^1/_2$ tablespoons oil
8 spring onions (scallions), cut into pieces
3 garlic cloves, crushed
8 cm (3 in) piece ginger, finely shredded
2 skinless chicken breasts, cut into strips
2 red capsicums (peppers), cut into strips
150 g (5$^1/_2$ oz) snow peas (mangetout)
100 g (3$^1/_2$ oz) cashews
2 tablespoons soy sauce
1$^1/_2$ teaspoons sesame oil

1 Heat the oil in a wok until it is smoking — this will only take a few seconds. Add the spring onion, garlic and ginger and stir them around for a few seconds. Next, add the chicken and stir it around until it has all turned white. Add the red capsicum and keep stirring, then throw in the snow peas and cashews and stir-fry for another minute or so.

2 Once the red capsicum has started to soften a little, add the soy sauce and sesame oil, toss everything together and then tip the stir-fry out into a serving dish.

3 Serve with rice or noodles and more soy sauce if you like.

STIR-FRIED CHICKEN WITH GINGER AND CASHEWS

SERVES 4

SICHUAN PRAWNS WITH SNOW PEAS

INGREDIENTS

2 teaspoons Sichuan pepper
750 g (1½ lb) raw prawns (shrimp) , peeled and deveined,
   tails intact
2 tablespoons grated fresh ginger
3 cloves garlic, finely chopped
2 tablespoons Chinese rice wine or dry sherry
oil, for cooking
2 eggs, lightly beaten
½ red capsicum (pepper), cut into strips
½ green capsicum (pepper), cut into strips
4 spring onions, cut into pieces
100 g (3½ oz) snow peas (mangetout)
½ teaspoon salt
75 g (2½ oz) roasted unsalted peanuts, roughly chopped
50 g (1¾ oz) snow pea (mangetout) sprouts

1   Heat the wok until very hot and dry-fry the Sichuan pepper until it is fragrant. Remove from the wok and crush with a mortar and pestle or in a spice grinder.

2   Combine the prawns with the Sichuan pepper, ginger, garlic and wine in a glass or ceramic dish. Cover and refrigerate for 20 minutes.

3   Heat the wok until very hot, add 1½ tablespoons of the oil and swirl it around to coat the side. Dip three or four prawns in the beaten eggs, then stir-fry for about 1 minute, or until the prawns just change colour and are cooked. Remove from the wok. Repeat with the remaining prawns, reheating the wok to very hot for each batch and adding a little oil when needed. Remove the prawns from the wok.

4   Add the capsicum, spring onion, snow peas and salt to the wok. Stir-fry for 2 minutes, or until the vegetables are just crisp and tender.

5   Return the prawns to the wok with the peanuts and toss gently to combine. Serve immediately on a bed of snow pea sprouts.

    SERVES 4

500 g (1 lb 2 oz) hokkien (egg) noodles

60 ml ($^1/_4$ cup) peanut oil

20 scallops, roe and beards removed

1 large onion, cut into thin wedges

3 garlic cloves, crushed

1 tablespoon grated ginger

1 tablespoon chilli bean paste

150 g (5$^1/_2$ oz) choy sum, cut into 5 cm (2 inch) lengths

60 ml ($^1/_4$ cup) chicken stock

2 tablespoons light soy sauce

2 tablespoons kecap manis

15 g ($^1/_2$ cup) coriander (cilantro) leaves

90 g (1 cup) bean sprouts

1 long red chilli, seeded and finely sliced

1 teaspoon sesame oil

1 tablespoon Chinese rice wine

1 Place the hokkien noodles in a heatproof bowl, cover with boiling water and soak for 1 minute until tender and separated. Drain, rinse under cold water, then drain again.

2 Heat a wok over high heat, add 2 tablespoons of the peanut oil and swirl to coat the side of the wok. Add the scallops in batches and sear for 20 seconds each side, or until sealed. Remove, then wipe the wok clean. Add the remaining oil and swirl to coat. Stir-fry the onion for 2 minutes, or until softened. Add the garlic and ginger and cook for 30 seconds. Stir in the chilli bean paste and cook for 1 minute, or until fragrant.

3 Add the choy sum to the wok with the noodles, stock, soy sauce and kecap manis. Stir-fry for 2–3 minutes, or until the choy sum has wilted and the noodles have absorbed most of the liquid. Return the scallops to the wok, add the coriander, bean sprouts, chilli, sesame oil and rice wine, tossing gently until combined.

SEARED SCALLOPS WITH CHILLI BEAN PASTE

SERVES 4

STIR-FRIED LAMB WITH MINT, CHILLI AND SHANGHAI NOODLES

400 g (14 oz) Shanghai noodles
1 teaspoon sesame oil
2 tablespoons peanut oil
220 g ($^1/_2$ lb) lamb fillet, cut into thin strips
2 cloves garlic, crushed
2 fresh red chillies, seeded and finely sliced
1 tablespoon oyster sauce
2 teaspoons palm sugar
2 tablespoons fish sauce
2 tablespoons lime juice
$^1/_2$ cup (10 g/$^1/_3$ oz) fresh mint, chopped
lime wedges, to garnish

1 Cook the noodles in a large saucepan of boiling water for 4–5 minutes. Drain, then rinse in cold water. Add the sesame oil and toss through.

2 Heat the peanut oil in a wok over high heat. Add the lamb and cook in batches for 1–2 minutes, or until just browned. Return all the meat to the wok and add the garlic and chilli. Cook for 30 seconds then add the oyster sauce, palm sugar, fish sauce, lime juice and noodles. Cook for another 2–3 minutes, or until the noodles are warm. Stir in the mint and serve immediately with the lime wedges.

SERVES 4-6

INGREDIENTS

3 bird's eye chillies, seeded and finely chopped
3 garlic cloves, crushed
2 tablespoons fish sauce
1 teaspoon grated palm sugar or soft brown sugar
2 tablespoons peanut or vegetable oil
400 g (14 oz) lean beef fillet, thinly sliced across the grain
150 g (5¹/₂ oz) snake beans, sliced into 3 cm (1¹/₄ inch) lengths
30 g (1 cup) Thai basil
thinly sliced bird's eye chilli, to garnish

1   Combine the chilli, garlic, fish sauce, palm sugar and 1 tablespoon of the oil in a
    large non-metallic bowl. Add the beef, toss well, then cover and marinate in the fridge
    for 2 hours.

2   Heat a wok to hot, add 2 teaspoons of the oil and swirl to coat. Stir-fry the beef in two
    batches over high heat for 2 minutes each batch, or until just browned. Remove from
    the wok.

3   Heat the remaining oil in the wok, then add the snake beans and 60 ml (¹/₄ cup) water
    and cook over high heat for 3–4 minutes, tossing regularly, until tender. Return the beef to
    the wok with the basil. Cook for a further 1–2 minutes, or until warmed through. Garnish
    with chilli and serve.

SERVES 4

PRAWNS WITH SPICY TAMARIND SAUCE

INGREDIENTS

¹/₂ cup (80 g/3 oz) raw cashew nuts
1¹/₄ cups (250 g/9 oz) jasmine rice
2 garlic cloves, finely chopped
1¹/₂ tablespoons fish sauce
1 tablespoon sambal oelek
1 tablespoon peanut oil
1 kg (2 lb) raw medium prawns (shrimp), peeled and deveined with tails intact
2 teaspoons tamarind concentrate
1¹/₂ tablespoons grated palm sugar
350 g choy sum, cut into 10 cm lengths

1 Preheat the oven to moderate 180°C (350°F/Gas 4). Spread the cashews on a baking tray and bake for 5–8 minutes, or until light golden—watch carefully, as they burn easily.

2 Meanwhile, bring a large saucepan of water to the boil. Add the rice and cook for 12 minutes, stirring occasionally. Drain well.

3 Place the garlic, fish sauce, sambal oelek and toasted cashews in a blender or food processor, adding 2–3 tablespoons of water, if needed, and blend to a rough paste.

4 Heat a wok until very hot, add the oil and swirl to coat. Add the prawns, toss for 1–2 minutes, or until starting to turn pink. Remove from the wok. Add the cashew paste and stir-fry for 1 minute, or until it starts to brown slightly. Add the tamarind, sugar and about ¹/₃ cup (80 ml) water, then bring to the boil, stirring well. Return the prawns to the wok and stir to coat. Cook for 2–3 minutes, or until the prawns are cooked through.

5 Place the choy sum in a paper-lined bamboo steamer and steam over a wok or saucepan of simmering water for 3 minutes, or until tender. Serve with the prawns and rice.

SERVES 4

STIR-FRIED SCALLOPS WITH SUGAR SNAP PEAS

2 tablespoons oil
2 large cloves garlic, crushed
3 teaspoons finely chopped fresh ginger
300 g sugar snap peas
500 g scallops without roe, membrane removed
2 spring onions, cut into 2 cm (1 inch) lengths
2$^1/_2$ tablespoons oyster sauce
2 teaspoons soy sauce
$^1/_2$ teaspoon sesame oil
2 teaspoons sugar

1 Heat a wok over medium heat, add the oil and swirl to coat the surface of the wok. Add the garlic and ginger, and stir-fry for 30 seconds, or until fragrant.

2 Add the peas to the wok and cook for 1 minute, then add the scallops and spring onion and cook for 1 minute, or until the spring onion is wilted. Stir in the oyster and soy sauces, sesame oil and sugar and heat for 1 minute, or until warmed through. Serve with rice.

SERVES 4

INGREDIENTS

1 tablespoon peanut oil
2 cloves garlic, crushed
1 tablespoon finely grated fresh ginger
2 tablespoons finely chopped lemon grass, white part only
8 spring onions, cut into short lengths
1 kg (2 lb) raw prawns (shrimp), peeled, deveined, tails intact
2 tablespoons lime juice
1 tablespoon soft brown sugar
2 teaspoons fish sauce
$^{1}/_{4}$ cup (60 ml/2 fl oz) chicken stock
1 teaspoon cornflour (cornstarch)
500 g (1 lb) baby bok choy, cut in half lengthways
$^{1}/_{4}$ cup (15 g/$^{1}/_{2}$ oz) chopped mint

1 Heat a wok until very hot, add the oil and swirl to coat. Add the garlic, ginger, lemon grass and spring onion, and stir-fry for 1 minute, or until fragrant. Add the prawns and stir-fry for 2 minutes.

2 Place the lime juice, sugar, fish sauce, chicken stock and cornflour in a small bowl. Mix well, then add to the wok and stir until the sauce boils and thickens. Cook for a further 1–2 minutes, or until the prawns are pink and just tender.

3 Add the bok choy and stir-fry for 1 minute, or until wilted. Stir in the mint and serve.

LEMON GRASS PRAWNS

SERVES 4

LAMB WITH HOKKIEN NOODLES AND SOUR SAUCE

INGREDIENTS

450 g (1 lb) hokkien (egg) noodles (see note)
2 tablespoons vegetable oil
375 g (13 oz) lamb backstrap, thinly sliced against the grain
70 g (2$^1/_2$ oz) red Asian shallots, peeled and thinly sliced
3 garlic cloves, crushed
2 teaspoons finely chopped ginger
1 small red chilli, seeded and finely chopped
1$^1/_2$ tablespoons red curry paste
125 g (4$^1/_2$ oz) snow peas (mangetout), trimmed and cut in half on the diagonal
1 small carrot, julienned
125 ml ($^1/_2$ cup) chicken stock
15 g ($^1/_2$ oz) palm sugar, grated, or soft brown sugar
1 tablespoon lime juice
small whole basil leaves, to garnish

1 Put the noodles in a bowl, cover with boiling water and soak for 1 minute. Drain and set aside.

2 Heat 1 tablespoon of the oil in a wok and swirl to coat the side. Stir-fry the lamb in batches over high heat for 2–3 minutes, or until it just changes colour. Remove to a side plate.

3 Add the remaining oil, then the shallots, garlic, ginger and chilli and stir-fry for 1–2 minutes. Stir in the curry paste and cook for 1 minute. Add the snow peas, carrot and the lamb and combine. Cook over high heat, tossing often, for 1–2 minutes.

4 Add the stock, palm sugar and lime juice, toss to combine and cook for 2–3 minutes. Add the noodles and cook for 1 minute, or until heated through. Divide among serving bowls and garnish with the basil.

NOTE Hokkien noodles are thick, fresh egg noodles that have been cooked and lightly oiled before packaging. They are usually sold vacuum packed.

SERVES 4-6

INGREDIENTS

1 1/2 cups (300 g/10 1/2 oz) long-grain rice
3 cloves garlic, finely chopped
1 tablespoon grated fresh ginger
4 stems lemon grass (white part only), finely chopped
2 1/2 tablespoons oil
600 g (21 oz) lean rump steak, trimmed and sliced thinly across the grain
1 tablespoon lime juice
1–2 tablespoons fish sauce
2 tablespoons kecap manis
1 large red onion, cut into small wedges
200 g (7 oz) green beans, sliced on the diagonal into 5 cm (2 inches) lengths

1 Bring a large saucepan of water to the boil. Add the rice and cook for 12 minutes, stirring occasionally. Drain well.

2 Meanwhile, combine the garlic, ginger, lemon grass and 2 teaspoons of the oil in a non-metallic bowl. Add the beef, then marinate for 10 minutes. Combine the lime juice, fish sauce and kecap manis.

3 Heat a wok until very hot, add 1 tablespoon oil and swirl to coat. Stir-fry the beef in batches for 2–3 minutes, or until browned. Remove from the wok.

4 Reheat the wok to very hot, heat the remaining oil, then add the onion and stir-fry for 2 minutes. Add the beans and cook for another 2 minutes, then return the beef to the wok. Pour in the fish sauce mixture and cook until heated through. Serve with the rice.

SERVES 4

HOT AND SWEET CHICKEN

125 ml ($^1/_2$ cup/4 oz) rice vinegar

160 g ($^2/_3$ cup/5$^1/_2$ oz) caster (superfine) sugar

6 garlic cloves, crushed

a large pinch of chilli flakes

1 teaspoon ground coriander (cilantro)

1 teaspoon ground white pepper

2 bunches coriander (cilantro), finely chopped, including roots and stems

3 tablespoons olive oil

2 tablespoons lemon juice

8 boneless and skinless chicken thighs, cut in half

2 tablespoons caster (superfine) sugar, extra

2 tablespoons fish sauce

1 small cucumber, peeled and sliced

1 Put the vinegar and sugar in a small saucepan, bring to the boil, then turn down the heat and simmer for a minute. Take the mixture off the heat and add two crushed garlic cloves, the chilli flakes and a pinch of salt. Leave the dressing to cool.

2 Heat a small frying pan for a minute, add the ground coriander and white pepper and stir it around for a minute. This will make the spices more fragrant. Add the rest of the garlic, the fresh coriander and a pinch of salt. Add 2 tablespoons of the oil and all the lemon juice and mix to a paste. Rub this all over the chicken pieces.

3 Heat the rest of the oil in a wok, add the chicken and fry it on both sides for 8 minutes, or until it is cooked through. Sprinkle in the extra sugar and the fish sauce and cook for another minute or two until any excess liquid has evaporated and the chicken pieces are sticky. Serve the chicken with the sliced cucumber and some rice. Dress with the sauce.

INGREDIENTS

1¹/₂ tablespoons peanut oil
1 large onion, finely chopped
2 garlic cloves, finely chopped
2 x 2 cm (³/₄ x ³/₄ inch) piece ginger, shredded
500 g (1 lb 2 oz) chicken thigh fillets, trimmed and cut into 2 cm (³/₄ inch) pieces
175 g (6 oz) Chinese cabbage, shredded
1 carrot, julienned
200 g (7 oz) Chinese barbecued pork (char sui), cut into 5 mm (¹/₄ inch) thick pieces
3 teaspoons Chinese rice wine
2 teaspoons sugar
150 g (5¹/₂ oz) snow peas (mangetout), trimmed
375 ml (1¹/₂ cups) chicken stock
1 tablespoon light soy sauce
225 g (8 oz) pancit canton (or Chinese e-fu) noodles (see note)
1 lemon, cut into wedges

1 Heat a wok over high heat, add the oil and swirl to coat. Add the onion and cook for 2 minutes, then add the garlic and ginger and cook for 1 minute. Add the chicken and cook for 2–3 minutes, or until browned. Stir in the cabbage, carrot, pork, rice wine and sugar and cook for a further 3–4 minutes, or until the pork is heated and the vegetables are soft. Add the snow peas and cook for 1 minute. Remove the mixture from the wok.

2 Add the chicken stock and soy sauce to the wok and bring to the boil. Add the noodles and cook, stirring, for 3–4 minutes, or until soft and almost cooked through.

3 Return the stir-fry mixture to the wok and toss with the noodles for 1 minute, or until combined. Divide among four warmed serving dishes and garnish with lemon wedges.

NOTE Pancit canton noodles are used mostly in the Philippines and China, where they are called 'birthday' or 'long-life' noodles — their length denotes a long life for those who eat them. These round cakes of pre-boiled, deep-fried noodles are delicate and break easily. They are available in Asian grocery stores.

SWEET CHILLI PRAWNS

1 kg (2 lb) raw medium prawns (shrimp)
2 tablespoons peanut oil
1 cm x 3 cm ($^1/_2$ inch x 1 inch) piece fresh ginger, cut into julienne strips
2 cloves garlic, finely chopped
5 spring onions, cut into 3 cm lengths
$^1/_3$ cup (80 ml/2$^3/_4$ oz) chilli garlic sauce
2 tablespoons tomato sauce
2 tablespoons Chinese rice wine
1 tablespoon Chinese black vinegar or rice vinegar
1 tablespoon soy sauce
1 tablespoon soft brown sugar
1 teaspoon cornflour (cornstarch) mixed with $^1/_2$ cup (125 ml/4 oz) water
finely chopped spring onion, to garnish

1 Peel and devein the prawns, leaving the tails intact. Heat a wok until very hot, then add the oil and swirl to coat the side. Heat over high heat until smoking, then quickly add the ginger, garlic and spring onion and stir-fry for 1 minute. Add the prawns and cook for 2 minutes, or until they are just pink and starting to curl. Remove the prawns from the wok with tongs or a slotted spoon.

2 Put the chilli garlic sauce, tomato sauce, rice wine, vinegar, soy sauce, sugar and cornflour paste in a small jug and whisk together. Pour the sauce into the wok and cook, stirring, for 1–2 minutes, or until it thickens slightly. Return the prawns to the wok for 1–2 minutes, or until heated and cooked through. Garnish with the finely chopped spring onion. Serve immediately with rice or thin egg noodles.

NOTE Chinese rice wine has a rich sweetish taste. Use dry sherry if unavailable. Chinese black vinegar is made from rice and has a sweet, mild taste. It is available in Asian food stores.

SERVES 4

350 g (12^1/$_2$ oz) pork fillet
^{1}/$_3$ cup (80 ml/2^3/$_4$ fl oz) soy sauce
^{1}/$_4$ cup (60 ml/ 2 fl oz) mirin
2 teaspoons grated fresh ginger
2 cloves garlic, crushed
1^1/$_2$ tablespoons soft brown sugar
500 g (17^1/$_2$ oz) Hokkien noodles
2 tablespoons peanut oil
1 onion, cut into thin wedges
1 red capsicum (pepper), cut into thin strips
2 carrots, finely sliced on the diagonal
4 spring onions, finely sliced on the diagonal
200 g fresh shiitake mushrooms, sliced

1 Trim the pork of any excess fat or sinew and slice thinly. Combine the soy sauce, mirin, ginger, garlic and sugar in a large non-metallic bowl, add the pork and coat. Cover with plastic wrap and refrigerate for 10 minutes.

2 Meanwhile, place the noodles in a bowl of hot water for 5 minutes to separate and soften.

3 Heat a large wok over high heat, add 1 tablespoon oil and swirl to coat. Drain the pork, reserving the marinade, and stir-fry in batches for 3 minutes, or until browned. Remove and keep warm.

4 Reheat the wok over high heat, add the remaining oil and swirl to coat. Add the onion, capsicum and carrot, and stir-fry for 2–3 minutes, or until just tender, then add the spring onion and shiitake mushrooms. Cook for another 2 minutes, then return the pork to the wok. Drain the noodles and add to the wok with the reserved marinade. Toss to combine and cook for another 1 minute, or until heated through, then serve.

JAPANESE PORK AND NOODLE STIR-FRY

SERVES 4

INGREDIENTS

1 tablespoon jasmine rice
2 teaspoons oil
400 g (14 oz) minced (ground) chicken
2 tablespoons fish sauce
1 stem lemon grass, white part only, finely chopped
$^1/_3$ cup (80 ml/2$^3/_4$ fl oz) chicken stock
3 tablespoons lime juice
4 spring onions, finely sliced on the diagonal
4 red Asian shallots, sliced
$^1/_2$ cup (25 g/$^3/_4$ oz) finely chopped fresh coriander (cilantro)
   leaves
$^1/_2$ cup (25 g/$^3/_4$ oz) shredded fresh mint
200 g (7 oz) lettuce leaves, shredded
$^1/_4$ cup (40 g) chopped roasted unsalted peanuts
1 small fresh red chilli, sliced
lime wedges, to serve

1 Heat a frying pan. Add the rice and dry-fry over low heat for 3 minutes, or until lightly golden. Grind in a mortar and pestle to a fine powder.

2 Heat a wok over medium heat. Add the oil and mince and cook for 4 minutes, or until it changes colour, breaking up any lumps. Add the fish sauce, lemon grass and stock and cook for a further 10 minutes. Cool.

3 Add the lime juice, spring onion, Asian shallots, coriander, mint and ground rice. Mix well.

4 Arrange the lettuce on a serving platter and top with the chicken mixture. Sprinkle with the nuts and chilli, and serve with lime wedges.

SERVES 6

ONE-POTS

INGREDIENTS

Chicken balls
500 g (1 lb 2 oz) minced (ground) chicken
1 small red chilli, finely chopped
2 garlic cloves, finely chopped
1/2 small red onion, finely chopped
1 stem lemon grass (white part only), finely chopped
2 tablespoons chopped coriander (cilantro) leaves

200 g (7 oz) dried rice vermicelli
1 tablespoon peanut oil
75 g (1/4 cup) good-quality laksa paste
1 litre (4 cups) chicken stock
500 ml (2 cups) coconut milk
8 fried tofu puffs, cut in half on the diagonal
90 g (1 cup) bean sprouts
2 tablespoons shredded Vietnamese mint
3 tablespoons shredded coriander (cilantro) leaves
lime wedges, to serve
fish sauce, to serve (optional)

1 To make the balls, process all the ingredients in a food processor until just combined. Roll tablespoons of mixture into balls with wet hands.

2 Place the vermicelli in a heatproof bowl, cover with boiling water and soak for 6–7 minutes. Drain well.

3 Heat the oil in a large saucepan over medium heat. Add the laksa paste and cook for 1–2 minutes, or until aromatic. Add the stock, reduce the heat and simmer for 10 minutes. Add the coconut milk and the chicken balls and simmer for 5 minutes, or until the balls are cooked through.

4 Divide the vermicelli, tofu puffs and bean sprouts among four serving bowls and ladle the soup over the top, dividing the balls evenly. Garnish with the mint and coriander leaves. Serve with the lime wedges and, if desired, fish sauce.

SERVES 4

LION'S HEAD MEATBALLS

INGREDIENTS

Chicken stock
1.5 kg (3 lb) chicken bones (chicken necks, backs, wings), washed
2 slices fresh ginger, cut into 1 cm (½ inch) thick slices
4 spring onions

6 dried Chinese mushrooms
100 g (3½ oz) mung bean vermicelli
600 g (1¼ lb) minced (ground) pork
1 egg white
4 cloves garlic, finely chopped
1 tablespoon finely grated fresh ginger
1 tablespoon cornflour (cornstarch)
1½ tablespoons Chinese rice wine
6 spring onions, thinly sliced
2 tablespoons peanut oil
¼ cup (60 ml/2 fl oz) light soy sauce
1 teaspoon sugar
400 g (13 oz) bok choy, halved lengthways, leaves separated

1 To make the stock, place the bones and 3.5 litres (15 cups) water in a large saucepan and bring to a simmer—do not let it boil. Remove the scum from the surface and continue doing so over the next 30 minutes. Add the ginger and spring onions, and cook, partially covered, keeping at a low simmer for 3 hours. Strain through a fine sieve. Cool. Cover and refrigerate overnight. Remove the layer of fat from the surface once it has solidified.

2 Soak the Chinese mushrooms in 1 cup (250 ml/8 fl oz) boiling water for 20 minutes. Drain. Discard the stems and thinly slice the caps. Meanwhile, place the vermicelli in a heatproof bowl, cover with boiling water and soak for 3–4 minutes, or until soft. Drain and rinse. Preheat the oven to hot 220°C (425°F/Gas 7).

3 Place the mince, egg white, garlic, ginger, cornflour, rice wine, two-thirds of the spring onion and salt, to taste, in a food processor. Using the pulse button, process until smooth and well combined. Divide the mixture into eight portions and shape into large balls with wet hands.

4 Place 2 cups (500 ml/16 fl oz) of the stock (freeze any remaining stock) in a large saucepan and bring to the boil over high heat, then remove from the heat and keep warm.

5 Heat the oil in a wok over high heat. Fry the meatballs in batches for 2 minutes each side, or until golden, but not cooked through. Drain.

6 Place the meatballs, mushrooms, soy sauce and sugar in a 2.5 litre (10 cup) ovenproof clay pot or casserole dish, and cover with the hot stock. Bake, covered, for 45 minutes. Add the bok choy and noodles and bake, covered, for another 10 minutes. Sprinkle with the remaining spring onion, and serve.

SERVES 4

INGREDIENTS

1 tablespoon ghee or oil
2 onions, chopped
1/2 cup (125 g/4 oz) plain yoghurt
1 teaspoon chilli powder
1 tablespoon ground coriander (cilantro)
2 teaspoons ground cumin
1 teaspoon ground cardamom
1/2 teaspoon ground cloves
1 teaspoon ground turmeric
3 cloves garlic, crushed
1 tablespoon grated fresh ginger
400 g (13 oz) can chopped tomatoes
1 kg (2 lb) boned leg of lamb, cut into 2.5 cm (1 inch) cubes
1/4 cup (30 g/1 oz) slivered almonds
1 teaspoon garam masala
chopped fresh coriander (cilantro) leaves, to garnish

1 Heat the ghee in a large saucepan, add the onion and cook, stirring, for 5 minutes, or until soft. Stir in the yoghurt, chilli powder, coriander, cumin, cardamom, cloves, turmeric, garlic and ginger. Add the tomato and 1 teaspoon salt, and simmer for 5 minutes.

2 Add the lamb and stir until coated. Cover and cook over low heat, stirring occasionally, for 1–1 1/2 hours, or until the lamb is tender. Uncover and simmer until the liquid thickens.

3 Meanwhile, toast the almonds in a dry frying pan over medium heat for 3–4 minutes, shaking the pan gently, until the nuts are golden brown. Remove from the pan at once to prevent them burning.

4 Add the garam masala to the curry and mix through well. Sprinkle the slivered almonds and coriander leaves over the top, and serve.

SERVES 4-6

INGREDIENTS

1 kg (2 lb 4 oz) asparagus
500 ml (2 cups) chicken stock
500 ml (2 cups) vegetable stock
4 tablespoons olive oil
1 small onion, finely chopped
360 g (1^2/$_3$ cups) risotto rice (arborio, vialone nano or carnaroli)
70 g (2^1/$_2$ oz) Parmesan cheese, grated
3 tablespoons thick (double/heavy) cream

1   Wash the asparagus and remove the woody ends (hold each spear at both ends and bend
    it gently — it will snap at its natural breaking point). Separate the tender spear tips from
    the stems.

2   Cook the asparagus stems in boiling water for 8 minutes, or until very tender. Drain and
    place in a blender with the chicken and vegetable stocks. Blend for 1 minute, then put in a
    saucepan, bring to the boil and maintain at a low simmer.

3   Cook the asparagus tips in boiling water for 1 minute, drain and refresh in iced water.

4   Heat the oil in a large wide heavy-based saucepan. Add the onion and cook until soft but
    not browned. Stir in the rice, season, and reduce the heat to low. Stir in a ladleful of the
    stock and cook over moderate heat, stirring continuously. When the stock has been
    absorbed, stir in another ladleful. Continue like this for about 20 minutes, until all the stock
    has been added and the rice is al dente. (You may not use all the stock, or you may need
    a little extra — every risotto will be slightly different.) Add the Parmesan and cream and
    gently stir in the asparagus tips. Season.

SERVES 4

600 g (1¼ lb) orange sweet potato (kumera)
2 tablespoons olive oil
1.5 kg (3 lb) chicken pieces
1 leek, cut into 2 cm (¾ inch) slices
2 cloves garlic, crushed
2 tablespoons plain (all-purpose) flour
2 cups (500 ml/16 fl oz) chicken stock
2 tablespoons fresh thyme

1 Preheat the oven to hot 220°C (425°F/Gas 7). Peel the sweet potato and cut it into chunks. Heat 1 tablespoon of the oil in a large flameproof casserole dish. Cook the chicken in batches for 3–4 minutes, or until browned. Set aside. Add the remaining oil and cook the leek and garlic for 2 minutes, or until soft.

2 Add the flour to the dish and cook, stirring, for about 1 minute to brown the flour. Gradually add the stock, stirring until the sauce boils and thickens. Remove from the heat. Return the chicken to the pan.

3 Add the sweet potato and half the thyme. Bake, covered, for 1½ hours, or until the chicken is cooked through and the sweet potato is tender. Season, and scatter with the remaining thyme. Serve with steamed rice.

CHICKEN, LEEK AND SWEET POTATO ONE-POT

SERVES 4

LAMB SHANKS IN TOMATO SAUCE ON POLENTA

2 tablespoons olive oil

1 large red onion, sliced

4 French-trimmed lamb shanks (about 250 g/8 oz each)

2 cloves garlic, crushed

400 g (13 oz) can peeled, chopped tomatoes

½ cup (125 ml/4 fl oz) red wine

2 teaspoons chopped fresh rosemary

1 cup (150 g/5 oz) instant polenta

50 g (1¾ oz) butter

½ cup (50 g/1¾ oz) grated fresh Parmesan

1 Preheat the oven to warm 160°C (315°F/Gas 2–3). Heat the oil in a 4 litre flameproof casserole dish over medium heat and sauté the onion for 3–4 minutes, or until softening and becoming transparent. Add the lamb shanks and cook for 2–3 minutes, or until lightly browned. Add the garlic, tomato and wine, then bring to the boil and cook for 3–4 minutes. Stir in the rosemary. Season with ¼ teaspoon each of salt and pepper.

2 Cover and bake for 2 hours. Remove the lid, return to the oven and simmer for a further 15 minutes, or until the lamb just starts to fall off the bone. Check periodically that the sauce is not too dry, adding water if needed.

3 About 20 minutes before serving, bring 1 litre (4 cups) water to the boil in a saucepan. Add the polenta in a thin stream, whisking continuously, then reduce the heat to very low. Simmer for 8–10 minutes, or until thick and coming away from the side of the pan. Stir in the butter and Parmesan. To serve, spoon the polenta onto serving plates, top with the shanks and tomato sauce.

SERVES 4

INGREDIENTS

2 tablespoons soy bean oil, or oil

500 g (1 lb) firm white fish (ling, perch), cut into 2 cm (¾ inch) cubes

250 g (8 oz) raw prawns (shrimp), peeled and deveined, tails intact

2 x 400 ml (13 fl oz) cans coconut milk

1 tablespoon red curry paste

4 fresh or 8 dried kaffir lime (makrut) leaves

2 tablespoons fish sauce

2 tablespoons finely chopped fresh lemon grass (white part only)

2 cloves garlic, crushed

1 tablespoon finely chopped fresh galangal

1 tablespoon shaved palm sugar or soft brown sugar

300 g (10 oz) silken firm tofu, cut into 1.5 cm (⅝ inch) cubes

½ cup (125 g/4 oz) bamboo shoots, julienned

1 large fresh red chilli, thinly sliced

2 teaspoons lime juice

spring onions, chopped, to garnish

fresh coriander (cilantro) leaves, chopped, to garnish

1   Heat the oil in a large frying pan or wok over medium heat. Sear the fish and prawns for 1 minute on each side. Remove the fish and prawns from the pan.

2   Place ¼ cup (60 ml/2 fl oz) of the coconut milk and the curry paste in the pan, and cook over medium heat for 2 minutes, or until fragrant and the oil separates. Add the remaining coconut milk, kaffir lime leaves, fish sauce, lemon grass, garlic, galangal, palm sugar and 1 teaspoon salt. Cook over low heat for 15 minutes.

3   Add the tofu cubes, bamboo shoots and sliced chilli. Simmer for a further 3–5 minutes. Return to medium heat, add the seafood and lime juice, and cook for a further 3 minutes, or until the seafood is just cooked. Remove from the heat.

4   Serve the curry with steamed rice and garnish with the spring onion and coriander leaves.

SERVES 4

INGREDIENTS

2 kg (4 lb) leg of lamb, boned
1 onion, chopped
2 teaspoons grated fresh ginger
3 cloves garlic
2 teaspoons ground coriander (cilantro)
2 teaspoons ground cumin
1 teaspoon cardamom seeds
large pinch cayenne pepper
2 tablespoons ghee or oil
1 onion, extra, sliced
2½ tablespoons tomato paste (purée)
½ cup (125 g/4 oz) plain yoghurt
½ cup (125 ml/4 fl oz) coconut cream
½ cup (95 g/3 oz) ground almonds
toasted slivered almonds, to serve

1 Trim any excess fat or sinew from the leg of lamb, then cut the meat into 3 cm (1¼ inch) cubes and place in a large bowl.

2 Place the onion, ginger, garlic, coriander, cumin, cardamom seeds, cayenne pepper and ½ teaspoon salt in a food processor, and process to a smooth paste. Add the spice mixture to the lamb and mix well to coat. Leave to marinate for 1 hour.

3 Heat the ghee in a large saucepan, add the extra sliced onion and cook, stirring, over low heat for 7 minutes, or until the onion is soft. Add the lamb mixture and cook, stirring constantly, for 8–10 minutes, or until the lamb changes colour. Stir in the tomato paste, yoghurt, coconut cream and ground almonds.

4 Reduce the heat and simmer, covered, stirring occasionally, for 50 minutes, or until the meat is tender. Add a little water if the mixture becomes too dry. Season with salt and pepper, and garnish with the slivered almonds. Serve with rice.

SERVES 4-6

BALTI CHICKEN

1 kg (2 lb) chicken thigh fillets
⅓ cup (80 ml/2¾ fl oz) oil
1 large red onion, finely chopped
4–5 cloves garlic, finely chopped
1 tablespoon grated fresh ginger
2 teaspoons ground cumin
2 teaspoons ground coriander (cilantro)
1 teaspoon ground turmeric
½ teaspoon chilli powder
425 g (14 oz) can chopped tomatoes
1 green capsicum (pepper), seeded and diced
1–2 small green chillies, seeded and finely chopped
4 tablespoons chopped fresh coriander (cilantro)
2 chopped spring onions, to garnish

1 Remove any excess fat or sinew from the chicken thigh fillets and cut into four or five even-sized pieces.

2 Heat a large wok over high heat, add the oil and swirl to coat the side. Add the onion and stir-fry over medium heat for 5 minutes, or until softened but not browned. Add the garlic and ginger and stir-fry for 3 more minutes.

3 Add the spices, 1 teaspoon salt and ¼ cup (60 ml/2 fl oz) water. Increase the heat to high and stir-fry for 2 minutes, or until the mixture has thickened. Take care not to burn.

4 Add the tomato and 1 cup (250 ml/8 fl oz) water and cook, stirring often, for a further 10 minutes, or until the mixture is thick and pulpy and the oil comes to the surface.

5 Add the chicken to the pan, reduce the heat and simmer, stirring often, for 15 minutes. Add the capsicum and chilli and simmer for 25 minutes, or until the chicken is tender. Add a little water if the mixture is too thick. Stir in the coriander and garnish with the spring onion.

SERVES 6

INGREDIENTS

Curry paste

2 tomatoes, peeled, seeded and roughly chopped

5 small fresh red chillies, seeded and chopped

5 cloves garlic, chopped

2 stems lemon grass (white part only), sliced

1 tablespoon coriander (cilantro) seeds, dry-roasted and ground

1 teaspoon shrimp powder, dry-roasted (see note)

1 tablespoon ground almonds

¼ teaspoon ground nutmeg

1 teaspoon ground turmeric

3 tablespoons tamarind purée

1 tablespoon lime juice

250 g (8 oz) swordfish, cut into 3 cm (1¼ inch) cubes

¼ cup (60 ml/2 fl oz) oil

2 red onions, chopped

2 small fresh red chillies, seeded and sliced

400 g (13 oz) raw medium prawns (shrimp), peeled and deveined, tails intact

250 g (8 oz) calamari (squid) tubes, cut into 1 cm (½ inch) rings

½ cup (125 ml/4 fl oz) fish stock

fresh Thai basil leaves, shredded, to garnish

1 To make the curry paste, place all the ingredients in a blender or food processor, and blend to a thick paste.

2 Place the lime juice in a bowl and season with salt and freshly ground black pepper. Add the swordfish, toss to coat well and leave to marinate for 20 minutes.

3 Heat the oil in a saucepan or wok, add the onion, sliced red chilli and curry paste, and cook, stirring occasionally, over low heat for 10 minutes, or until fragrant.

4 Add the swordfish and prawns, and stir to coat in the curry paste mixture. Cook for 3 minutes, or until the prawns just turn pink, then add the calamari and cook for 1 minute.

5 Add the stock and bring to the boil, then reduce the heat and simmer for 2 minutes, or until the seafood is cooked and tender. Season to taste with salt and freshly ground black pepper. Garnish with the shredded fresh basil leaves.

SERVES 6

INGREDIENTS

Curry paste

2 red onions, chopped

4 small fresh red chillies, seeded and sliced

4 cloves garlic, sliced

2 stems lemon grass (white part only), sliced

3 cm x 2 cm (1¹/₄ inch x ³/₄ inch) piece fresh galangal, sliced

8 kaffir lime (makrut) leaves, roughly chopped

1 teaspoon ground turmeric

¹/₂ teaspoon shrimp paste, dry-roasted

2 tablespoons oil

750 g (1¹/₂ lb) chicken thigh fillets, cut into bite-size pieces

400 ml (13 fl oz) can coconut milk

3 tablespoons tamarind purée

1 tablespoon fish sauce

3 kaffir lime (makrut) leaves, shredded

1 To make the curry paste, place all the ingredients in a food processor or blender and process to a thick paste.

2 Heat a wok or large saucepan over high heat, add the oil and swirl to coat the side. Add the curry paste and cook, stirring occasionally, over low heat for 8–10 minutes, or until fragrant. Add the chicken and stir-fry with the paste for 2–3 minutes.

3 Add the coconut milk, tamarind purée and fish sauce to the wok, and simmer, stirring occasionally, for 15–20 minutes, or until the chicken is tender. Garnish with the lime leaves. Serve with rice and steamed bok choy.

SERVES 4

INGREDIENTS

2 x 270 ml (9 fl oz) cans coconut cream (do not shake the cans)
3 tablespoons chu chee curry paste
500 g (1 lb) scallops, with roe removed
500 g (1 lb) raw medium king prawns (shrimp), peeled and deveined, tails intact
2–3 tablespoons fish sauce
2–3 tablespoons palm sugar or soft brown sugar
8 kaffir lime (makrut) leaves, finely shredded
2 fresh red chillies, thinly sliced
1 cup (30 g/1 oz) fresh Thai basil leaves

1 Place 1 cup (250 ml/8 fl oz) of the thick coconut cream from the top of the can in a wok. Heat until just boiling, then stir in the curry paste, reduce the heat and simmer for 10 minutes, or until fragrant and the oil begins to separate.

2 Stir in the remaining coconut cream, scallops and prawns, and cook for 5 minutes, or until tender. Add the fish sauce, palm sugar, kaffir lime leaves and chilli, and cook for 1 minute. Stir in half the basil and garnish with the remaining leaves.

CHU CHEE SEAFOOD

SERVES 4

INGREDIENTS

1 cup (250 ml/8 fl oz) coconut cream (do not shake the can)
2 tablespoons red curry paste
500 g (1 lb) round or topside steak, cut into strips (see note)
2 tablespoons fish sauce
1 tablespoon palm sugar or soft brown sugar
5 kaffir lime (makrut) leaves, halved
2 cups (500 ml/16 fl oz) coconut milk
8 Thai eggplants, halved
2 tablespoons finely shredded fresh Thai basil leaves

1 Place the thick coconut cream from the top of the can in a wok and bring to the boil. Boil for 10 minutes, or until the oil starts to separate. Add the curry paste and simmer, stirring to prevent it sticking to the bottom, for 5 minutes, or until fragrant.

2 Add the meat and cook, stirring, for 3–5 minutes, or until it changes colour. Add the fish sauce, palm sugar, lime leaves, coconut milk and remaining coconut cream, and simmer for 1 hour, or until the meat is tender and the sauce has slightly thickened.

3 Add the eggplant and cook for 10 minutes, or until tender. If the sauce is too thick, add a little water. Stir in half the shredded basil leaves. Garnish with the remaining basil leaves and serve with rice.

NOTE Cut the meat into 5 x 5 x 2 cm (2 x 2 x ³/₄ inch) pieces, then cut across the grain at a 45° angle into 5 mm (¹/₄ inch) thick slices.

SERVES 4

INGREDIENTS

2 garlic cloves, crushed

3 small green chillies, seeded and finely chopped

$^{1}/_{2}$ teaspoon ground turmeric

$^{1}/_{2}$ teaspoon ground cloves

$^{1}/_{2}$ teaspoon ground cinnamon

$^{1}/_{2}$ teaspoon ground cayenne pepper

1 tablespoon tamarind purée

170 ml ($^{2}/_{3}$ cup) oil

800 g (1 lb 12 oz) pomfret, sole or leatherjacket fillets, skinned

310 ml (1$^{1}/_{4}$ cups) coconut cream

2 tablespoons chopped coriander (cilantro) leaves

1 Mix together the garlic, chilli, spices, tamarind and 125 ml ($^{1}/_{2}$ cup) of the oil. Place the fish fillets in a shallow dish and spoon the marinade over them. Turn the fish over, cover and refrigerate for 30 minutes.

2 Heat the remaining oil in a large heavy-based frying pan and add the fish in batches. Cook for 1 minute on each side. Return all the fish to the pan, then reduce the heat to low and add any remaining marinade and the coconut cream. Season with salt and gently cook for 3–5 minutes, or until the fish is cooked through and flakes easily. If the sauce is too runny, lift out the fish, simmer the sauce for a few minutes, then pour it over the fish. Garnish with the coriander leaves.

SERVES 4

INGREDIENTS

Curry paste
10–12 large dried red chillies
1 teaspoon white pepper
4 red Asian shallots, chopped
4 garlic cloves, sliced
1 stem lemon grass, white part only, sliced
1 tablespoon finely chopped galangal
2 small coriander (cilantro) roots, chopped
1 tablespoon finely chopped ginger
1 tablespoon shrimp paste, dry roasted

1 tablespoon peanut oil
1 garlic clove, crushed
1 tablespoon fish sauce
30 g (¼ cup) ground candlenuts
310 ml (1¼ cups) fish stock
1 tablespoon whisky
3 kaffir lime (makrut) leaves, torn
600 g (1 lb 5 oz) raw prawns (shrimp), peeled and deveined, with tails intact
1 small carrot, quartered lengthways and sliced thinly on the diagonal
150 g (5½ oz) snake beans (yard-long beans), cut into 2 cm (¾ inch) lengths
50 g (¼ cup) bamboo shoots
Thai basil leaves, to garnish

1 To make the curry paste, soak the chillies in boiling water for 15 minutes. Drain and chop. Place in a food processor with the white pepper, shallots, garlic, lemon grass, galangal, coriander roots, ginger, shrimp paste and 1 teaspoon salt and blend until smooth — add a little water, if necessary, to form a paste.

2 Heat a wok over medium heat, add the oil and swirl to coat the side. Add the garlic and 3 tablespoons of the curry paste and cook, stirring, for 5 minutes. Add the fish sauce, ground candlenuts, fish stock, whisky, lime leaves, prawns, carrot, beans and bamboo shoots. Bring to the boil, then reduce the heat and simmer for 5 minutes, or until the prawns and vegetables are cooked.

3 Garnish with Thai basil and freshly ground black pepper.

SERVES 6

INGREDIENTS

Paste

8–10 large dried red chillies

6 red Asian shallots, chopped

6 garlic cloves, chopped

1 teaspoon ground coriander (cilantro)

1 tablespoon ground cumin

1 teaspoon white pepper

2 stems lemon grass, white part only, bruised and sliced

1 tablespoon chopped galangal

6 coriander (cilantro) roots

2 teaspoons shrimp paste

2 tablespoons roasted peanuts

1 tablespoon peanut oil

400 ml (14 fl oz) can coconut cream

1 kg (2 lb 4 oz) round or blade steak, cut into 1 cm ($\frac{1}{2}$ inch) slices

400 ml (14 fl oz) can coconut milk

90 g ($\frac{1}{3}$ cup) crunchy peanut butter

4 kaffir lime (makrut) leaves

3 tablespoons lime juice

2$\frac{1}{2}$ tablespoons fish sauce

3–4 tablespoons grated palm sugar or soft brown sugar

1 tablespoon chopped roasted peanuts, extra, to garnish

Thai basil, to garnish

1 To make the paste, soak the chillies in a bowl of boiling water for 15 minutes, or until soft. Remove the seeds and chop. Place in a food processor with the shallots, garlic, ground coriander, ground cumin, white pepper, lemon grass, galangal, coriander roots, shrimp paste and peanuts and process until smooth — add a little water if the paste is too thick.

2 Place the peanut oil and the thick coconut cream from the top of the can (reserve the rest) in a saucepan and cook over medium heat for 10 minutes, or until the oil separates. Add 6–8 tablespoons of the paste and cook, stirring, for 5–8 minutes, or until fragrant.

3 Add the beef, coconut milk, peanut butter, lime leaves and the reserved coconut cream. Cook for 8 minutes, or until the beef just starts to change colour. Reduce the heat and simmer for 1 hour, or until the beef is tender.

4 Stir in the lime juice, fish sauce and sugar. Serve garnished with the peanuts and Thai basil.

SERVES 4-6

TERIYAKI BEEF WITH GREENS AND CRISPY NOODLES

INGREDIENTS

450 g (1 lb) sirloin steak, cut into thin strips
125 ml ($\frac{1}{2}$ cup) teriyaki marinade
vegetable oil, for deep-frying
100 g ($3\frac{1}{2}$ oz) dried rice vermicelli
2 tablespoons peanut oil
1 onion, sliced
3 garlic cloves, crushed
1 red chilli, seeded and finely chopped
200 g (7 oz) carrots, julienned
600 g (1 lb 5 oz) choy sum, cut into 3 cm ($1\frac{1}{4}$ inch) lengths
1 tablespoon lime juice

1 Combine the beef and teriyaki marinade in a non-metallic bowl and marinate for 2 hours.

2 Fill a wok one-third full of oil and heat to 190°C (375°F), or until a cube of bread browns in 10 seconds. Separate the vermicelli noodles into small bundles and deep-fry until they sizzle and puff up. Drain well on paper towels. Drain the oil and carefully pour it into a heatproof bowl to cool before discarding.

3 Heat 1 tablespoon of the peanut oil in the wok. When the oil is nearly smoking, add the beef (reserving the marinade) and cook in batches over high heat for 1–2 minutes. Remove to a plate. Heat the remaining oil. Add the onion and stir-fry for 3–4 minutes. Add the garlic and chilli and cook for 30 seconds. Add the carrot and choy sum and stir-fry for 3–4 minutes, or until tender.

4 Return the beef to the wok with the lime juice and reserved marinade and cook over high heat for 3 minutes. Add the noodles, toss well briefly, and serve immediately.

SERVES 4

INGREDIENTS

Sauce

1/2–1 teaspoon dashi granules

1/3 cup (80 ml/2 3/4 fl oz) soy sauce

2 tablespoons sake

2 tablespoons mirin

1 tablespoon caster sugar

300 g (10 oz) shirataki noodles

50 g (1 3/4 oz) lard

5 large spring onions, cut into 1 cm (1/2 inch) slices on the diagonal

16 fresh shiitake mushrooms, cut into smaller pieces if large

800 g (1 lb 10 oz) rump steak, thinly sliced across the grain

100 g (3 1/2 oz) watercress, trimmed

4 eggs (optional)

1   To make the sauce, dissolve the dashi granules in 1/2 cup (125 ml/4 fl oz) water. Add the soy sauce, sake, mirin and sugar, and stir until combined.

2   Drain the noodles, then soak them in boiling water for 2 minutes. Rinse in cold water and drain well.

3   Melt the lard in a large frying pan over medium heat. Cook the spring onion, mushrooms and beef in batches, stirring, for 1–2 minutes each batch, or until just brown. Return the meat, spring onion and mushrooms to the pan, then add the sauce and watercress. Cook for 1 minute, or until heated through and the watercress has wilted—the sauce needs to just cover the ingredients but not drown them.

4   To serve, divide the noodles among four serving bowls and spoon the sauce evenly over the top. If desired, crack an egg into each bowl and break up through the sauce using chopsticks until it partially cooks.

SERVES 4

CATALAN FISH STEW

300 g (10 oz) red mullet fillets
400 g (13 oz) firm white fish fillets
300 g (10 oz) cleaned calamari (squid)
1.5 litres (6¼ cups) fish stock
⅓ cup (80 ml/2¾ fl oz) olive oil
1 onion, chopped
6 cloves garlic, chopped
1 small fresh red chilli, chopped
1 teaspoon paprika
pinch saffron threads
150 ml (5 fl oz) white wine
425 g (14 oz) can crushed tomatoes
16 raw medium prawns (shrimp), peeled and deveined, tails
   intact
2 tablespoons brandy
24 black mussels, cleaned
1 tablespoon chopped fresh parsley

Picada
2 tablespoons olive oil
2 slices day-old bread, cubed
2 cloves garlic
5 blanched almonds, toasted
2 tablespoons fresh flat-leaf parsley

1   Cut the fish and calamari into 4 cm (1½ inch) pieces. Place the stock in a large saucepan, bring to the boil and boil for 15 minutes, or until reduced by half.

2   To make the picada, heat the oil in a frying pan, add the bread and cook, stirring, for 2–3 minutes, or until golden, adding the garlic for the last minute. Place the almonds, bread, garlic and parsley in a food processor and process, adding enough of the stock to make a smooth paste.

3   Heat 2 tablespoons of the oil in a large saucepan, add the onion, garlic, chilli and paprika, and cook, stirring, for 1 minute. Add the saffron, wine, tomato and stock. Bring to the boil, then reduce the heat and simmer.

4   Heat the remaining oil in a frying pan and quickly fry the fish and calamari for 3–5 minutes. Remove from the pan. Add the prawns, cook for 1 minute and then pour in the brandy. Carefully ignite the brandy with a match and let the flames burn down. Remove from the pan.

5   Add the mussels to the stock and simmer, covered, for 2–3 minutes, or until opened. Discard any that do not open. Add all the seafood and the picada to the pan, stirring until the sauce has thickened and the seafood has cooked through. Season to taste, sprinkle with the parsley, and serve.

SERVES 6-8

INGREDIENTS

500 g (1 lb 2 oz) tiger prawns (shrimp)
1½ tablespoons lemon juice
3 tablespoons oil
½ onion, finely chopped
½ teaspoon ground turmeric
5 cm (2 inch) piece of cinnamon stick
4 cloves
7 cardamom pods
5 Indian bay leaves (cassia leaves)
2 cm (¾ inch) piece of ginger, grated
3 garlic cloves, chopped
1 teaspoon chilli powder
170 ml (⅔ cup) coconut milk

1 Peel and devein the prawns, leaving the tails intact. Put them in a bowl, add the lemon juice, then toss together and leave for 5 minutes. Rinse the prawns under running cold water and pat dry with paper towels.

2 Heat the oil in a heavy-based frying pan and fry the onion until lightly browned. Add the turmeric, cinnamon, cloves, cardamom, bay leaves, ginger and garlic and fry for 1 minute. Add the chilli powder, coconut milk and salt, to taste, and slowly bring to the boil. Reduce the heat and simmer for 2 minutes.

3 Add the prawns, return to the boil, then reduce the heat and simmer for 5 minutes, or until the prawns are cooked through and the sauce is thick. (Care should be taken not to overcook the prawns or they will become rubbery.)

SERVES 4

GREEK OCTOPUS STEW

INGREDIENTS

1 kg (2 lb) baby octopus
2 tablespoons olive oil
1 large onion, chopped
3 cloves garlic, crushed
1 bay leaf
3 cups (750 ml/24 fl oz) red wine
$\frac{1}{4}$ cup (60 ml/2 fl oz) red wine vinegar
400 g (13 oz) can crushed tomatoes
1 tablespoon tomato paste(purée)
1 tablespoon chopped fresh oregano
$\frac{1}{4}$ teaspoon ground cinnamon
small pinch ground cloves
1 teaspoon sugar
2 tablespoons finely chopped fresh flat-leaf parsley

1   Cut between the head and tentacles of the octopus, just below the eyes. Grasp the body and push the beak out and up through the centre of the tentacles with your fingers. Cut the eyes from the head by slicing off a small round. Discard the eye section. Carefully slit through one side, avoiding the ink sac, and remove any gut from inside. Rinse the octopus well under running water.

2   Heat the oil in a large saucepan, add the onion and cook over medium heat for 5 minutes, or until starting to brown. Add the garlic and bay leaf, and cook for 1 minute further. Add the octopus and stir to coat in the onion mixture.

3   Stir in the wine, vinegar, tomato, tomato paste, oregano, cinnamon, cloves and sugar. Bring to the boil, then reduce the heat and simmer for 1 hour, or until the octopus is tender and the sauce has thickened slightly. Stir in the parsley and season with salt and ground black pepper. Serve with a Greek salad and crusty bread to mop up the delicious juices.

SERVES 4-6

INGREDIENTS

1.5 kg (3 lb) leg or shoulder of lamb, cut into 2.5 cm (1 inch) pieces
3 cloves garlic, chopped
⅓ cup (80 ml/2¾ fl oz) olive oil
2 teaspoons ground cumin
1 teaspoon ground ginger
1 teaspoon ground turmeric
1 teaspoon paprika
½ teaspoon ground cinnamon
2 onions, thinly sliced
600 ml (20 fl oz) beef stock
¼ preserved lemon, pulp discarded, rind rinsed and cut into thin strips
425 g (14 oz) can chickpeas, drained
35 g (1¼ oz) cracked green olives
¼ cup (15 g/½ oz) chopped fresh coriander (cilantro) leaves

1 Place the lamb pieces in a non-metallic bowl, add the chopped garlic, 2 tablespoons of the olive oil and the ground cumin, ginger, turmeric, paprika, cinnamon, and ½ teaspoon ground black pepper and 1 teaspoon salt. Mix well to coat, then leave to marinate for 1 hour.

2 Heat the remaining olive oil in a large saucepan, add the lamb in batches and cook over high heat for 2–3 minutes, or until browned. Remove from the pan. Add the onion and cook for 2 minutes, then return the meat to the pan and add the beef stock. Reduce the heat and simmer, covered, for 1 hour.

3 Add the preserved lemon strips, drained chickpeas and olives, and cook, uncovered, for a further 30 minutes, or until the lamb is tender and the sauce has reduced and thickened. Stir in the coriander. Serve in bowls with couscous.

SERVES 6-8

CHILLI CON POLLO

1 tablespoon olive oil
1 onion, finely chopped
500 g (1 lb) minced (ground) chicken
1–2 teaspoons mild chilli powder
440 g (14 oz) can chopped tomatoes
2 tablespoons tomato paste (purée)
1–2 teaspoons soft brown sugar
425 g (14 oz) can red kidney beans, rinsed and drained

1 Heat the oil in a large saucepan. Add the chopped onion and cook over medium heat for 3 minutes, or until soft. Increase the heat to high and add the chicken mince. Cook until the chicken has browned, breaking up any lumps with a wooden spoon.

2 Add the chilli powder to the chicken and cook for 1 minute. Stir in the tomato, tomato paste and $^1/_2$ cup (125 ml/4 fl oz) water.

3 Bring to the boil, then reduce the heat and simmer for 30 minutes. Stir through the sugar to taste and the kidney beans. Season. Serve with corn chips or in taco shells with sour cream.

SERVES 4

INGREDIENTS

¼ cup (60 ml/2 fl oz) olive oil

4 chicken thighs and 6 drumsticks

1 large red onion, finely chopped

1 large green capsicum (pepper), two-thirds diced and one-third julienned

3 teaspoons sweet paprika

400 g (13 oz) can diced tomatoes

1¼ cups (275 g/9 oz) paella or arborio rice (see note)

½ teaspoon ground saffron

1 Heat 2 tablespoons of the oil in a large deep frying pan over high heat. Season the chicken pieces well and brown in batches. Remove the chicken from the pan.

2 Reduce the heat to medium and add the remaining oil. Add the onion and the diced capsicum, and cook gently for 5 minutes. Stir in the sweet paprika and cook for 30 seconds. Add the tomato and simmer for 1–3 minutes, or until it thickens.

3 Stir in 3½ cups (875 ml/28 fl oz) boiling water, then add the rice and saffron. Return the chicken to the pan and stir to combine. Season to taste. Bring to the boil, then cover, reduce the heat to medium–low and simmer for 20–30 minutes, or until the liquid has been absorbed and the chicken is tender. Stir in the julienned capsicum, then allow to stand, covered, for 3–4 minutes before serving.

NOTE Paella rice is a medium round grain from Spain. Calasparra is the most commonly available variety and can be purchased from fine food stores or Spanish delicatessens.

SPANISH CHICKEN AND RICE STEW

SERVES 4

STUFFED SQUID STEW

INGREDIENTS

100 ml (3¹/₂ fl oz) olive oil
1 large onion, finely chopped
2 cloves garlic, crushed
1 cup (80 g/2³/₄ oz) fresh breadcrumbs
1 egg, lightly beaten
60 g (2 oz) kefalotyri cheese, grated
60 g (2 oz) haloumi cheese, grated
4 large or 8 small squid (1 kg/2 lb), cleaned (see note)
1 small onion, finely chopped, extra
2 cloves garlic, crushed, extra
500 g (1 lb) firm ripe tomatoes, peeled and diced
150 ml (5 fl oz) red wine
1 tablespoon chopped fresh oregano
1 tablespoon chopped fresh flat-leaf parsley

1 Heat 2 tablespoons of the oil in a frying pan, add the onion and cook over medium heat for 3 minutes. Remove. Combine with the garlic, breadcrumbs, egg and cheese. Season.

2 Pat the squid hoods dry with paper towels and, using a teaspoon, fill them three-quarters full with the stuffing. Do not pack them too tightly or the stuffing mixture will swell and burst out during cooking. Secure the ends with wooden toothpicks.

3 Heat the remaining oil in a large frying pan, add the squid and cook for 1–2 minutes on all sides. Remove. Add the extra onion and cook over medium heat for 3 minutes, or until soft, then add the extra garlic and cook for a further 1 minute. Stir in the tomato and wine, and simmer for 10 minutes, or until thick and pulpy, then stir in the oregano and parsley. Return the squid to the pan and cook, covered, for 20–25 minutes, or until tender. Serve warm with the tomato sauce or cool with a salad.

NOTE Ask the fishmonger to clean the squid. Or, discard the tentacles and cartilage. Rinse the hoods under running water and pull off the skin.

SERVES 4

INGREDIENTS

350 g (11 oz) dried white haricot beans

150 g (5 oz) tocino, speck or pancetta, unsliced

$\frac{1}{2}$ leek, thinly sliced

2 cloves garlic

1 bay leaf

1 small fresh red chilli, halved and seeded

1 small onion

2 cloves

1 sprig fresh rosemary

3 sprigs fresh thyme

1 sprig fresh parsley

$\frac{1}{4}$ cup (60 ml/2 fl oz) olive oil

8 pork sausages

$\frac{1}{2}$ onion, finely chopped

1 green capsicum (pepper), finely chopped

$\frac{1}{2}$ teaspoon paprika

$\frac{1}{2}$ cup (125 ml/4 fl oz) tomato paste (purée)

1 teaspoon cider vinegar

1 Soak the beans overnight in cold water. Drain and rinse the beans under cold water. Put them in a large saucepan with the tocino, leek, garlic, bay leaf and chilli. Stud the onion with the cloves and add to the saucepan. Tie the rosemary, thyme and parsley together, and add to the saucepan. Pour in 3 cups (750 ml/24 fl oz) cold water and bring to the boil. Add 1 tablespoon of the oil, reduce the heat and simmer, covered, for about 1 hour, or until the beans are tender. When necessary, add a little more boiling water to keep the beans covered.

2 Prick each sausage 5 or 6 times and twist tightly in opposite directions in the middle to give 2 short fat sausages joined in the middle. Put in a single layer in a large frying pan and add enough cold water to reach halfway up their sides. Bring to the boil and simmer, turning two or three times, until all the water has evaporated and the sausages brown lightly in the little fat that is left in the pan. Remove from the pan and cut the short sausages apart. Add the remaining oil, the chopped onion and green capsicum to the pan, and fry over medium heat for 5–6 minutes. Stir in the paprika, cook for 30 seconds, then add the tomato purée. Season to taste. Cook, stirring, for 1 minute.

3 Remove the tocino, herb sprigs and any loose large pieces of onion from the bean mixture. Leave in any loose leaves from the herbs and any small pieces of onion. Add the sausages and sauce to the pan, and stir the vinegar through. Bring to the boil. Adjust the seasoning.

SERVES 4

PORK SAUSAGE AND WHITE BEAN STEW

INGREDIENTS

60 ml (¹/₄ cup) olive oil
1 large red capsicum (pepper), seeded and cut into 5 mm (¹/₄ inch) strips
600 g (1 lb 5 oz) chicken thigh fillets, cut into 3 cm (1¹/₄ inch) cubes
200 g (7 oz) chorizo sausage, cut into 2 cm (³/₄ inch) slices
200 g (7 oz) mushrooms, thinly sliced
3 garlic cloves, crushed
1 tablespoon lemon zest
700 g (1 lb 9 oz) tomatoes, roughly chopped
200 g (7 oz) green beans, cut into 3 cm (1¹/₄ inch) lengths
1 tablespoon chopped rosemary
2 tablespoons chopped flat-leaf (Italian) parsley
¹/₄ teaspoon saffron threads dissolved in 60 ml (¹/₄ cup) hot water
440 g (2 cups) short-grain rice
750 ml (3 cups) hot chicken stock
6 lemon wedges

1 Heat the oil in a large deep frying pan or paella pan over medium heat. Add the capsicum and cook for 6 minutes, or until soft. Remove from the pan.

2 Add the chicken to the pan and cook for 10 minutes, or until brown on all sides. Remove. Add the sausage to the pan and cook for 5 minutes, or until golden on all sides. Remove.

3 Add the mushrooms, garlic and lemon zest and cook over medium heat for 5 minutes. Stir in the tomato and capsicum and cook for a further 5 minutes, or until the tomato is soft.

4 Add the beans, rosemary, parsley, saffron mixture, rice, chicken and sausage. Stir briefly and then add the stock. Do not stir at this point. Reduce the heat and simmer for 30 minutes. Remove the pan from the heat, cover and leave to stand for 10 minutes. Serve with lemon wedges.

NOTE Paellas are not stirred right to the bottom of the pan during cooking in the hope that a thin crust of crispy rice will form. This is considered one of the best parts of the paella. For this reason, do not use a non-stick frying pan. Paellas are traditionally served at the table from the pan.

SERVES 6

INGREDIENTS

2 tablespoons olive oil
8 (1.2 kg/2 lb 6½ oz) chicken pieces
½ cup (125 ml/4 fl oz) chicken stock
½ cup (125 ml/4 fl oz) dry white wine
½ cup (125 ml/4 fl oz) balsamic vinegar
40 g (1¼ oz) chilled butter

1 Heat the oil in a large casserole dish over medium heat and cook the chicken, in batches, for 7–8 minutes, until browned. Pour off any excess fat.

2 Add the stock, bring to the boil, then reduce the heat and simmer, covered, for 30 minutes, or until the chicken is cooked through.

3 Add the white wine and vinegar and increase the heat to high. Boil for 1 minute, or until the liquid has thickened. Remove from the heat, stir in the butter until melted, and season. Spoon the sauce over the chicken to serve, accompanied by roast potatoes and salad.

NOTE Use a good-quality balsamic vinegar, as the cheaper varieties can be too acidic.

CHICKEN WITH BALSAMIC VINEGAR

SERVES 4

PROVENCALE OCTOPUS

INGREDIENTS

1 kg (2 lb) baby octopus
$^1/_4$ cup (60 ml/2 fl oz) olive oil
1 large brown onion, chopped
2 cloves garlic
500 g (1 lb) ripe tomatoes, peeled, seeded and chopped
$1^1/_3$ cups (330 ml/11 fl oz) dry white wine
$^1/_4$ teaspoon saffron threads
2 sprigs fresh thyme
2 tablespoons roughly chopped fresh flat-leaf parsley

1 To clean the octopus, use a small sharp knife and cut each head from the tentacles. Remove the eyes by cutting a round of flesh from the base of each head. To clean the heads, carefully slit them open and remove the gut. Rinse thoroughly. Cut the heads in half. Push out the beaks from the centre of the tentacles from the cut side. Cut the tentacles into sets of four or two, depending on the size of the octopus.

2 Blanch all the octopus in boiling water for 2 minutes, then drain and allow to cool slightly. Pat dry with paper towels.

3 Heat the olive oil in a heavy-based frying pan and cook the onion for 7–8 minutes over medium heat until lightly golden. Add the octopus and garlic to the pan, and cook for another 2–3 minutes. Add the tomato, wine, saffron and thyme. Add just enough water to cover the octopus.

4 Simmer, covered, for 1 hour. Uncover and cook for another 15 minutes, or until the octopus is tender and the sauce has thickened a little. The cooking time will vary depending upon the size of the octopus. Season to taste. Serve hot or at room temperature, sprinkled with chopped parsley.

SERVES 6

INGREDIENTS

¼ cup (60 ml/2 fl oz) oil
1 kg (2 lb) veal shoulder, diced
1 large onion, thinly sliced
3 cloves garlic, finely chopped
¼ cup (60 g/2 oz) Hungarian paprika
½ teaspoon caraway seeds
2 x 400 g (13 oz) cans chopped tomatoes, one drained
350 g (11 oz) fresh fettuccine
40 g (1¼ oz) butter, softened

1   Heat half the oil in a large saucepan over medium–high heat, then brown the veal in batches for 3 minutes per batch. Remove the veal from the pan and set aside with any pan juices.

2   Add the remaining oil to the pan and sauté the onion and garlic over medium heat for 5 minutes, or until softened. Add the paprika and ¼ teaspoon of the caraway seeds, and stir for 30 seconds.

3   Add the chopped tomatoes and their liquid plus ½ cup (125 ml/4 fl oz) water. Return the veal to the pan with any juices, increase the heat to high and bring to the boil. Reduce the heat to low, then cover and simmer for 1¼ hours, or until the meat is tender and the sauce has thickened.

4   About 15 minutes before the veal is ready, cook the pasta in a large saucepan of rapidly boiling salted water according to the packet instructions until al dente. Drain, then return to the pan. Stir in the butter and the remaining caraway seeds. Serve immediately with the paprika veal.

PAPRIKA VEAL WITH CARAWAY NOODLES

SERVES 4

CHICKEN MARSALA

¼ cup (60 ml/2 fl oz) olive oil
3 leeks, thinly sliced
1 teaspoon finely chopped fresh rosemary
3 bay leaves, torn
1 kg (2 lb) chicken pieces
seasoned plain (all-purpose) flour
1 large eggplant (aubergine), cut into cubes
2 zucchini (courgettes), roughly chopped
½ cup (125 ml/4 fl oz) Marsala
300 ml (10 fl oz) chicken stock
2 cups (500 ml/16 fl oz) tomato paste (purée)
200 g (6½ oz) button mushrooms, halved

1 Heat the oil in a large, heavy-based saucepan. Fry the leek, rosemary and bay leaves over low heat for 5 minutes, or until soft, stirring occasionally. Remove with a slotted spoon, leaving as much oil in the pan as possible.

2 Toss the chicken pieces in the seasoned flour. Add the chicken to the pan and brown well in batches over medium heat. Return all the chicken to the pan with the leek mixture.

3 Add the eggplant and zucchini, and cook, stirring, for 2–3 minutes, or until softened, turning the chicken over. Add the Marsala and stock, and cook for 15 minutes over medium–high heat.

4 Add the tomato purée and season well with salt and pepper. Bring to the boil, turning the chicken pieces in the sauce. Reduce the heat to a very gentle simmer, then cover and cook for 35 minutes. Add the mushrooms and cook, uncovered, for 5 minutes.

NOTE Marsala is a famous Italian fortified wine. It has a smoky, rich flavour and ranges from dry to sweet.

SERVES 4

INGREDIENTS

300 g (10 oz) skinless firm white fish fillets (see note)
250 g (8 oz) black mussels
500 g (1 lb) raw medium prawns (shrimp), peeled and
  deveined, tails intact
200 g (6 1/2 oz) calamari (squid) rings
1/4 cup (60 ml/2 fl oz) olive oil
1 large onion, diced
3 cloves garlic, finely chopped
1 small red capsicum (pepper), thinly sliced
1 small fresh red chilli, seeded and chopped (optional)

2 teaspoons paprika
1 teaspoon ground turmeric
2 tomatoes, peeled and diced
1 tablespoon tomato paste (purée)
2 cups (400 g/13 oz) long-grain rice
1/2 cup (125 ml/4 fl oz) white wine
1.25 litres fish stock
1/4 cup (7 g/1/4 oz) chopped fresh flat-leaf parsley, for
  serving
lemon wedges, for serving

1 Cut the fish fillets into 2.5 cm (1 inch) cubes. Scrub the mussels and pull out the hairy beards. Discard any broken mussels or those that don't close when tapped. Refrigerate the seafood, covered, until ready to use.

2 Heat the oil in a paella pan or a large deep frying pan with a lid. Add the onion, garlic, capsicum and chilli to the pan, and cook over medium heat for 2 minutes, or until the onion and capsicum are soft. Add the paprika, turmeric and 1 teaspoon salt, and stir-fry for 1–2 minutes, or until aromatic.

3 Add the tomato and cook for 5 minutes, or until softened. Add the tomato paste. Stir in the rice until it is well coated.

4 Pour in the wine and simmer until almost absorbed. Add all the fish stock and bring to the boil. Reduce the heat and simmer for 20 minutes, or until almost all the liquid is absorbed into the rice. There is no need to stir the rice, but you may occasionally wish to fluff it up with a fork to separate the grains.

5 Add the mussels to the pan, poking the shells into the rice, cover and cook for 2–3 minutes over low heat. Add the prawns and cook for 2–3 minutes. Add the fish, cover and cook for 3 minutes. Finally, add the calamari rings and cook for 1–2 minutes. By this time, the mussels should have opened—discard any unopened ones. The prawns should be pink and the fish should flake easily when tested with a fork. The calamari should be white, moist and tender. Cook for another 2–3 minutes if the seafood is not quite cooked, but avoid overcooking as the seafood will toughen and dry out.

6 Serve with parsley and lemon wedges. Delicious with a tossed salad.

NOTE You can use just fish, or other seafood such as scampi, octopus and crabs. If using just fish, choose one with few bones and chunky flesh, such as ling, blue-eye or warehou.

SERVES 4

CHINESE BRAISED CHICKEN

1 cup (250 ml/8 fl oz) soy sauce
1 cinnamon stick
⅓ cup (90 g/3 oz) sugar
⅓ cup (80 ml/2¾ fl oz) balsamic vinegar
2.5 cm (1 inch) piece fresh ginger, thinly sliced
4 cloves garlic
¼ teaspoon dried chilli flakes
1.5 kg (3 lb) chicken pieces (skin removed)
1 tablespoon sesame seeds, toasted

1 Combine 1 litre water with the soy sauce, cinnamon stick, sugar, balsamic vinegar, ginger, garlic and chilli flakes in a saucepan. Bring to the boil, then reduce the heat and simmer for 5 minutes.

2 Add the chicken pieces and simmer, covered, for 50 minutes, or until cooked through. Serve the chicken on a bed of steamed greens, drizzled with the poaching liquid and sprinkled with toasted sesame seeds.

SERVES 4-6

CHILLI CON CARNE

185 g (6 oz) dried black eye beans
650 g (1 lb 5 oz) tomatoes
1½ tablespoons oil
900 g (1 lb 13 oz) trimmed chuck steak, cut into chunks
3 onions, thinly sliced
2 cloves garlic, chopped
2 teaspoons ground cumin
1 tablespoon paprika
½ teaspoon ground allspice
1–2 teaspoons chilli powder
1 tablespoon soft brown sugar
1 tablespoon red wine vinegar

1 Put the beans in a bowl, cover with plenty of water and leave overnight to soak. Drain well. Score a cross in the base of each tomato. Put the tomatoes in a bowl of boiling water for 30 seconds, then transfer to a bowl of cold water. Drain and peel the skin away from the cross. Halve the tomatoes and remove the seeds with a teaspoon. Chop the flesh finely.

2 Heat 1 tablespoon of the oil in a large heavy-based pan and add half the meat. Cook over medium-high heat for 2 minutes, or until well browned. Remove from the pan and repeat with the remaining meat, then remove from the pan.

3 Add the rest of the oil to the pan and add the onion. Cook over medium heat for 5 minutes, or until softened. Add the garlic and spices and cook, stirring, for 1 minute, or until aromatic. Add 2 cups (500 ml/16 fl oz) water and stir. Return the meat to the pan with the beans and tomatoes. Bring to the boil, then reduce the heat to low and simmer, partially covered, for 2 hours, or until the meat is tender and the chilli con carne is thick and dryish, stirring occasionally. Towards the end of the cooking time the mixture may start to catch, so add a little water if necessary. Stir through the sugar and vinegar, and season with salt to taste. Serve with flour tortillas, grated low-fat cheese and lime wedges.

60 ml ($^{1}/_{4}$ cup) olive oil
4 chicken thighs and 6 drumsticks
1 large red onion, finely chopped
1 large green capsicum (pepper), two-thirds diced and one-third julienned
3 teaspoons sweet paprika
400 g (14 oz) can chopped tomatoes
250 g (1$^{1}/_{4}$ cups) long-grain rice
$^{1}/_{2}$ teaspoon ground saffron

1 Heat 2 tablespoons of the oil in a deep frying pan over high heat. Season the chicken pieces well and brown in batches. Remove the chicken from the pan.

2 Reduce the heat to medium and add the remaining oil. Add the onion and diced capsicum, and cook gently for 5 minutes. Stir in the paprika and cook for about 30 seconds. Add the tomato and simmer for 1–3 minutes, or until the mixture thickens.

3 Stir 875 ml (3$^{1}/_{2}$ cups) of boiling water into the pan, then add the rice and saffron. Return the chicken to the pan and stir to combine. Season with salt and pepper. Bring to the boil, cover, reduce the heat to medium–low and simmer for 20 minutes, or until all the liquid has been absorbed and the chicken is tender. Stir in the julienned capsicum, then allow it to stand, covered, for 3–4 minutes before serving.

SAFFRON CHICKEN AND RICE

SERVES 4

PORK, PAPRIKA AND POTATO STEW

1 tablespoon paprika
4 thick pork loin cutlets
2 tablespoons olive oil
¼ cup (60 ml/2 fl oz) sherry vinegar
¼ teaspoon cayenne pepper
½ cup (125 ml/4 fl oz) tomato purée
400 g (13 oz) potatoes, cut into 2 cm (¾ inch) cubes
8 French shallots, peeled
200 g (6½ oz) rocket leaves

1 Combine the paprika with ¼ teaspoon each of salt and freshly ground black pepper. Sprinkle over both sides of the pork. Heat the oil over medium heat in a deep frying pan large enough to fit the cutlets in a single layer, and cook the cutlets until brown on both sides.

2 Pour the sherry vinegar into the pan and stir well to scrape up any sediment stuck to the base. Stir in the cayenne pepper, tomato purée and 1 cup (250 ml/8 fl oz) hot water. Bring to the boil, then add the potato and shallots. Reduce the heat and simmer, covered, for 30 minutes, or until the sauce has thickened and reduced by half—check the liquid level once or twice, and add a little more water if necessary. Season.

3 To serve, divide the rocket leaves among four serving plates and place a cutlet on top. Spoon the sauce and potato over the top.

SERVES 4

INGREDIENTS

70 g (2¹/₂ oz) cellophane noodles (mung bean vermicelli)
250 g (9 oz) Chinese cabbage
1 litre (4 cups) chicken stock
2.5 x 2.5 cm (1 x 1 inch) piece ginger, thinly sliced
350 g (12 oz) Chinese roast pork, skin removed and reserved (see note)
2 spring onions (scallions), thinly sliced on the diagonal
2 tablespoons light soy sauce
1 tablespoon Chinese rice wine
¹/₂ teaspoon sesame oil

1 Soak the noodles in boiling water for 3–4 minutes. Drain and rinse, then drain again.

2 Separate the cabbage leaves and cut the leafy ends from the stems. Cut both the cabbage stems and leaves into 2–3 cm (³/₄–1¹/₄ inch) squares.

3 Place the stock and ginger slices in a 2 litre (8 cup) flameproof casserole dish and bring to the boil over high heat. Add the cabbage stems and cook for 2 minutes, then add the cabbage leaves and cook for 1 minute. Reduce the heat to medium, add the noodles and cook, covered, for 4–5 minutes, stirring occasionally.

4 Meanwhile, cut the pork into 2 cm (³/₄ inch) cubes and add the spring onion, soy sauce, rice wine and sesame oil. Stir to combine, then cook, covered, for 3–4 minutes and then serve.

NOTE If desired, grill (broil) the reserved pork skin for 1 minute, or until crispy, and arrange on top of each serving.

SERVES 4

MEE GROB

INGREDIENTS

4 Chinese dried mushrooms
oil, for deep-frying
100 g (3¹/₂ oz) dried rice vermicelli
100 g (3¹/₂ oz) fried tofu, cut into matchsticks
4 garlic cloves, crushed
1 onion, chopped
1 chicken breast fillet, thinly sliced
8 green beans, sliced on the diagonal
6 spring onions (scallions), thinly sliced on the diagonal
8 raw prawns (shrimp), peeled and deveined, with tails
    intact
30 g (¹/₃ cup) bean sprouts
coriander (cilantro) leaves, to garnish

Sauce
1 tablespoon soy sauce
3 tablespoons white vinegar
5 tablespoons sugar
3 tablespoons fish sauce
1 tablespoon sweet chilli sauce

1 Soak the mushrooms in boiling water for 20 minutes. Drain, discard the stems and thinly slice.

2 Fill a wok one-third full of oil and heat to 180°C (350°F), or until a cube of bread browns in 15 seconds. Cook the vermicelli in small batches for 5 seconds, or until puffed and crispy. Drain. Add the tofu to the wok in batches and deep-fry for 1 minute, or until crisp. Drain. Carefully remove all but 2 tablespoons of oil.

3 Reheat the wok until very hot and add the garlic and onion and stir-fry for 1 minute. Add the chicken pieces, mushrooms, beans and half the spring onion. Stir-fry for 2 minutes, or until the chicken has almost cooked through. Add the prawns and stir-fry for a further 2 minutes, or until they just turn pink.

4 Combine all the sauce ingredients and add to the wok. Stir-fry for 2 minutes, or until the meat and prawns are tender and the sauce is syrupy.

5 Remove from the heat and stir in the vermicelli, tofu and bean sprouts. Garnish with the coriander and remaining sliced spring onion.

SERVES 4-6

16 mussels

12 large prawns (shrimp)

435 ml (1³/₄ cups) cider or dry white wine

50 g (1³/₄ oz) butter

1 garlic clove, crushed

2 shallots, finely chopped

2 celery stalks, finely chopped

1 large leek, white part only, thinly sliced

250 g (9 oz) small chestnut mushrooms, sliced

1 bay leaf

300 g (10¹/₂ oz) salmon fillet, skinned and cut into chunks

400 g (14 oz) sole fillet, skinned and cut into thick strips widthways

300 ml (10¹/₂ fl oz) thick (double/heavy) cream

3 tablespoons finely chopped parsley

1 Scrub the mussels and remove their beards. Throw away any that are open and don't close when tapped on the bench. Peel and devein the prawns.

2 Pour the cider into a large saucepan and bring to a simmer. Add the mussels, cover the pan and cook for 3–5 minutes, shaking the pan every now and then. Place a fine sieve over a bowl, tip in the mussels, then transfer them to a plate, throwing away any that haven't opened. Strain the cooking liquid again through the sieve.

3 Add the butter to the cleaned saucepan and melt over moderate heat. Add the garlic, shallot, celery and leek and cook for 7–10 minutes, or until the vegetables are just soft. Add the mushrooms and cook for a further 4–5 minutes until softened. While the vegetables are cooking, remove the mussels from their shells.

4 Add the strained liquid to the vegetables in the saucepan, add the bay leaf and bring to a simmer. Add the salmon, sole and prawns and cook for 3–4 minutes until the fish is opaque and the prawns are pink. Stir in the cream and cooked mussels and simmer for 2 minutes. Season and stir in the parsley.

SERVES 6

SHELLFISH STEW

INGREDIENTS

10 pieces veal shank, about 4 cm (1$^1/_2$ inch) thick
plain (all-purpose) flour, seasoned with salt and pepper
60 ml ($^1/_4$ cup) olive oil
60 g (2$^1/_4$ oz) butter
1 garlic clove
1 small carrot, finely chopped
1 large onion, finely chopped
$^1/_2$ celery stalk, finely chopped
250 ml (1 cup) dry white wine
375 ml (1$^1/_2$ cups) veal or chicken stock
400 g (14 oz) can chopped tomatoes
bouquet garni

1 Tie each piece of veal shank around its girth to secure the flesh, then dust with the seasoned flour. Heat the oil, butter and garlic in a large heavy saucepan big enough to hold the shanks in a single layer. Put the shanks in the saucepan and cook for 12–15 minutes until well browned. Remove the shanks from the pan and set aside. Discard the garlic.

2 Add the carrot, onion and celery to the pan and cook over moderate heat for 5–6 minutes, without browning. Increase the heat to high, add the wine and cook for 2–3 minutes. Add the stock, tomatoes and bouquet garni. Season with salt and pepper.

3 Return the veal shanks to the pan, standing them up in a single layer. Cover the pan, reduce the heat and simmer for 1 hour, or until the meat is tender and you can cut it with a fork.

4 If you prefer a thicker sauce, remove the veal shanks and increase the heat. Boil the sauce until reduced and thickened, then return the veal to the saucepan. Discard the bouquet garni, and taste for salt and pepper. If desired, serve with mashed potato.

SERVES 4

INGREDIENTS

1¹/₂ tablespoons peanut oil
1 kg (2 lb 4 oz) stewing beef (such as chuck), cut into 3 cm (1¹/₄ inch) cubes
1 tablespoon finely chopped ginger
1 tablespoon finely chopped garlic
1 litre (4 cups) good-quality beef stock
80 ml (¹/₃ cup) Chinese rice wine
80 ml (¹/₃ cup) hoisin sauce
5 cm (2 inch) piece cassia bark
1 piece dried tangerine peel
1 star anise
1 teaspoon Sichuan peppercorns, lightly crushed
2 teaspoons soft brown sugar
300 g (10¹/₂ oz) daikon, cut into 3 cm (1¹/₄ inch) chunks
3 spring onions (scallions), cut into 3 cm (1¹/₄ inch) lengths, plus extra, to garnish
50 g (1³/₄ oz) sliced bamboo shoots
a few drops sesame oil (optional)

1 Heat a wok until very hot, add the peanut oil and swirl to coat the side. Stir-fry the beef in four batches for 1–2 minutes for each batch, or until the meat is browned all over. Remove from the wok.

2 Add the ginger and garlic to the wok and stir-fry for a few seconds. Add the stock, rice wine, hoisin sauce, cassia bark, tangerine peel, star anise, Sichuan peppercorns, sugar, daikon and 875 ml (3¹/₂ cups) water, then return the beef to the wok.

3 Bring to the boil, skimming any scum that forms on the surface, then reduce to a simmer and cook, stirring occasionally, for 1¹/₂ hours, or until the beef is tender and the sauce has thickened slightly. Add the spring onion and bamboo shoots 5 minutes before the end of the cooking time. Stir in a few drops of sesame oil, if desired, and garnish with extra spring onion. Serve with rice.

NOTE You can remove the star anise, cassia bark and tangerine peel before serving or leave them in the serving dish for presentation.

HOISIN BEEF STEW

CHICKEN CASSEROLE WITH MUSTARD AND TARRAGON

$^1/_4$ cup (60 ml/2 fl oz) olive oil

1 kg (2 lb) chicken thigh fillets, halved, then quartered

1 onion, finely chopped

1 leek, sliced

1 clove garlic, finely chopped

350 g (12$^1/_2$ oz) button mushrooms, sliced

$^1/_2$ teaspoon dried tarragon

1$^1/_2$ cups (375 ml/12$^1/_2$ fl oz) chicken stock

$^3/_4$ cup (185 ml/6$^1/_4$ fl oz) cream

2 teaspoons lemon juice

2 teaspoons Dijon mustard

1 Preheat the oven to moderate 180°C (350°F/ Gas 4). Heat 1 tablespoon of the oil in a flameproof casserole dish over medium heat, and cook the chicken in two batches for 6–7 minutes each, or until golden. Remove from the dish.

2 Add the remaining oil to the casserole dish and cook the onion, leek and garlic over medium heat for 5 minutes, or until soft. Add the mushrooms and cook for 5–7 minutes, or until they are soft and browned, and most of the liquid has evaporated. Add the tarragon, chicken stock, cream, lemon juice and mustard, bring to the boil and cook for 2 minutes. Return the chicken pieces to the dish and season well. Cover.

3 Place the casserole in the oven and cook for 1 hour, or until the sauce has reduced and thickened. Season to taste with salt and pepper, and serve with potatoes and a green salad.

SERVES 4-6

INGREDIENTS

4 pieces (500 g/1 lb 2 oz) veal schnitzel
plain (all-purpose) flour, seasoned
50 g (1¾ oz) butter
1 tablespoon oil
185 ml (¾ cup) dry Marsala
3 teaspoons cream
30 g (1 oz) butter, chopped, extra

1 Using a meat mallet or the heel of your hand, flatten the schnitzel pieces to 5 mm (¼ inch) thick. Dust the veal in the flour, shaking off any excess. Heat the butter and oil in a large frying pan and cook the veal over medium–high heat for 1–2 minutes on each side, or until almost cooked through. Remove and keep warm.

2 Add the Marsala to the pan and bring to the boil, scraping the base of the pan to loosen any sediment. Reduce the heat and simmer for 1–2 minutes, or until slightly reduced. Add the cream and simmer for 2 minutes, then whisk in the extra butter until the sauce thickens slightly. Return the veal to the pan and simmer for 1 minute, or until the meat is warmed through. Serve immediately. Delicious with a creamy garlic mash and a tossed green salad.

NOTE Purchase veal that is pale in colour and free of sinew. Sinew will make the meat tough.

VEAL MARSALA

BEEF STROGANOFF

400 g (14 oz) beef fillet, cut into 1 x 5 cm ($^1/_2$ x 2 inch) strips
2 tablespoons plain (all-purpose) flour
50 g (1$^3/_4$ oz) butter
1 onion, thinly sliced
1 garlic clove, crushed
250 g (9 oz) small Swiss brown mushrooms, sliced
60 ml ($^1/_4$ cup) brandy
250 ml (1 cup) beef stock
1$^1/_2$ tablespoons tomato paste (purée)
185 g ($^3/_4$ cup) sour cream
1 tablespoon chopped flat-leaf (Italian) parsley

1 Dust the beef strips in flour, shaking off any excess.

2 Melt half the butter in a large frying pan and cook the meat in small batches for 1–2 minutes, or until seared all over. Remove. Add the remaining butter to the pan and cook the onion and garlic over medium heat for 2–3 minutes, or until they soften. Add the mushrooms and cook for 2–3 minutes.

3 Pour in the brandy and simmer until nearly all of the liquid has evaporated, then stir in the beef stock and tomato paste. Cook for 5 minutes to reduce the liquid slightly. Return the beef strips to the pan with any juices and stir in the sour cream. Simmer for 1 minute, or until the sauce thickens slightly. Season with salt and freshly ground black pepper.

4 Garnish with the chopped parsley and serve immediately with fettucine or steamed rice.

SERVES 4

CHICKEN

INGREDIENTS

12 large chicken wings
2 teaspoons garlic salt
2 teaspoons onion powder
oil, for deep-frying
125 ml (1/2 cup) tomato sauce (ketchup)
2 tablespoons Worcestershire sauce
50 g (1 3/4 oz) butter, melted
Tabasco sauce, to taste

Ranch dressing
1 small garlic clove, crushed
185 g (3/4 cup) mayonnaise
125 ml (1/2 cup) buttermilk
2 tablespoons finely chopped flat-leaf (Italian) parsley
1 tablespoon finely chopped chives
1 1/2 teaspoons lemon juice
1 1/2 teaspoons Dijon mustard
1 teaspoon onion powder

1 Pat the wings dry with paper towels, remove and discard the tip of each wing, then cut them in half at the joint. Combine the garlic salt, onion powder and 2 teaspoons of ground black pepper, and rub the spice mixture into each chicken piece.

2 Deep-fry the chicken in batches for 2–3 minutes without letting it brown, then remove from the oil and drain on crumpled paper towels. When the chicken has cooled a little, put it in a non-metallic bowl with the combined tomato sauce, Worcestershire sauce, butter and Tabasco, and toss so that all of the pieces are well coated in the marinade. Cover and refrigerate for at least 2 hours, or overnight.

3 To make the ranch dressing, mash the garlic and 1/4 teaspoon salt to a paste then add the mayonnaise, buttermilk, parsley, chives, lemon juice, mustard and onion powder, and whisk it all together. Season well, cover and chill for at least 1 hour before serving.

4 Preheat a barbecue to medium direct heat. Cook the chicken for 6–8 minutes on each side, or until it is caramelised and sticky, turning and basting with the marinade as it cooks. Serve hot with the ranch dressing.

SPICY BUFFALO WINGS WITH RANCH DRESSING

SERVES 4

CRISPY CHICKEN WINGS

INGREDIENTS

12 chicken wings
3 tablespoons soy sauce
3 tablespoons hoisin sauce
125 g ($^1/_2$ cup) tomato sauce (ketchup)
2 tablespoons honey
1 tablespoon soft brown sugar
1 tablespoon cider vinegar
2 garlic cloves, crushed
$^1/_4$ teaspoon Chinese five-spice powder
2 teaspoons sesame oil

1 Tuck the chicken wing tips to the underside and place in a non-metallic bowl. Mix together all the remaining ingredients and pour over the wings, tossing to coat. Cover and leave in the fridge for at least 2 hours, turning occasionally. Drain, reserving the marinade.

2 Cook the wings on a hot, lightly oiled barbecue grill or flat plate for 5 minutes, or until cooked through, brushing with the reserved marinade several times.

SERVES 6

INGREDIENTS

500 g (1 lb) chicken mince
1 red onion, finely chopped
3 cloves garlic, crushed
2 tablespoons chopped fresh mint
2 tablespoons chopped fresh parsley
2 tablespoons lime juice
2 eggs, lightly beaten
2 cups (160 g/5$\frac{1}{2}$ oz) fresh white breadcrumbs
2 teaspoons chicken stock powder
1$\frac{1}{2}$ cups (150 g/5 oz) dry breadcrumbs
oil, for shallow-frying
4 large flour tortillas
lettuce leaves, to serve
1 large ripe avocado, sliced

Lime Hummus
300 g (10 oz) can chickpeas, drained
2–3 tablespoons tahini
2 teaspoons sesame oil
2 cloves garlic, crushed
$\frac{1}{2}$ cup (60 ml/2 fl oz) lime juice
1 tablespoon finely chopped fresh mint
$\frac{1}{2}$ teaspoon sweet paprika

1 In a bowl, combine the chicken mince, onion, garlic, herbs, lime juice, 1 egg, fresh bread-crumbs, stock powder and some freshly ground black pepper. Use your hands to mix thoroughly. Shape 2 tablespoons of the mixture at a time into round patties, dip in the remaining beaten egg, then toss in the dry breadcrumbs, pressing them on firmly.

2 Arrange the patties on a tray, cover and refrigerate for 30 minutes. Just before serving, shallow-fry the patties in moderately hot oil for 2–3 minutes each side, or until golden and cooked through. Drain on paper towels.

3 To make the lime hummus, process the chickpeas, tahini, sesame oil, garlic, lime juice and a little salt and pepper in a food processor until the mixture is a smooth, thick paste. Stir in the mint and paprika.

4 To serve, toast the tortillas under a grill or place in a dry pan until heated and lightly browned on both sides. Arrange lettuce leaves, a few chicken patties and some sliced avocado on each and top with the lime hummus.

SERVES 4

CHICKEN QUESADILLAS

4 large green chillies
3 large red chillies
2 chicken breast fillets
3 tablespoons wholegrain mustard
2 tablespoons honey
4 flour tortillas
3 cups (375 g/12 oz) grated Cheddar
6 spring onions, thinly sliced
1–2 small red chillies, thinly sliced, optional
1–2 small green chillies, thinly sliced, optional
oilve oil, for cooking

Green Chilli Salsa
3 long green chillies, thinly sliced
2 tomatoes, peeled, seeded and chopped
1 onion, finely chopped
$1/3$ cup (10 g/$1/4$ oz) fresh coriander (cilantro) leaves, finely
   chopped
2 tablespoons lime juice

1 Place the large chillies under a hot grill and cook for 5–8 minutes, turning frequently, until the skins are blackened. Place the chillies in a plastic bag and leave to cool. Remove the skin and seeds. Cut them in half, then slice the flesh into thin strips.

2 Place the chicken in a deep dish. Combine the mustard and honey and add to the chicken. Turn the meat until well coated with the mixture. Cover and refrigerate for 1 hour. Place the chicken under a hot grill and cook for 4 minutes each side, or until tender. Cool slightly, then cut into thin strips.

3 To make the green chilli salsa, combine the chilli, tomato, onion, coriander and lime juice in a bowl and mix well, adding a little more lime juice if desired. Set aside to allow the flavours to combine.

4 Lightly grease a large, heavy-based frying pan and warm over medium heat. Place one tortilla in the pan and sprinkle with a quarter of the Cheddar and half the spring onion, roasted chilli, chicken and sliced chilli. Sprinkle with a third of the remaining Cheddar and top with another tortilla.

5 Brush lightly with a little oil, invert the quesadilla onto a plate and then slide back into the pan so that the top becomes the bottom. Cook for a few minutes longer, just until the Cheddar has melted and the underside looks golden and crisp. Slide the quesadilla onto a plate and keep warm.

6 Repeat with another tortilla, adding half of the remaining Cheddar, the remaining spring onion, roasted chilli, chicken and sliced chilli. Top with the rest of the Cheddar and the last tortilla. Serve immediately, cut into halves or triangles, with the salsa.

SERVES 4

1 kg (2 lb) chicken thigh fillets
$^1/_2$ cup (125 ml/4 fl oz) sake
$^3/_4$ cup (185 ml/6 fl oz) shoyu (Japanese soy sauce)
$^1/_2$ cup (125 ml/4 fl oz) mirin
2 tablespoons sugar
10 spring onions, diagonally cut into 2 cm ($^3/_4$ inch) pieces

1 Soak 25 wooden skewers in water for about 20 minutes to prevent burning. Drain and set aside.

2 Cut the chicken thigh fillets into bite-sized pieces. Combine the sake, shoyu, mirin and sugar in a small pan. Bring the mixture to the boil and then set aside.

3 Thread the chicken pieces onto the wooden skewers alternately with the spring onion pieces. Place the chicken skewers on a foil-lined tray and cook them under a preheated grill, turning and brushing frequently with the sauce, for 7–8 minutes, or until the chicken is cooked through. Serve immediately, garnished with a few spring onion pieces.

YAKITORI

MAKES 25 skewers

INGREDIENTS

Laksa paste

1 large onion, roughly chopped

5 cm (2 inch) piece fresh ginger, chopped

8 cm (3 inch) piece galangal, peeled and chopped

1 stem lemon grass, white part only, roughly chopped

2 cloves garlic

1 fresh red chilli, seeded and diced

2 teaspoons vegetable oil

2 tablespoons mild curry paste

500 g (1 lb) chicken breast fillets, cut into cubes

2 cups (500 ml/16 fl oz) chicken stock

60 g (2 oz) rice vermicelli

50 g ($1^3/_4$oz) dried egg noodles

400 ml (13 fl oz) light coconut milk

10 snow peas (mangetout), halved

3 spring onions, finely chopped

1 cup (90 g/3 oz) bean sprouts

$^1/_2$ cup (15 g/$^1/_2$ oz) fresh coriander (cilantro) leaves

1   To make the laksa paste, process the onion, ginger, galangal, lemon grass, garlic and chilli in a food processor until finely chopped. Add the oil and process until the mixture has a paste-like consistency. Spoon into a large wok, add the curry paste and stir over low heat for 1–2 minutes, until aromatic. Take care not to burn.

2   Increase the heat to medium, add the chicken and stir for 2 minutes, or until the chicken is well coated. Stir in the chicken stock and mix well. Bring slowly to the boil, then simmer for 10 minutes, or until the chicken is cooked through.

3   Meanwhile, cut the vermicelli into shorter lengths. Cook the vermicelli and egg noodles separately in large pans of boiling water for 5 minutes each. Drain and rinse in cold water.

4   Just prior to serving, add the light coconut milk and snow peas to the chicken and heat through. To serve, divide the vermicelli and noodles among four warmed serving bowls. Pour the hot laksa over the top and garnish with the spring onion, bean sprouts and coriander leaves.

HINT   If you prefer a more fiery laksa, use a medium or hot brand of curry paste or increase the amount of chillies in your laksa paste.

  SERVES 4-6

INGREDIENTS

Garlic Croutons
1 thin baguette
45 g (1¹/₂ oz) unsalted butter
¹/₂ cup (125 ml/4 fl oz) olive oil
4 cloves garlic, crushed

1 cos lettuce, tough outer leaves discarded
1 large smoked chicken (about 950 g/1 lb 14 oz)
1¹/₂ cups (150 g/5 oz) Parmesan shavings

Dressing
2 eggs
2 cloves garlic, crushed
2 tablespoons lemon juice
2 teaspoons Dijon mustard
45 g (1¹/₂ oz) can anchovy fillets, drained
1 cup (250 ml/8 fl oz) olive oil
¼ teaspoon salt
1 teaspoon freshly ground black pepper

1 To make the garlic croutons, slice the baguette diagonally into 1 cm (½ inch) thick slices. Melt the butter and olive oil in a large frying pan over moderate heat. Stir in the crushed garlic. Fry the bread slices, a few at a time, until golden. Remove from the pan and drain on paper towels.

2 Separate the lettuce leaves, wash and dry thoroughly. Tear the larger leaves into pieces and refrigerate until well chilled. Cut the chicken into bite-sized chunks. Refrigerate while preparing the dressing.

3 To make the dressing, blend or process the eggs, garlic, lemon juice, mustard and anchovies. With the motor running, gradually pour in the oil in a thin stream and process until thick. Season with the salt and pepper.

4 In a large bowl, combine the torn lettuce leaves, chicken, about half of the croutons and half the Parmesan. Add the dressing and toss well. Arrange 2–3 whole lettuce leaves in each individual serving bowl, spoon in the salad and sprinkle with the remaining croutons and Parmesan. Season liberally with freshly ground black pepper and serve immediately.

SERVES 4

SAGE AND RICOTTA STUFFED CHICKEN

250 g (1 cup) fresh ricotta cheese, well drained
1 tablespoon shredded sage leaves
2 garlic cloves, crushed
$1^{1}/_{2}$ teaspoons grated lemon zest
40 g ($1^{1}/_{2}$ oz) finely grated Parmesan cheese
4 chicken breast fillets, tenderloin removed
8 thin slices prosciutto
olive oil, for brushing

1 Mix together the ricotta, sage, garlic, zest and Parmesan until they are well combined. Use a sharp knife to cut a large pocket into the side of each chicken breast and fill each pocket with a quarter of the ricotta mixture. Pin the pockets closed with toothpicks and wrap each breast in two slices of prosciutto, securing it with a toothpick.

2 Heat a barbecue flat plate to medium direct heat, brush the chicken parcels with olive oil and season them with freshly ground black pepper. Cook them for 8 minutes on each side, or until they are cooked through. This is delicious served with baby spinach salad.

SERVES 4

INGREDIENTS

5 cm (2 inch) piece galangal (see hint)
2 cups (500 ml/16 fl oz) coconut milk
1 cup (250 ml/8 fl oz) chicken stock
3 chicken breast fillets, cut into thin strips
1–2 teaspoons finely chopped red chilli
2 tablespoons fish sauce
1 teaspoon soft brown sugar
1/4 cup (7 g/1/4 oz) fresh coriander (cilantro) leaves
fresh coriander (cilantro) sprigs, to serve

1   Peel the galangal and cut it into thin slices. Combine the galangal, coconut milk and stock in a medium pan. Bring to the boil and simmer, uncovered, over low heat for 10 minutes, stirring occasionally.

2   Add the chicken strips and chilli to the pan and simmer for 8 minutes.

3   Stir in the fish sauce and brown sugar. Add the coriander leaves and serve immediately, garnis

HINT   If fresh galangal is not available, you can use 5 large slices of dried galangal instead. Prepare by soaking the slices in a little boiling water for 10 minutes and then cutting them into shreds. Add the soaking liquid to the chicken stock to make 1 cup (250 ml/8 fl oz) and use it in the recipe.

SERVES 4

CHILLI CHICKEN AND CASHEW SALAD

3 tablespoons sweet chilli sauce

2 tablespoons lime juice

2 teaspoons fish sauce

2 tablespoons chopped coriander (cilantro)

1 garlic clove, crushed

1 small red chilli, finely chopped

11/2 teaspoons grated fresh ginger

2 tablespoons olive oil

600 g chicken breast fillets

100 g salad leaves

250 g cherry tomatoes, halved

100 g Lebanese cucumber, cut into bite-sized chunks

50 g snow pea (mangetout) sprouts, trimmed

80 g (1/2 cup) cashew nuts, roughly chopped

1 Combine the chilli sauce, lime juice, fish sauce, coriander, garlic, chilli, ginger and 1 tablespoon of the oil in a large bowl.

2 Heat the remaining oil in a frying or chargrill pan over medium heat until hot, and cook the chicken for 5–8 minutes on each side or until cooked through. While still hot, slice each breast widthways into 1 cm (1/2 inch) slices and toss in the bowl with the dressing. Leave to cool slightly.

3 Combine the salad leaves, cherry tomatoes, cucumber chunks and snow pea sprouts in a serving bowl. Add the chicken and all of the dressing, and toss gently until the leaves are lightly coated. Scatter with chopped cashews and serve.

SERVES 4

INGREDIENTS

60 ml ('/₄ cup) lemon juice

1'/₂ teaspoons garam masala

1 teaspoon ground turmeric

1 tablespoon finely grated fresh ginger

2 garlic cloves, finely chopped

3'/₂ tablespoons vegetable oil

3 chicken breast fillets (650 g/23 oz)

1 onion, thinly sliced

2 zucchini (courgettes), thinly sliced on the diagonal

100 g watercress leaves

150 g freshly shelled peas

2 ripe tomatoes, finely chopped

30 g (1 cup) coriander (cilantro) leaves

Dressing

1 teaspoon cumin seeds

'/₂ teaspoon coriander (cilantro) seeds

90 g ('/₃ cup) natural yoghurt

2 tablespoons chopped mint

2 tablespoons lemon juice

1   Combine the lemon juice, garam masala, turmeric, ginger, garlic and 2 teaspoons oil in a large bowl. Add the chicken fillets and onion, toss to coat in the marinade, cover, and refrigerate for 1 hour.

2   Remove and discard the onion then heat 2 tablespoons of oil in a large, frying pan. Cook the chicken for about 4–5 minutes on each side or until it is cooked through. Remove the chicken from the pan and leave for 5 minutes. Cut each breast across the grain into 1 cm ('/₂ inch) slices.

3   Heat the remaining oil in the pan and cook the zucchini for 2 minutes, or until lightly golden and tender. Toss with the watercress in a large bowl. Cook the peas in boiling water for 5 minutes, or until tender, then drain. Rinse under cold water to cool. Add to the salad with the tomato, chicken and coriander.

4   For the dressing, gently roast the cumin and coriander seeds in a dry frying pan for 1–2 minutes, or until fragrant. Remove, then pound the seeds to a powder. Mix with the yoghurt, mint and lemon juice, then gently fold through the salad.

SERVES 4

INDIAN MARINATED CHICKEN SALAD

SMOKED CHICKEN AND PASTA SALAD WITH MUSTARD DRESSING

INGREDIENTS

1 tablespoon balsamic vinegar
150 ml (5 fl oz) olive oil
1 tablespoon lemon juice
3 tablespoons wholegrain mustard
200 g (7 oz) bucatini
450 g (16 oz) good-quality smoked chicken breast
8 small radishes
2 small Fuji apples
4 spring onions, finely sliced
35 g (1 oz) rocket

1 Combine the vinegar, olive oil, lemon juice and mustard in a screw-top jar, and shake well to combine. Season to taste with salt and pepper. Bring a large saucepan of salted water to the boil, and cook the bucatini according to the packet instructions until al dente. Drain, rinse under cold water and drain again. Toss one-third of the dressing through the bucatini and set aside for 30 minutes.

2 Cut the chicken breast on the diagonal and place in a large bowl. Thinly slice the radishes and add to the chicken. Quarter, core and cube the apples without peeling them, and add to the chicken with the sliced spring onion and rocket. Pour in the remaining dressing and toss lightly.

3 Gently mix the pasta with the smoked chicken until well combined. Divide the salad among four serving dishes and serve with fresh, crusty bread. May be served cold as a light meal.

NOTE Bucatini is a thick, spaghetti-like pasta with a hollow centre. It has a chewy texture. Smoked chicken often has a dark skin. You may wish to remove this to improve the appearance of the salad.

SERVES 4

INGREDIENTS

375 g (13 oz) penne
100 ml (3^1/$_3$ fl oz) olive oil
4 long, thin eggplants (aubergines), thinly sliced on the diagonal
2 chicken breast fillets
2 teaspoons lemon juice
15 g (^{1}/$_2$ cup) chopped flat-leaf parsley
270 g (9^1/$_2$ oz) chargrilled red capsicum (pepper), drained and sliced (see note)
155 g (5^1/$_2$ oz) fresh asparagus spears, trimmed, blanched and cut into 5 cm (2 inch) lengths
85 g (3 oz) semi-dried (sun-blushed) tomatoes, finely sliced
grated Parmesan cheese (optional)

1 Cook the pasta in a large saucepan of boiling water until al dente. Drain, return to the pan and keep warm. Heat 2 tablespoons of the oil in a large frying pan over high heat and cook the eggplant for 4–5 minutes, or until golden and cooked through.

2 Heat a lightly oiled chargrill pan over high heat and cook the chicken for 5 minutes each side, or until browned and cooked through. Cut into thick slices. Combine the lemon juice, parsley and the remaining oil in a small jar and shake well. Return the pasta to the heat, toss through the dressing, chicken, eggplant, capsicum, asparagus and tomato until well mixed and warmed through. Season with black pepper. Serve warm with a scattering of grated Parmesan, if desired.

NOTE Jars of chargrilled capsicum can be bought at the supermarket; otherwise, visit your local deli.

SERVES 4

INGREDIENTS

250 g (9 oz) cotelli pasta
125 ml (¹/₂ cup) olive oil
1 large red capsicum (pepper)
3 chicken breast fillets
6 spring onions, cut into 2 cm (1 inch) lengths
4 garlic cloves, thinly sliced
35 g (³/₄ cup) chopped mint
80 ml (¹/₃ cup) cider vinegar
100 g baby English spinach leaves

1 Cook the pasta in a large saucepan of boiling water until al dente, drain, stir in 1 table-spoon of the oil and set aside. Meanwhile, cut the capsicum into quarters, removing the seeds and membrane. Place, skin-side-up, under a hot grill for 8–10 minutes, or until the skin blackens and blisters. Cool in a plastic bag, then peel away the skin. Cut into thin strips. Place the chicken between two sheets of plastic wrap and press with the palm of your hand until slightly flattened.

2 Heat 1 tablespoon of the oil in a large frying pan, add the chicken and cook over medium heat for 2–3 minutes each side, or until light brown and cooked through. Remove from the pan and cut into 5 mm slices.

3 Add another tablespoon of the oil to the pan and add the spring onion, sliced garlic and capsicum and cook, stirring, for 2–3 minutes, or until starting to soften. Add 25 g (¹/₂ cup) of the mint, the vinegar and the remaining oil and stir until warmed through. In a large bowl, combine the pasta, chicken, spinach, onion mixture and remaining mint and toss well, seasoning to taste. Serve warm.

SERVES 4

INGREDIENTS

4 tablespoons coconut cream
1 tablespoon fish sauce
1 tablespoon palm sugar
2 chicken breasts, skinned and cut into shreds
120 g (4^1/$_2$ oz) glass noodles
2 stems lemon grass
4 kaffir lime (makrut) leaves
1 red onion, finely chopped
a large handful coriander (cilantro) leaves, chopped
a large handful mint, chopped
1–2 red chillies, sliced
3 green bird's eye chillies, finely sliced
2 tablespoons roasted peanuts, chopped
1–2 limes, cut in halves or quarters

1   Mix the coconut cream in a small saucepan or a wok with the fish sauce and palm sugar and bring to the boil, then add the chicken and simmer until the chicken is cooked through. This should only take a minute if you stir it a couple of times. Leave the chicken to cool in the sauce. Soak the noodles in boiling water for a minute or two — they should turn translucent and soft when they are ready. Drain them, then, using a pair of scissors, cut them into shorter lengths.

2   Peel the lemon grass until you reach the first purplish ring, then trim off the root. Make two or three cuts down through the bulb-like root, finely slice across it until it starts to get harder, then throw the hard top piece away. Pull the stems out of the lime leaves by folding the leaves in half, with the shiny side inwards, and pulling down on the stalk. Roll up the leaves tightly, then slice them very finely across.

3   Put all the ingredients, except the lime, in a bowl with the noodles and chicken, with its sauce, and toss everything together. Now squeeze the lime pieces over the dish and toss again.

THAI CHICKEN WITH GLASS NOODLES

SERVES 4

INGREDIENTS

2 cups (500 ml/16 fl oz) coconut cream (do not shake the can—see note)
4 tablespoons green curry paste
2 tablespoons grated palm sugar or soft brown sugar
2 tablespoons fish sauce
4 kaffir lime (makrut) leaves, finely shredded
1 kg (2 lb) chicken thigh or breast fillets, cut into thick strips
200 g (6$^1/_2$ oz) bamboo shoots, cut into thick strips
100 g (3$^1/_2$ oz) snake beans, cut into 5 cm (2 inch) lengths
$^1/_2$ cup (15 g/$^1/_2$ oz) fresh Thai basil leaves

1   Place $^1/_2$ cup (125 ml/4 fl oz) of the thick coconut cream from the top of the can in a wok, and bring to the boil. Add the curry paste, then reduce the heat and simmer for 15 minutes, or until fragrant and the oil starts to separate from the cream. Add the palm sugar, fish sauce and kaffir lime leaves to the pan.

2   Stir in the remaining coconut cream and the chicken, bamboo shoots and beans, and simmer for 15 minutes, or until the chicken is tender. Stir in the Thai basil and serve with rice.

NOTE   Do not shake the can of coconut cream because good-quality coconut cream has a layer of very thick cream at the top that has separated from the rest of the cream. This has a higher fat content, which causes it to split or separate more readily than the rest of the coconut cream or milk.

SERVES 4-6

CHIANG MAI NOODLES

250 g (9 oz) fresh thin egg noodles
2 tablespoons oil
6 red Asian shallots, finely chopped
3 cloves garlic, crushed
1–2 small fresh red chillies, seeded and finely chopped
2–3 tablespoons red curry paste
375 g (13 oz) chicken breast fillet, cut into thin strips
2 tablespoons fish sauce
1 tablespoon grated palm sugar
750 ml (3 cups/25 fl oz) coconut milk
1 tablespoon lime juice
250 ml (1 cup/8$^1/_2$ fl oz) chicken stock
4 spring onions, sliced, to garnish
$^1/_3$ cup (10 g/$^1/_3$ oz) fresh coriander (cilantro) leaves, to garnish
fried red Asian shallot flakes, to garnish
purchased fried noodles, to garnish
fresh red chilli, finely diced, to garnish

1 Cook the noodles in a saucepan of boiling water according to the packet instructions. Drain, cover and set aside.

2 Heat a large wok over high heat, add the oil and swirl to coat. Add the shallots, garlic and chilli, and stir-fry for 3 minutes. Stir in the curry paste and stir-fry for 2 minutes. Add the chicken and stir-fry for 3 minutes, or until it changes colour.

3 Stir in the fish sauce, palm sugar, coconut milk, lime juice and stock. Reduce the heat and simmer over low heat for 5 minutes—do not boil.

4 To serve, divide the noodles among four deep serving bowls and spoon in the chicken mixture. Garnish with the spring onion, coriander, shallot flakes, noodles and chilli.

SERVES 4

BACON-WRAPPED CHICKEN

2 tablespoons olive oil

2 tablespoons lime juice

$1/4$ teaspoon ground coriander (cilantro)

6 chicken breast fillets

4 tablespoons fruit chutney

3 tablespoons chopped pecan nuts

6 rashers bacon

1 Mix together the olive oil, lime juice, coriander and salt and pepper. Using a sharp knife, cut a pocket in the thickest section of each fillet. Mix together the chutney and nuts. Spoon 1 tablespoon of the chutney mixture into each chicken breast pocket.

2 Turn the tapered ends of the fillets to the underside. Wrap a slice of bacon around each fillet to enclose the filling and secure with a toothpick.

3 Put the chicken parcels on a hot, lightly oiled barbecue grill or flat plate and cook for 5 minutes on each side, or until cooked through, turning once. Brush with the lime juice mixture several times during cooking and drizzle with any leftover lime juice mixture to serve.

NOTE This recipe also works well with prosciutto, which is an Italian equivalent of bacon.

SERVES 6

INGREDIENTS

1.8 kg (4 lb) chicken
1 tablespoon soy sauce
2 garlic cloves, crushed
1 teaspoon finely grated fresh ginger
1 tablespoon honey
1 tablespoon rice wine
1 teaspoon five-spice
1 tablespoon peanut oil

1 Wash the chicken and pat it thoroughly dry inside and out with paper towels. Whisk the soy sauce, garlic, ginger, honey, rice wine and five-spice together in a small bowl and brush it all over the chicken, ensuring every bit of skin is well coated. Put the chicken on a wire rack over a baking tray and refrigerate it, uncovered, for at least 8 hours, or overnight.

2 Preheat a kettle or covered barbecue to medium indirect heat and put a drip tray under the rack. Brush the chicken liberally with the peanut oil and put it breast-side up in the middle of the barbecue over the drip tray. Cover the barbecue and roast the chicken for 1 hour 10 minutes, or until the juices run clear when you pierce it with a skewer between the thigh and body. Check the chicken every so often, and if it appears to be over-browning, cover it loosely with foil. Leave it to rest, covered, for 10 minutes before carving and serving. The flavours in this style of chicken go particularly well with steamed Asian greens and fried rice.

FIVE-SPICE ROAST CHICKEN

SERVES 4

HONEY MUSTARD CHICKEN

175 g ($^1/_2$ cup) honey
60 g ($^1/_4$ cup) Dijon mustard
2 tablespoons oil
2 tablespoons white wine vinegar
3 garlic cloves, crushed
2 tablespoons chopped parsley leaves
1.8 kg (4 lb) chicken, cut into 10 serving pieces

1 Put the honey, mustard, oil, white wine vinegar, garlic, parsley and $^1/_4$ teaspoon freshly ground black pepper in a large, non-metallic bowl. Mix it all together well, and put aside 60 ml ($^1/_4$ cup) of the marinade to baste the chicken during cooking. Add the chicken pieces to the rest of the marinade and turn them so that they are thoroughly coated. Cover the bowl and refrigerate it for at least 4 hours, or overnight.

2 Preheat a covered or kettle barbecue to medium indirect heat and cook the chicken pieces for 20–30 minutes, or until they are cooked through. The breast pieces may take as little as 15 minutes, while dark meat will take longer. Baste the chicken with the reserved marinade during the last 5–8 minutes of cooking, but no earlier or it is likely to burn. The chicken is delicious served on a bed of spring onion mash.

SERVES 4-6

INGREDIENTS

250 g (1 cup) plain Greek-style yoghurt
2 teaspoons soft brown sugar
4 garlic cloves, crushed
3 teaspoons ground cumin
1$^1/_2$ teaspoons ground coriander (cilantro)
7 g ($^1/_4$ cup) chopped flat-leaf (Italian) parsley
60 ml ($^1/_4$ cup) lemon juice
1 x 1.8 kg (4 lb) chicken, cut into 10 serving pieces
cooking oil spray

1   Put the yoghurt, brown sugar, garlic, cumin, coriander, chopped parsley and lemon juice in
    a large non-metallic bowl and mix them together. Add the chicken pieces to the marinade
    and turn them so that they are completely coated, then cover and refrigerate for at least 2
    hours, or overnight.

2   Lightly spray the barbecue plates with oil, then preheat the barbecue to medium direct
    heat. Take the chicken pieces out of the marinade and season them with salt and pepper.
    Cook the chicken pieces on the flat plate, turning them frequently, for 20–30 minutes, or
    until they are cooked through. If you have a barbecue with a lid, cover the barbecue while
    the chicken is cooking. This way, the breast pieces will take only 15 minutes to cook, while
    the pieces on the bone will take about 10 minutes longer.

SERVES 4-6

MARGARITA CHICKEN

4 chicken breasts, skin on, tenderloin and any excess fat removed
60 ml ($\frac{1}{4}$ cup) tequila
60 ml ($\frac{1}{4}$ cup) lime juice
2 small chillies, finely chopped
3 garlic cloves, crushed
15 g ($\frac{1}{4}$ cup) finely chopped coriander (cilantro) leaves
1 tablespoon olive oil
lime wedges

1 Put the chicken, tequila, lime juice, chilli, garlic, coriander and olive oil in a non-metallic bowl and mix it all together so that the chicken is coated in the marinade. Cover the bowl and refrigerate for at least 2 hours, or preferably overnight.

2 Preheat a barbecue chargrill to medium–high direct heat. Remove the chicken breasts from the marinade, season them with salt and pepper, and grill for 7–8 minutes on each side or until they are cooked through.

3 Slice the chicken breasts on the diagonal and serve with lime wedges.

SERVES 4

INGREDIENTS

4 large chicken breast fillets
2 tablespoons mirin
2 tablespoons sake
1 tablespoon oil
5 cm (2 inch) piece of fresh ginger, very finely sliced
3 teaspoons soy sauce
salad leaves, to serve

1   Put the chicken in a non-metallic dish. Combine the mirin, sake and oil and pour over the chicken. Marinate for 15 minutes, then drain the chicken, reserving the marinade.

2   Cook the chicken on a hot, lightly oiled barbecue grill or flat plate for 4 minutes each side, or until tender.

3   Put the ginger in a pan and add the reserved marinade. Boil for about 7 minutes, or until thickened. Drizzle the soy sauce over the chicken and top with the ginger. Serve immediately on a bed of salad leaves.

MIRIN AND SAKE CHICKEN

SERVES 4

THAI SPICED CHICKEN WITH POTATO ROSTI

600 g (1 lb 5 oz) chicken breast fillet, cut into strips
1 tablespoon chopped lemon grass
2 tablespoons lime juice
1¹/₂ tablespoons oil
2 garlic cloves, crushed
1 tablespoon grated fresh ginger
2 teaspoons sweet chilli sauce
2 spring onions (scallions), chopped
1 lime, cut into 6 wedges

Potato rosti
600 g (1 lb 5 oz) potatoes
3 tablespoons plain (all-purpose) flour
1 egg, lightly beaten

1 Remove any excess fat or sinew from the chicken and put the chicken in a shallow, non-metallic dish. Mix together the lemon grass, lime juice, oil, garlic, ginger, sweet chilli sauce and spring onion. Pour over the chicken pieces, cover and refrigerate for at least 2 hours.

2 To make the potato rosti, peel and grate the potatoes. Squeeze the excess moisture from the potato with your hands until it feels quite dry. Mix the potato with the flour and egg and season well. Divide into six equal portions. Cook on a hot, lightly oiled barbecue flat plate for 10 minutes, or until golden brown on both sides, flattening them down with the back of a spatula during cooking.

3 Drain the chicken and reserve the marinade. Cook on a barbecue grill or flat plate for 3 minutes each side, or until tender and golden brown. Brush with the reserved marinade while cooking. Serve with the rosti and a squeeze of lime juice.

SERVES 6

INGREDIENTS

1 kg (2 lb) chicken thigh fillets, cut into 2 cm ($^3/_4$ inch) cubes
$1^1/_2$ tablespoons finely chopped fresh thyme
1 tablespoon oil
90 g (3 oz) butter
3 French shallots, thinly sliced
$1^1/_2$ cups (375 ml/12 fl oz) apple cider
1 kg (2 lb) potatoes, cubed
2 large green apples, peeled, cored and sliced into eighths
$^2/_3$ cup (170 ml/$5^1/_2$ fl oz) cream

1   Season the chicken thighs with 2 teaspoons of the thyme and salt and black pepper.
    Heat the oil and 20 g ($^3/_4$ oz) of the butter in a large saucepan over medium–high heat.
    Cook the chicken in two batches for 2–3 minutes, or until evenly browned. Remove
    from the pan.

2   Add the French shallots and the remaining thyme to the pan, and sauté for 2 minutes.
    Pour in the cider, then bring to the boil, scraping off any sediment that has stuck to the
    bottom of the pan. Return the chicken to the pan and cover. Reduce the heat to
    medium–low and cook for 35–40 minutes, or until the chicken is tender and the sauce
    has reduced (check occasionally to see if any water needs to be added).

3   Meanwhile, cook the potato and apple in a saucepan of boiling water for 15–20 minutes,
    or until tender. Drain and return to the pan over low heat for 1 minute to allow any water
    to evaporate. Remove from the heat, and mash with a potato masher. Stir in 2 tablespoons
    of the cream and the remaining butter with a wooden spoon, then season with salt and
    pepper.

4   Gently stir the remaining cream into the chicken stew and cook for a further 2–4 minutes,
    or until the sauce has thickened. Serve at once with the potato and apple mash and a
    crisp green salad.

SERVES 4

CHICKEN, ARTICHOKE AND BROAD BEAN STEW

1 cup (155 g/5 oz) frozen broad beans
8 chicken thighs (skin removed, optional)
$^1/_2$ cup (60 g/2 oz) seasoned plain flour
2 tablespoons oil
1 large red onion, cut into small wedges
$^1/_2$ cup (125 ml/4 fl oz) dry white wine
$1^1/_4$ cups (310 ml/10 fl oz) chicken stock
2 teaspoons finely chopped fresh rosemary
340 g (11 oz) marinated artichokes, well drained and quartered
800 g (1 lb 10 oz) potatoes, cut into large cubes
60 g (2 oz) butter

1 Remove the skins from the broad beans. Coat the chicken in the flour, shaking off the excess. Heat the oil in a saucepan or flameproof casserole dish, then brown the chicken in two batches on all sides over medium heat. Remove and drain on paper towels.

2 Add the onion to the pan and cook for 3–4 minutes, or until soft but not brown. Increase the heat to high, pour in the wine and boil for 2 minutes, or until reduced to a syrup. Stir in 1 cup (250 ml/8 fl oz) of the stock and bring just to the boil, then return the chicken to the pan with the rosemary. Reduce the heat to low and simmer, covered, for 45 minutes.

3 Add the artichokes to the pan, increase the heat to high and return to the boil. Reduce to a simmer and cook, uncovered, for 10–15 minutes. Add the beans and cook for a further 5 minutes.

4 Meanwhile, cook the potato in a saucepan of boiling water for 15–20 minutes, or until tender. Drain, then return to the pan. Add the butter and the remaining stock, and mash with a potato masher. Serve on the side of the stew.

SERVES 4

1 stem lemon grass, white part only, chopped
5 cm (2 inch) piece ginger, peeled and chopped
2–3 small red chillies, seeded and chopped
1 teaspoon grated kaffir lime (makrut) or lime rind
2–3 cloves garlic, chopped
$^1/_2$ teaspoon ground black pepper
2 tablespoons oil
375 g (12 oz) chicken breast fillets, cut into thin strips
250 g (8 oz) green beans, cut into short pieces
1 celery stick, cut into thick slices
185 g (6 oz) snow peas (mangetout), halved
200 g (6$^1/_2$ oz) asparagus, cut into short pieces
270 ml (9 fl oz) can coconut cream
2 tablespoons sweet chilli sauce
20 small fresh basil leaves

1 Place the lemon grass, ginger, chilli, lime rind, garlic, pepper and oil in a food processor or blender, and process until the mixture forms a rough paste. Combine the paste and chicken strips in a glass or ceramic bowl, cover and refrigerate for at least 15 minutes.

2 Briefly blanch the beans, celery, snow peas and asparagus in a pan of boiling water. Drain and plunge into iced water. Drain again.

3 Heat the wok until very hot and stir-fry the chicken mixture in batches over high heat for 3–4 minutes, or until the chicken is cooked through. Stir constantly so the paste doesn't burn. Return all of the chicken to the wok with the vegetables, coconut cream, sweet chilli sauce, to taste, and basil leaves. Stir-fry until heated through. Serve with rice or noodles.

CHICKEN WITH BEANS AND ASPARAGUS

SERVES 4

SICHUAN CHICKEN

INGREDIENTS

$1/4$ teaspoon five-spice powder
750 g ($1^1/2$ lb) chicken thigh fillets, halved
2 tablespoons peanut oil
1 tablespoon julienned fresh ginger
1 teaspoon Sichuan peppercorns, crushed
1 teaspoon chilli bean paste (toban djan)
2 tablespoons light soy sauce
1 tablespoon Chinese rice wine
$1^1/4$ cups (250 g/8 oz) jasmine rice
600 g ($1^1/4$ lb) baby bok choy, leaves separated

1 Sprinkle the five-spice powder over the halved chicken fillets. Heat a wok until very hot, add half the oil and swirl to coat the side. Add the chicken pieces and cook for 2 minutes each side, or until browned. Remove from the wok.

2 Reduce the heat to medium. Add the julienned ginger to the wok and cook for 30 seconds. Add the crushed Sichuan peppercorns and chilli bean paste. Return the chicken pieces to the wok, add the soy sauce, wine and $1/2$ cup (125 ml/4 fl oz) water, then simmer for 15–20 minutes, or until the chicken is cooked through.

3 Meanwhile, bring a large saucepan of water to the boil. Add the rice and cook for 12 minutes, stirring occasionally. Drain well.

4 Heat the remaining peanut oil in a saucepan. Add the baby bok choy and toss gently for 1 minute, or until the leaves wilt and the stems are tender. Serve with the chicken and boiled rice.

SERVES 4

INGREDIENTS

750 g (1 1/2 lb) chicken thigh fillets, cut into 5 cm (2 inch)
  pieces
plain flour, for coating
2 tablespoons oil
2 teaspoons red curry paste
2 spring onions, sliced
415 g (13 oz) can apricot halves in light syrup
1/2 cup (125 ml/4 fl oz) chicken stock
200 g (6 1/2 oz) plain yoghurt
2 tablespoons chopped fresh coriander (cilantro) leaves
fresh coriander (cilantro) leaves, extra, to garnish

1 Lightly coat the chicken in the flour. Heat the oil in a saucepan, add the curry paste and stir over low heat for 1 minute. Add the spring onion and chicken, and cook, stirring, over medium heat for 2–3 minutes, or until the chicken is golden.

2 Drain the apricots and reserve 1/2 cup (125 ml/4 fl oz) apricot juice. Add the reserved juice, apricots and stock to the pan. Bring to the boil, then reduce the heat and simmer for 10 minutes, or until the chicken is tender.

3 Mix together the yoghurt and coriander, and place a spoonful of the mixture over each serving of chicken. Garnish with extra coriander leaves. Serve with couscous or rice.

SPICY APRICOT CHICKEN

SERVES 4

CHICKEN AND LEEK PIE

INGREDIENTS

50 g (1³/₄ oz) butter
2 large leeks, washed and thinly sliced
4 spring onions, sliced
1 clove garlic, crushed
¹/₄ cup (30 g/1 oz) plain flour
1¹/₂ cups (375 ml/12 fl oz) chicken stock
¹/₂ cup (125 ml/4 fl oz) cream
1 medium barbecued chicken, chopped
2 sheets puff pastry, thawed
¹/₄ cup (60 ml/2 fl oz) milk

1 Preheat the oven to moderately hot 200°C (400°F/Gas 6). In a pan, melt the butter and add the leek, spring onion and garlic. Cook over low heat for 6 minutes, or until the leek is soft but not browned. Sprinkle in the flour and mix well. Pour in the stock gradually and cook, stirring well, until the mixture is thick and smooth.

2 Stir in the cream and the chicken. Put the mixture in a shallow 20 cm (8 inch) pie dish and set aside to cool.

3 Cut a circle out of one of the sheets of pastry to cover the top of the pie. Brush around the rim of the pie dish with a little milk. Put the pastry on top and seal around the edge firmly. Trim off any overhanging pastry and decorate the edge with the back of a fork. Cut the other sheet into 1 cm (¹/₂ inch) strips and roll each strip up loosely into a spiral. Arrange the spirals on top of the pie, starting from the middle and leaving a gap between each one. The spirals may not cover the whole surface of the pie. Make a few small holes between the spirals to let out any steam, and brush the top of the pie lightly with milk. Bake for 25–30 minutes, or until the top is brown and crispy. Make sure the spirals look well cooked and are not raw in the middle.

NOTE Make small pies by placing the mixture into 4 greased 1¹/₄ cup (315 ml/10 fl oz) round ovenproof dishes. Cut the pastry into 4 rounds to fit. Bake for 15 minutes, or until crisp.

SERVES 4

INGREDIENTS

Pastry	Filling
2 cups (250 g/8 oz) self-raising flour	1 barbecued chicken
125 g (4 oz) butter, chopped	30 g (1 oz) butter
1 egg	1 onion, finely chopped
	310 g (10 oz) can creamed corn
	1¼ cups (315 ml/10 fl oz) cream

1 To make the pastry, process the flour and butter in a food processor for 15 seconds, or until the mixture is fine and crumbly. Add the egg and 2–3 tablespoons water and process for 30 seconds, or until the mixture just comes together. Turn onto a lightly floured surface and gather together into a smooth ball. Cover with plastic wrap and refrigerate for 20 minutes.

2 Meanwhile, to make the filling, remove the meat from the chicken carcass and shred finely. Heat the butter in a pan and cook the onion over medium heat for 3 minutes. Add the chicken, corn and cream. Bring to the boil, then reduce the heat and simmer for 10 minutes. Remove from the heat and allow to cool slightly.

3 Preheat the oven to moderate 180°C (350°F/Gas 4). Roll half the pastry between two sheets of plastic wrap to cover the base and side of a 23 cm (9 inch) pie dish. Spoon the chicken mixture into the pastry-lined dish.

4 Roll the remaining pastry to cover the top of the pie. Brush with milk. Press the edges together to seal. Trim the edges with a sharp knife. Roll the excess pastry into two long ropes and twist together. Brush the pie edge with a little milk and place the pastry rope around the rim. Bake for 45 minutes.

FAMILY CHICKEN PIE

SERVES 6

GINGER CHICKEN WITH MUSHROOMS AND WHEAT NOODLES

4 dried Chinese mushrooms
2 teaspoons cornflour (cornstarch)
2 tablespoons soy sauce
2 tablespoons oyster sauce
1 tablespoon mirin or sweet sherry
200 g (6^1/$_2$ oz) dried wheat noodles
1 teaspoon sesame oil
oil, for cooking
2–3 cloves garlic, crushed

8 cm (3 inch) piece fresh ginger, cut into matchsticks
375 g (12 oz) chicken breast fillets or tenderloins, cut into
thin strips
1 red onion, cut into thin wedges
6 spring onions, cut into short lengths
185 g (6 oz) small field mushrooms, thickly sliced
1 cup (90 g/3 oz) bean sprouts
^{1}/$_3$ cup (20 g/^{3}/$_4$ oz) chopped fresh mint

1 Place the dried mushrooms in a small bowl and cover with hot water. Leave to soak for 10 minutes, or until softened. Drain and squeeze dry, then discard the hard centre stem and chop the mushrooms finely.

2 Combine the cornflour with ^{1}/$_4$ cup (60 ml/2 fl oz) water and mix to a fine paste. Add the soy sauce, oyster sauce and mirin.

3 Cook the noodles in a large pan of boiling salted water for 1–2 minutes, or according to the manufacturer's instructions. Drain and set aside.

4 Heat the wok until very hot, add the sesame oil and 1 tablespoon of the oil, and swirl it around to coat the side. Stir-fry the garlic, ginger and chicken strips in batches over high heat for 2–3 minutes, or until the chicken has cooked through. Remove from the wok and set aside.

5 Reheat the wok, add 1 tablespoon of the oil and stir-fry the red onion and spring onion for 1–2 minutes, or until softened. Add the dried and field mushrooms, then stir-fry the mixture for 1–2 minutes, or until tender. Remove from the wok and set aside.

6 Add the soy sauce mixture to the wok and stir for 1–2 minutes, or until the sauce is well heated and slightly thickened. Return the chicken and vegetables to the wok with the bean sprouts, noodles and chopped mint. Stir until the noodles are well coated with the sauce. Serve at once.

SERVES 4

INGREDIENTS

2 x 800 g (1 lb 10 oz) chickens
100 g (3^1/$_2$ oz) butter, softened
2 cloves garlic, crushed
1 tablespoon finely grated orange rind
^{1}/$_2$ cup (60 ml/2 fl oz) orange juice

1 Preheat the oven to hot 220°C (425°F/Gas 7). Using kitchen scissors, cut the chickens in half through the backbone and breastbone. Pat dry with paper towels and wipe the inside.

2 Combine the butter, garlic and orange rind and beat well. Gently loosen the skin of the chickens by sliding your fingers between the flesh and the skin. Push the orange butter under the skin as evenly as possible. Put the chickens onto a ceramic dish and pour on the orange juice. Cover and refrigerate for 3 hours, or preferably overnight.

3 Drain the chicken pieces well and arrange cut-side down on roasting racks inside two baking dishes. Pour 2 tablespoons of water into each baking dish.

4 Roast for 30–40 minutes, or until the chickens are golden brown. Cover with foil and allow to rest for 15 minutes. Cut into quarters to serve.

NOTE If you can, use freshly squeezed orange juice.

ORANGE ROASTED CHICKENS

SERVES 8

RICE WITH CHICKEN AND SEAFOOD

500 g (1 lb) raw medium prawns (shrimp)
500 g (1 lb) mussels
200 g (6$^1/_2$ oz) calamari (squid) tubes
$^1/_4$ cup (60 ml/2 fl oz) oil
2 chorizo sausages, thickly sliced
500 g (1 lb) chicken pieces
300 g (10 oz) pork fillet, thickly sliced
4 cloves garlic, crushed
2 red onions, chopped
$^1/_4$ teaspoon saffron threads, soaked in hot water
$^1/_4$ teaspoon turmeric
4 large tomatoes, peeled, seeded and chopped
2 cups (440 g/14 oz) short-grain rice
1.25 litres hot chicken stock
125 g (4 oz) green beans, cut into 4 cm (1$^1/_2$ inch) lengths
1 red capsicum (peppers), cut into thin strips
1 cup (155 g/5 oz) fresh peas

1 Peel the prawns. Devein, leaving the tails intact. Scrub the mussels and remove the beards. Cut the calamari tubes into 5 mm ($^1/_4$ inch) thin slices. Heat 1 tablespoon of the oil in a large, heavy-based pan and add the chorizo. Cook over medium heat for 5 minutes, or until browned. Drain on paper towels. Add the chicken pieces and cook for 5 minutes, or until golden, turning once. Drain on paper towels.

2 Add the pork to the pan and cook for 3 minutes, or until browned, turning once. Drain on paper towels. Heat the remaining oil in the pan, add the garlic, onion, drained saffron and turmeric, and cook over medium heat for 3 minutes, or until the onion is soft. Add the tomato and cook for 3 minutes, or until soft.

3 Add the rice and stir for 5 minutes, or until the rice is translucent. Stir in the hot chicken stock, bring to the boil, cover and simmer for 10 minutes. Add the chicken, cover and cook for 20 minutes. Add the pork, prawns, mussels, calamari, chorizo and vegetables. Cover and cook for 10 minutes, or until the liquid has been absorbed.

SERVES 4-6

1 tablespoon olive oil
1 onion, finely chopped
2 cloves garlic, crushed
100 g (3^1/$_2$ oz) ham, finely chopped
1 green capsicum (pepper), finely chopped
2 tablespoons finely chopped pitted black olives
^{1}/$_3$ cup (35 g/1^1/$_4$ oz) grated Parmesan
6 chicken breast fillets
plain flour, to coat
2 eggs, lightly beaten
1^1/$_2$ cups (150 g/5 oz) dry breadcrumbs
^{1}/$_4$ cup (60 ml/2 fl oz) olive oil

1 Heat the oil in a pan and add the onion, garlic, ham and capsicum. Cook, stirring, over medium heat for 5 minutes, or until the onion is soft. Remove and place in a heatproof bowl. Add the olives and Parmesan.

2 Cut a deep pocket in the side of each chicken fillet, cutting almost through to the other side.

3 Fill each fillet with the ham mixture and secure with toothpicks along the opening of the pocket. Coat each fillet with the flour, shaking off any excess. Dip into the beaten egg and then coat with the breadcrumbs. Heat the oil in a large pan and cook the fillets, in batches, over medium-high heat for 15–20 minutes, turning halfway through, until golden and cooked through. To serve, remove the toothpicks, then cut diagonally into thin slices.

STUFFED CHICKEN BREASTS

SERVES 4

VIETNAMESE CHICKEN AND NOODLE CASSEROLE

1 stem lemon grass
4 kaffir lime (makrut) leaves
4 cups (1 litre/5$^1/_3$ pt) chicken stock
400 ml (13 fl oz) coconut cream
$^1/_4$ cup (30 g/1 oz) coconut milk powder
2 tablespoons peanut oil
400 g (13 oz) chicken breast fillets, cut into strips
12 raw king prawns (jumbo shrimp), peeled and deveined, tails intact
8 spring onions, sliced
2 teaspoons finely chopped fresh ginger
4 cloves garlic, finely chopped
2 small red chillies, seeded and finely chopped
500 g (1 lb) Hokkien noodles
1 teaspoon dried shrimp paste
2 tablespoons lime juice
1 cup (90 g/3 oz) bean sprouts
fresh mint leaves, to garnish
fresh coriander (cilantro) leaves, to garnish

1 Finely chop the white stem of the lemon grass. Remove the centre stem from the kaffir lime leaves, then finely shred the leaves.

2 Place the lemon grass and lime leaves in a large, heavy-based pan with the stock, coconut cream and coconut milk powder. Bring to the boil, stirring constantly to dissolve the coconut milk powder. Reduce the heat and simmer, covered, for 15 minutes.

3 Heat a wok over high heat and add the peanut oil. Add the chicken, prawns, spring onion, ginger, garlic and chilli. Stir-fry for 5–10 minutes, or until the chicken and prawns are cooked through.

4 Place the noodles in the simmering coconut cream, then add the chicken and prawn mixture from the wok. Add the shrimp paste and lime juice. Allow the noodles to heat through.

5 Divide the sprouts among warmed deep bowls and place the noodles, chicken and prawns on top. Ladle the sauce over, scatter with mint and coriander and serve at once.

SERVES 6

4 vine-ripened tomatoes, cut into 1 cm ($^1/_2$ inch) slices
1 teaspoon caster sugar
1 red onion, sliced
150 ml olive oil
1 ripe avocado
60 g ($^1/_4$ cup) sour cream
100 ml (3$^1/_2$ fl oz) milk
2 tablespoons lime juice
2 x 16 cm corn tortillas
1 teaspoon dried oregano
2$^1/_2$ teaspoons ground cumin
1$^1/_4$ teaspoons garlic salt
$^1/_2$ teaspoon cayenne pepper
4 small skinless chicken breast fillets (about 600 g/21 oz)
15 g ($^1/_2$ cup) coriander (cilantro) leaves

1 Place the tomato slices in a wide dish, sprinkle with sugar and season well. Layer the onion over the top and drizzle with 60 ml ($^1/_4$ cup) of oil. Chill for 20 minutes.

2 Blend the avocado, sour cream, milk, lime juice and 80 ml ($^1/_3$ cup) water in a food processor for 1 minute or until smooth. Season.

3 Cut each of the corn tortillas into eight 2 cm (1 inch) strips. Combine the oregano, cumin, garlic salt and cayenne pepper, and coat the chicken breasts in the spice mixture, pressing down firmly with your fingers. Heat 1$^1/_2$ tablespoons of oil over medium– high heat in a large, non-stick frying pan until hot. Cook the chicken breasts for 4–5 minutes on each side, or until cooked through. Cool, then refrigerate. In the same pan add 60 ml ($^1/_4$ cup) of oil. Fry the tortilla strips until golden, turning once during cooking.

4 On each plate arrange the tomato and onion slices in a small circle. Slice each chicken breast on the diagonal into 2 cm (1 inch) pieces and arrange over the tomato. Spoon the dressing over the chicken and arrange four tortilla strips over the top. Sprinkle with coriander leaves and serve immediately.

BLACKENED CHICKEN WITH CRISPY TORTILLA

SERVES 4

CHARGRILLED CHICKEN WITH SPINACH AND RASPBERRIES

60 ml ($^1/_4$ cup) raspberry vinegar
2 tablespoons lime juice
2 garlic cloves, crushed
2 tablespoons chopped oregano
1 teaspoon soft brown sugar
2 small red chillies, finely chopped
125 ml ($^1/_2$ cup) virgin olive oil
4 chicken breast fillets
1 teaspoon Dijon mustard
200 g baby English spinach leaves
250 g fresh raspberries

1 Mix 2 tablespoons of the raspberry vinegar, the lime juice, crushed garlic, 1 tablespoon of the oregano, the sugar, chilli and 60 ml ($^1/_4$ cup) of the oil in a large bowl. Immerse the chicken in the marinade, cover and refrigerate for 2 hours.

2 Preheat the oven to 180°C (350°F/Gas 4). Heat a chargrill pan and cook the chicken for 3 minutes on each side, then place on a baking tray and bake for a further 5 minutes, or until cooked through. Allow the chicken to rest for 5 minutes, then cut each breast into five strips on the diagonal.

3 To make the dressing, combine the remaining oil, vinegar and oregano with the mustard, $^1/_4$ teaspoon salt and freshly ground black pepper and mix well. Toss the spinach and raspberries with half of the dressing. Top with the chicken and drizzle with the remaining dressing.

SERVES 4

INGREDIENTS

3 tablespoons yellow or red miso paste
2 tablespoons sugar
60 ml ($^1/_4$ cup) sake
2 tablespoons mirin
1 kg (2 lb 3 oz) chicken thighs, boned (skin on)
1 cucumber
2 spring onions, cut into 2 cm ($^3/_4$ inch) pieces

1 Soak 12 long wooden bamboo skewers in cold water for at least 10 minutes. Place the miso, sugar, sake and mirin in a small saucepan over medium heat and cook, stirring well, for 2 minutes, or until the sauce is smooth and the sugar has dissolved completely.

2 Cut the chicken into 2.5 cm (1 inch) cubes. Seed the cucumber and cut into 2 cm ($^3/_4$ inch) batons. Thread the chicken, cucumber and spring onion pieces alternately onto the skewers — you should have three pieces of chicken, three pieces of cucumber and three pieces of spring onion per skewer.

3 Cook on a chargrill plate over high heat, turning occasionally, for 10 minutes, or until the chicken is almost cooked. Brush with the miso sauce and continue cooking, then turn and brush the other side. Repeat this process once or twice until the chicken and vegetables are cooked. Serve immediately with rice and salad.

MISO YAKITORI CHICKEN

SERVES 4

WILD RICE AND ROAST CHICKEN WITH ASIAN DRESSING

190 g (1 cup) wild rice
200 g (1 cup) jasmine rice
1 Chinese barbecue roast chicken (see note)
15 g ($^1/_4$ cup) chopped mint
15 g ($^1/_4$ cup) chopped coriander (cilantro)
1 large Lebanese cucumber
6 spring onions
80 g ($^1/_2$ cup) roasted peanuts, roughly chopped
80 ml ($^1/_3$ cup) mirin
2 tablespoons Chinese rice wine
1 tablespoon soy sauce
1 tablespoon lime juice
2 tablespoons sweet chilli sauce, plus extra, to serve

1 Bring a large saucepan of water to the boil and add 1 teaspoon of salt and the wild rice. Cook for 30 minutes, add the jasmine rice and cook for a further 10 minutes, or until tender. Drain the rice, refresh under cold water and drain again.

2 Shred the chicken (the skin as well) into bite-sized pieces, place in a large bowl and add the mint and coriander. Cut the cucumber through the centre (do not peel) and slice thinly on the diagonal. Slice the spring onions on the diagonal. Add the cucumber, spring onion, rice and peanuts to the bowl with the chicken.

3 Mix together the mirin, rice wine, soy, lime juice and sweet chilli sauce in a small jug, pour over the salad and toss to combine. Pile the salad onto serving platters and serve with extra chilli sauce.

NOTE It is important to use a Chinese barbecued chicken, available from Chinese barbecue shops. The flavours of five-spice and soy used to cook it will add to the flavour of the dish.

SERVES 8

INGREDIENTS

4 chicken breasts (about 200 g/7 oz each)
2 tablespoons oil
1 clove garlic, crushed
$^1/_4$ cup (60 ml) dry white wine
2 tablespoons wholegrain mustard
2 teaspoons chopped fresh thyme
300 ml (10 fl oz) cream
240 g (8$^1/_2$ oz) green beans, topped and tailed
320 g (11$^1/_4$ oz) baby yellow squash, halved

1   Pound each chicken breast between sheets of plastic wrap with a mallet or rolling pin until
about 1 cm ($^1/_2$ inch) thick.

2   Heat the oil in a frying pan over high heat. Brown the chicken breasts for 4–5 minutes on
each side, or until brown. Remove and cover with foil.

3   Add the garlic to the frying pan and cook for 1 minute over medium heat, then stir in the
wine, mustard and thyme. Increase the heat to medium–high and pour in the cream.
Simmer for about 5 minutes, or until the sauce has reduced and thickened slightly, then
season to taste.

4   Meanwhile, bring a saucepan of lightly salted water to the boil, add the beans and squash
and cook for 2–4 minutes, or until just tender. Season to taste. To serve, pour a little of the
sauce over the chicken and serve with the vegetables on the side.

SERVES 4

MEXICAN CHICKEN BAKE

$^3/_4$ cup (165 g) short-grain rice
300 g (10$^1/_2$ oz) can red kidney beans, drained and thoroughly rinsed
3$^1/_2$ tablespoons chopped fresh coriander (cilantro) leaves
1 tablespoon oil
600 g skinless chicken thigh fillets, unrolled
2 x 200 g (7 oz) jars spicy taco sauce
2 cups (250 g/9 oz) grated Cheddar
$^1/_2$ cup (125 g/4$^1/_2$ oz) sour cream

1 Preheat the oven to moderate 180°C (350°F/Gas 4). Lightly grease a deep (7 cm/3 inch) round (21 cm/8 inch) ceramic casserole dish. Bring a large saucepan of water to the boil, add the rice and cook for 10–12 minutes, stirring occasionally. Drain.

2 In the prepared dish, combine the beans and 1$^1/_2$ tablespoons of the coriander, then add the rice and toss together. Lightly press the mixture so the beans are mixed into the rice and the mixture is flat.

3 Heat the oil in a large frying pan over medium–high heat. Sauté the chicken thighs for 3 minutes, then turn over. Add the spicy taco sauce, and cook for another 3 minutes.

4 To assemble, spread half the cheese over the rice. Arrange the thighs and sauce on top in a star shape, sprinkle with 1$^1/_2$ tablespoons coriander, then sprinkle with cheese. Cover with foil.

5 Bake for 35–40 minutes, or until the mixture is bubbling and the cheese is melted and slightly browned—remove the foil for the last 5 minutes. Cut into four servings with a knife and scoop out carefully, keeping the layers intact. Serve sprinkled with the remaining coriander and a dollop of sour cream.

SERVES 4

INGREDIENTS

¹/₄ cup (60 ml/2 fl oz) olive oil
4 chicken thighs and 6 drumsticks
1 large red onion, finely chopped
1 large green capsicum (pepper), two thirds diced and one third julienned
3 teaspoons sweet paprika
400 g (14 oz) can diced tomatoes
1¹/₄ cups (275 g/9³/₄ oz) paella or arborio rice
¹/₂ teaspoon ground saffron

1 Heat 2 tablespoons of the oil in a large deep frying pan over high heat. Season the chicken pieces well and brown in batches. Remove the chicken from the pan.

2 Reduce the pan to medium heat and add the remaining oil. Add the onion and the diced capsicum and cook gently for 5 minutes. Stir in the paprika and cook for 30 seconds. Add the tomato and simmer for 1–3 minutes, or until it thickens.

3 Stir 3¹/₂ cups (875 ml) boiling water into the pan, then add the rice and saffron. Return the chicken to the pan and stir to combine. Season, to taste. Bring to the boil, then cover, reduce the heat to medium–low and simmer for 20–30 minutes, or until all the liquid has been absorbed and the chicken is tender. Stir in the julienned capsicum, then allow to stand, covered, for 3–4 minutes before serving.

SPANISH SAFFRON CHICKEN AND RICE

SERVES 4

STUFFED CHICKEN BREAST WITH TOMATO, GOAT'S CHEESE AND ASPARAGUS

INGREDIENTS

4 large chicken breast fillets
100 g (3^1/$_2$ oz) semi-dried (sun-blushed) tomatoes
100 g (3^1/$_2$ oz) goat's cheese, sliced
200 g (7 oz) asparagus spears, trimmed, halved and blanched
50 g butter
1^1/$_2$ cups (375 ml/12^1/$_2$ fl oz) chicken stock
2 zucchini (courgettes), cut into 5 cm (2 inch) batons
1 cup (250 ml/8^1/$_2$ fl oz) cream
8 spring onions, thinly sliced

1   Pound each chicken breast between two sheets of plastic wrap with a mallet or rolling pin until 1 cm (^{1}/$_2$ inch) thick. Divide the tomato, goat's cheese and 155 g (5^1/$_2$ oz) of the asparagus pieces among the breasts. Roll up tightly lengthways, securing along the seam with toothpicks.

2   Heat the butter in a large frying pan over medium heat. Add the chicken, then brown on all sides. Pour in the stock, then reduce the heat to low. Cook, covered, for 10 minutes, or until the chicken is cooked through. Remove the chicken and keep warm.

3   Meanwhile, bring a saucepan of lightly salted water to the boil. Add the zucchini and remaining asparagus and cook for 2 minutes, or until just tender. Remove from the pan. Whisk the cream into the frying pan. Add the spring onion and simmer over medium–low heat for 4 minutes, or until reduced and thickened. To serve, cut each chicken roll in half on the diagonal and place on serving plates. Spoon on the sauce and serve with the greens.

SERVES 4

4 small chicken breast fillets, skin on (about 170 g/6 oz each)
$1/4$ cup (60 ml/ 2 fl oz) Japanese soy sauce
2 tablespoons sake
$1^1/_2$ tablespoons mirin
$1^1/_2$ tablespoons soft brown sugar
3 teaspoons finely grated fresh ginger
$1^1/_2$ cups (300 g/10$^1/_2$ oz) long-grain rice
2 tablespoons finely chopped fresh chives
2 tablespoons oil

1 Pound each breast between sheets of plastic wrap with a mallet until 1 cm ($1/_2$ inch) thick. Put the soy sauce, sake, mirin, sugar and 1 teaspoon ginger in a flat non-metallic dish and stir until the sugar has dissolved. Add the chicken and turn to coat. Cover and refrigerate for 1 hour, turning once halfway through.

2 Bring a large saucepan of water to the boil. Add the rice and cook for 12 minutes, stirring occasionally. Drain. Stir in the chives and remaining ginger, then cover until ready to serve.

3 Drain the chicken, reserving the marinade. Heat the oil in a deep frying pan and cook the chicken, skin-side-down over medium heat for 5 minutes, until the skin is crisp. Turn and cook for 4 minutes (not quite cooked).

4 Add the marinade and $1/4$ cup (60 ml) water to the pan and scrape up any sediment. Bring to the boil over high heat, then add the chicken (skin-side-up) and juices. Cook for 5–6 minutes, until cooked through, turning once. (If the sauce is runny, remove the chicken and boil the sauce until syrupy.) Serve the chicken whole or sliced, drizzled with the sauce.

TERIYAKI CHICKEN WITH GINGER CHIVE RICE

SERVES 4

CHICKEN CASSEROLE WITH OLIVES AND TOMATO

1 tablespoon olive oil
1 large onion, chopped
2 garlic cloves, crushed
8 pieces chicken, skin on
1 tablespoon tomato paste (purée)
375 ml (1^1/$_2$ cups) white wine
a pinch of sugar
8 large ripe tomatoes, chopped
4 tablespoons parsley, chopped
180 g (6^1/$_2$ oz) green beans, topped, tailed and halved
130 g (4^1/$_2$ oz) olives

1 Heat the oil in a large flameproof casserole and fry the onion for a minute or two. Add the garlic and the chicken and fry for as long as it takes to brown the chicken all over.

2 Add the tomato paste and white wine, along with the sugar, and stir everything together. Add the tomato and any juices, the parsley and the beans and bring to the boil. Turn down the heat, season well and simmer for 40 minutes.

3 Add the olives and simmer for another 5 minutes. The sauce should be thick by now and the chicken fully cooked. Add more salt and pepper, if necessary. Serve with potatoes, pasta or rice.

SERVES 4

INGREDIENTS

375 g (13 oz) fusilli, or other pasta shapes such as ruote, conchiglie or penne

2 tablespoons virgin olive oil

350 g (12 oz) chicken tenderloins, cut into 2 cm (³/₄ inch) pieces

20 g (³/₄ oz) butter

400 g (14 oz) Swiss brown or button mushrooms, sliced

2 garlic cloves, finely chopped

125 ml (¹/₂ cup) dry white wine

185 ml (³/₄ cup) cream

1 teaspoon finely grated lemon zest

2 tablespoons lemon juice

1 tablespoon chopped tarragon

2 tablespoons chopped parsley

25 g (¹/₄ cup) grated Parmesan cheese, plus extra, to serve

1 Cook the pasta in a large saucepan of boiling salted water until al dente.

2 Meanwhile, heat 1 tablespoon of the oil in a large frying pan, add the chicken and cook over high heat for 3–4 minutes, or until lightly browned. Remove from the pan.

3 Heat the butter and the remaining oil, add the mushrooms and cook, stirring, over high heat for 3 minutes. Add the garlic and cook for a further 2 minutes.

4 Pour in the wine, then reduce the heat to low and simmer for 5 minutes, or until nearly evaporated. Add the cream and chicken and simmer for about 5 minutes, or until thickened.

5 Stir the lemon zest, lemon juice, tarragon, parsley and Parmesan into the sauce. Season with salt and pepper, then add the hot pasta, tossing until well combined. Serve with the extra Parmesan.

SERVES 4

PASTA WITH ROAST CHICKEN, PINE NUTS AND LEMON

1.3 kg (3 lb) chicken
1 garlic bulb, cloves separated and left unpeeled
60 ml ($^1/_4$ cup) olive oil
30 g (1 oz) butter, softened
1 tablespoon finely chopped thyme
125 ml ($^1/_2$ cup) lemon juice
500 g (1 lb 2 oz) bavette or spaghetti
2 tablespoons currants
1 teaspoon finely grated lemon zest
50 g ($^1/_3$ cup) pine nuts, toasted
15 g ($^1/_2$ cup) finely chopped flat-leaf (Italian) parsley

1 Preheat the oven to 200°C (400°F/Gas 6). Remove the neck from the inside of the chicken and place the neck in a roasting tin. Rinse the inside of the chicken with cold water and shake out any excess. Insert the garlic cloves into the cavity, then put the chicken in the roasting tin.

2 Combine the oil, butter, thyme and lemon juice, then rub over the chicken. Season the chicken. Roast for 1 hour, or until the skin is golden and the juices run clear when the thigh is pierced with a skewer. Transfer the chicken to a bowl to catch any juices while resting. Remove the garlic from the cavity, cool, then squeeze the garlic cloves out of their skins and finely chop.

3 Cook the pasta in a large pan of boiling salted water until al dente. Meanwhile, pour the juices from the roasting tin into a saucepan and discard the neck. Add the currants, zest and chopped garlic, then simmer over low heat. Remove all the meat from the chicken and shred into bite-size pieces. Add the resting juices to the pan.

4 Add the chicken meat, pine nuts, parsley and the sauce to the hot pasta and toss well. Season with salt and pepper and serve.

SERVES 4-6

INGREDIENTS

oil, for cooking
500 g (1 lb) chicken thigh fillets, cut into cubes
1 egg white, lightly beaten
$^1/_3$ cup (40 g/1$^1/_4$ oz) cornflour (cornstarch)
2 onions, thinly sliced
1 green capsicum (pepper), cubed
2 carrots, cut into batons
100 g (3$^1/_2$ oz) snow peas, sliced
$^1/_4$ cup (90 g/3 oz) honey
2 tablespoons toasted almonds

1   Heat a wok until very hot, add 1$^1/_2$ tablespoons of the oil and swirl it around to coat the side. Dip half of the chicken into the egg white, then lightly dust with the cornflour. Stir-fry over high heat for 4–5 minutes, or until the chicken is golden brown and just cooked. Remove from the wok and drain on paper towels. Repeat with the remaining chicken, then remove all the chicken from the wok.

2   Reheat the wok, add 1 tablespoon of the oil and stir-fry the sliced onion over high heat for 3–4 minutes, or until slightly softened. Add the capsicum and carrot, and cook, tossing, for 3–4 minutes, or until tender. Stir in the snow peas and cook for 2 minutes.

3   Increase the heat, add the honey and toss the vegetables until well coated. Return the chicken to the wok and toss until it is heated through and is well coated in the honey. Remove from the heat and season well with salt and pepper. Serve immediately, sprinkled with the almonds.

SERVES 4

LIME AND GINGER GLAZE

In a small pan combine 1/2 cup (160 g/51/2 oz) lime marmalade, 1/4 cup (60 ml/2 fl oz) lime juice, 2 tablespoons sherry, 2 tablespoons soft brown sugar and 2 teaspoons finely grated fresh ginger. Stir over low heat until it reaches a liquid consistency. Pour over 1 kg (2 lb) chicken wings and toss well to combine. Cover and refrigerate for 2 hours or overnight. Cook in a moderately hot 190°C (375°F/Gas 5) oven for 40 minutes, or until cooked through. Makes 1 cup (250 ml/8 fl oz).

HONEY SOY MARINADE

Combine 1/4 cup (90 g/3 oz) honey, 1/4 cup (60 ml/2 fl oz) soy sauce, 1 crushed garlic clove, 2 tablespoons sake and 1/2 teaspoon Chinese five-spice powder. Remove excess fat from 500 g (1 lb) chicken thigh fillets. Pour on the marinade and toss well. Cover and refrigerate for 2 hours or overnight. Cook on a hot barbecue for 10 minutes, turning once, or until cooked through. Makes 2/3 cup (170 ml/51/2 fl oz).

REDCURRANT GLAZE

In a small saucepan combine a 340 g (11 oz) jar redcurrant jelly, 2 tablespoons lemon juice, 2 tablespoons brandy and 1 teaspoon chopped fresh thyme, and stir over low heat until it reaches a liquid consistency. Pour the marinade over 500 g (1 lb) chicken breast fillets and toss well to combine. Cover and refrigerate for 2 hours or overnight. Cook in a moderately hot 190°C (375°F/Gas 5) oven for 20 minutes, or until cooked through. Makes 1 cup (250 ml/8 fl oz).

TANDOORI MARINADE

Soak 8 bamboo skewers in water for 30 minutes to prevent burning. Combine 2 tablespoons tandoori paste, 1 cup (250 g/8 oz) plain yoghurt and 1 tablespoon lime juice. Cut 500 g (1 lb) tenderloins in half lengthwise and thread onto skewers. Pour over the marinade and toss well to combine. Cover and refrigerate for 1–2 hours. Place under a hot grill and cook, basting with the marinade, until cooked through. Makes 11/4 cups (315 ml/10 fl oz).

MEXICAN MARINADE

Combine 440 g (14 oz) bottled taco sauce, 2 tablespoons lime juice and 2 tablespoons chopped fresh coriander leaves. Pour the marinade over 1 kg (2 lb) scored chicken drumsticks and toss well to combine. Cover and refrigerate for 2 hours or overnight. Cook in a moderately hot 190°C (375°F/Gas 5) oven for 30 minutes, or until cooked through. Makes 11/4 cups (315 ml/10 fl oz).

THAI MARINADE

Combine 2 tablespoons fish sauce, 2 tablespoons lime juice, 1 crushed garlic clove, 1 finely chopped lemon grass stem, 2 teaspoons soft brown sugar, 1/2 cup (125 g/4 oz) coconut cream and 2 tablespoons chopped fresh coriander leaves. Pour the marinade over 1 kg (2 lb) chicken drumettes and toss well to combine. Cover and refrigerate for 2 hours or overnight. Cook in a moderately hot 190°C (375°F/Gas 5) oven for 30 minutes, or until cooked through. Makes 3/4 cup (185 ml/6 fl oz).

GRILLING

GARLIC DIP WITH CRUDITES

4 cloves garlic, crushed
2 egg yolks
300 ml (10 fl oz) light olive or vegetable oil
1 tablespoon lemon juice
pinch ground white pepper
12 asparagus spears, trimmed
26 radishes, trimmed
$1/2$ telegraph cucumber, seeded, halved and cut into batons
1 head witlof (chicory), leaves separated

1 Place the garlic, egg yolks and a pinch of salt in the bowl of a food processor. Process for 10 seconds.

2 With the motor running, add the oil in a thin, slow stream. The mixture will start to thicken. When this happens you can add the oil a little faster. Process until all the oil is incorporated and the mayonnaise is thick and creamy. Transfer to a bowl and stir in the lemon juice and a pinch of pepper.

3 Bring a saucepan of water to the boil, add the asparagus and cook for 1 minute. Remove and plunge into a bowl of iced water. Arrange the asparagus, radish, cucumber and witlof on a platter and place the garlic dip in a bowl on the platter.

NOTE Should the mayonnaise start to curdle as the oil is added, beat in 1–2 teaspoons boiling water. If this fails, put another egg yolk in a clean bowl and very slowly whisk in the curdled mixture, one drop at a time, then continue as above.

SERVES 4

INGREDIENTS

2 eggplants
3 cloves garlic, crushed
$^1/_2$ teaspoon ground cumin
$^1/_3$ cup (80 ml/2$^3/_4$ fl oz) lemon juice
2 tablespoons tahini
pinch cayenne pepper
1$^1/_2$ tablespoons olive oil
1 tablespoon finely chopped fresh flat-leaf parsley
black olives, to garnish

BABA GHANNOUJ

1 Preheat the oven to 200°C (400°F/Gas 6). Pierce the eggplants several times with a fork, then cook over an open flame for about 5 minutes, or until the skin is black and blistering, then place in a roasting tin and bake for 40–45 minutes, or until the eggplants are very soft and wrinkled. Place in a colander over a bowl to drain off any bitter juices and leave to stand for 30 minutes, or until cool.

2 Carefully peel the skin from the eggplant, chop the flesh and place in a food processor with the garlic, cumin, lemon, tahini, cayenne and olive oil. Process until smooth and creamy. Alternatively, use a potato masher or fork. Season with salt and stir in the parsley. Spread onto a flat bowl or plate and garnish with the olives. Serve with flatbread or pide.

NOTE If you prefer, you can simply roast the eggplant in a roasting tin in a 200°C (400°F/Gas 6) oven for 1 hour, or until very soft and wrinkled. Eggplants are also known as aubergines. The name baba ghannouj can be roughly translated as 'poor man's caviar'.

SERVES 10

GRILLED HALOUMI AND ROAST VEGETABLE SALAD

4 slender eggplants (aubergines), cut in half and then halved lengthways

1 red capsicum (pepper), halved, thickly sliced

4 small zucchini (courgettes), cut in half and then halved lengthways

$^1/_3$ cup (80 ml/$2^3/_4$ fl oz) olive oil

2 cloves garlic, crushed

200 g ($6^1/_2$ oz) haloumi cheese, thinly sliced

150 g (5 oz) baby English spinach leaves, trimmed

1 tablespoon balsamic vinegar

1 Preheat the oven to hot 220°C (425°F/Gas 7). Place the vegetables in a large bowl, add $^1/_4$ cup (60 ml/2 fl oz) of the olive oil and the garlic, season and toss well to combine. Place the vegetables in an ovenproof dish in a single layer. Roast for 20–30 minutes, or until tender and browned around the edges.

2 Meanwhile, cook the haloumi slices on a hot, lightly oiled barbecue grill for 1–2 minutes each side.

3 Top the spinach with the roast vegetables and haloumi. Whisk together the remaining oil and vinegar to make a dressing.

SERVES 4

INGREDIENTS

Tomato Relish
400 g (14 oz) can peeled tomatoes
$^2/_3$ cup (170 ml/$5^1/_2$ fl oz) white vinegar
$^1/_2$ cup (125 g/4 oz) sugar
1 clove garlic, finely chopped
2 spring onions, finely chopped
4 sun-dried (sun-blushed) tomatoes, finely chopped
1 small fresh red chilli, finely chopped

$^1/_2$ teaspoon salt
$^1/_2$ teaspoon cracked black pepper
6 large fresh cobs corn
1–2 tablespoons olive or vegetable oil
60 g (2 oz) butter
salt, to serve

1 To make the tomato relish, roughly chop the tomatoes by hand or in a food processor. Put the vinegar and sugar in a pan and stir over heat until the sugar dissolves. Bring to the boil, then reduce the heat and simmer for 2 minutes.

2 Add the tomatoes, garlic, spring onions, sun-dried tomatoes and chilli. Bring to the boil, reduce the heat and simmer, stirring often, for 35 minutes or until thickened. Season, remove from the heat and allow to cool.

3 Brush the corn with oil and cook on a hot, lightly oiled barbecue grill for 10 minutes, or until the corn is soft and flecked with brown in places. Transfer to the flatplate and add a knob of butter and salt to each cob. Serve at once with the relish.

SERVES 6

CORN ON THE COB WITH TOMATO RELISH

TABBOULEH

³/₄ cup (120 g/4 oz) burghul (cracked wheat)
3 ripe tomatoes
1 telegraph cucumber
4 spring onions, sliced
4 cups (120 g/4 oz) chopped fresh flat-leaf parsley
¹/₂ cup (15 g/¹/₂ oz) fresh mint, chopped

Dressing
¹/₃ cup (80 ml/2³/₄ fl oz) lemon juice
3 tablespoons olive oil
1 tablespoon extra virgin olive oil

1 Place the burghul in a bowl, cover with 2 cups (500 ml/16 fl oz) water and leave for 1 hour 30 minutes.

2 Cut the tomatoes in half, squeeze gently to remove the seeds and dice the flesh. Cut the cucumber in half lengthways, remove the seeds with a teaspoon and dice the flesh.

3 To make the dressing, whisk the lemon juice and 1¹/₂ teaspoons salt. Slowly whisk in the olive oil and extra virgin olive oil. Season with pepper.

4 Drain the burghul and squeeze out any excess water. Spread on paper towels and leave to dry for 30 minutes. Mix with the tomato, cucumber, spring onion and herbs. Add the dressing and toss together well.

SERVES 6

INGREDIENTS

3 large vine-ripened tomatoes
250 g (8 oz) bocconcini or mozzarella
12 fresh basil leaves
3 tablespoons extra virgin olive oil

1 Slice the tomatoes thickly (you will need roughly 12 slices). Slice the bocconcini into about 24 slices.

2 Arrange the tomato slices on a serving plate, alternating them with 2 slices of bocconcini. Place the basil leaves between the bocconcini slices.

3 Drizzle with the oil and season well with salt and ground black pepper.

TOMATO AND BOCCONCINI SALAD

SERVES 4

WHITE BEAN SALAD WITH TUNA

1 cup (200 g/7 oz) dried cannellini beans or 1 x 425 g (15 oz) can cannellini beans, rinsed and drained well

2 fresh bay leaves

1 large clove garlic, smashed

350 g green beans, trimmed

2 small baby fennel, thinly sliced

$1/2$ small red onion, very thinly sliced

1 cup (30 g/1 oz) fresh flat-leaf parsley, roughly chopped

1 tablespoon olive oil

2 fresh tuna steaks (400 g/14 oz)

$1/3$ cup (80 ml/$2^3/_4$ fl oz) lemon juice

1 clove garlic, extra, finely chopped

1 small fresh red chilli, seeds removed, finely chopped

1 teaspoon sugar

1 tablespoon lemon zest

$1/2$ cup (125 ml/$4^1/_4$ fl oz) extra virgin olive oil

1 Put the beans in a bowl, cover with cold water, allowing room for the beans to expand, and leave for at least 8 hours.

2 Rinse the beans well and transfer them to a saucepan. Cover with cold water, add the torn bay leaves and smashed garlic, and simmer for 20–25 minutes, or until tender. Drain.

3 Cook the green beans in boiling water for 1–2 minutes, or until tender, and refresh under cold water. Mix with the fennel, onion and parsley in a bowl.

4 Brush the oil over the tuna fillets and grill under high heat for 2 minutes on each side or until still pink in the centre. Remove, rest for 2–3 minutes, then cut into 3 cm (1 inch) chunks. Add to the green bean mixture and toss.

5 Mix the lemon juice, garlic, chilli, sugar and lemon zest together. Whisk in the extra virgin olive oil and season with salt and pepper. Toss gently through the salad.

SERVES 4-6

INGREDIENTS

700 g (1 lb 9 oz) rump steak, cut into 2.5 cm (1 inch) cubes
2 small garlic cloves, crushed
3 teaspoons grated ginger
1 tablespoon fish sauce
2 small red chillies, seeded and julienned

Satay sauce
1 tablespoon peanut oil
8 red Asian shallots, finely chopped
8 garlic cloves, crushed
4 small red chillies, finely chopped
1 tablespoon finely chopped ginger
250 g (1 cup) crunchy peanut butter
400 ml (14 fl oz) coconut milk
1 tablespoon soy sauce
60 g ($\frac{1}{3}$ cup) grated palm sugar or soft brown sugar
3 tablespoons fish sauce
1 kaffir lime (makrut) leaf
4 tablespoons lime juice

1 Combine the steak with the garlic, ginger and fish sauce and marinate, covered, in the refrigerator for at least 3 hours. Soak eight wooden skewers in cold water for 1 hour.

2 To make the satay sauce, heat the peanut oil in a saucepan over medium heat. Cook the shallots, garlic, chilli and ginger, stirring occasionally, for 5 minutes, or until the shallots are golden. Reduce the heat to low and add the peanut butter, coconut milk, soy sauce, palm sugar, fish sauce, lime leaf and lime juice. Simmer for 10 minutes, or until thickened, then remove the lime leaf.

3 Thread the beef onto the skewers and cook on a barbecue or chargrill pan (griddle) over high heat for 6–8 minutes, or until cooked through, turning halfway through the cooking time. Top with the satay sauce and garnish with the julienned chilli. Serve with rice.

LAMB KEBABS

5 garlic cloves, roughly chopped
5 cm (2 inch) piece of ginger, roughly chopped
3 green chillies, roughly chopped
1 onion, roughly chopped
3 tablespoons thick natural yoghurt
3 tablespoons coriander (cilantro) leaves
$1/_2$ teaspoon ground black pepper
500 g (1 lb 2 oz) minced (ground) lamb
red onion rings, to garnish
lemon wedges, to serve

1 Combine the garlic, ginger, chilli, onion, yoghurt and coriander leaves in a food processor to form a thick smooth paste. If you don't have a processor, chop the vegetables more finely and use a mortar and pestle. Add the pepper, season with salt, then mix in the mince. If you are using a mortar and pestle, mix the mince with the paste in a bowl.

2 Divide the meat into 16 portions, about 2 tablespoons each. Shape each portion into an oval patty, cover and chill for 20 minutes.

3 Heat the grill (broiler) to high. Using four metal skewers, thread four meatballs onto each. Grill (broil) for 7 minutes, or until brown on top. Turn over and brown the other side. Check that the meatballs are cooked. Serve with onion rings and lemon wedges.

SERVES 4

INGREDIENTS

800 g (1 lb 12 oz) rump steak

2 teaspoons ground cumin

1 teaspoon ground oregano

1 teaspoon paprika

2 tablespoons Worcestershire sauce

1 tablespoon soy sauce

3 garlic cloves

60 ml ($^1/_4$ cup) lime juice

1 large onion, thinly sliced

1 red capsicum (pepper), cut into 5 mm ($^1/_4$ inch) strips

1 green capsicum (pepper), cut into 5 mm ($^1/_4$ inch) strips

1 tablespoon olive oil

8 flour tortillas

1 ripe avocado, diced

2 ripe Roma (plum) tomatoes, diced

60 g ($^1/_2$ cup) grated Cheddar cheese

90 g ($^1/_3$ cup) sour cream

1 Trim the steak of any fat and give it a good pounding with a meat mallet on both sides. Mix the cumin, oregano, paprika, Worcestershire sauce, soy sauce, garlic and lime juice in a shallow, non-metallic dish and add the beef. Turn until well coated in the marinade, then cover and refrigerate for at least 4 hours, or overnight.

2 Drain the steak, reserving the marinade, and pat it dry with paper towels. Simmer the marinade in a small saucepan over medium heat for 5 minutes, or until it is reduced by about half, and keep it warm.

3 Preheat a barbecue to high direct heat. Toss the onion and capsicum with the oil then spread them across the flat plate, turning every so often, for 10 minutes, or until cooked through and caramelized. While the vegetables are cooking, grill the steak on the chargrill plate for 3 minutes each side, or until cooked to your liking. Remove it from the heat and let it rest, covered, for 5 minutes. Thinly slice the steak and arrange it on a plate with the onion and capsicum strips and serve with the tortillas, avocado, tomato, cheese, sour cream and marinade sauce. Let everyone fill their own tortillas.

BEEF FAJITAS

SERVES 4-6

CHILLI BEEF BURGERS

INGREDIENTS

500 g (1 lb 2 oz) minced (ground) beef
6 red Asian shallots, finely chopped
25 g (¼ cup) crisp fried onion flakes (see note)
3 garlic cloves, finely chopped
2 long red chillies, seeded and finely chopped
20 g (⅓ cup) finely chopped coriander (cilantro) leaves (include some stems)
2–2½ tablespoons chilli garlic sauce (see note)
1 egg, lightly beaten
160 g (2 cups/5½ oz) fresh breadcrumbs
olive oil, for brushing
1 loaf Turkish bread, cut into 4 pieces, or 4 round Turkish rolls
100 g (3 handfuls) mignonette or green oak lettuce leaves

1 To make the burgers, put the beef, shallots, onion flakes, garlic, chilli, coriander, chilli garlic sauce, egg, breadcrumbs and 1½ teaspoons of salt in a large bowl, and knead well with your hands until the ingredients are thoroughly combined. Cover the bowl and refrigerate for 2 hours.

2 Using wet hands, divide the beef mixture into four equal portions, roll each portion into a ball, then flatten it slightly to form patties. Preheat the chargrill plate to medium direct heat. Brush the patties lightly with oil and grill them for 5–6 minutes, then flip them over and cook for another 5–6 minutes, or until they are well browned and cooked through. A few minutes before the patties are done, toast the bread, cut-side down, on the chargrill plate for 1–2 minutes, or until it is marked and golden.

3 Divide the lettuce among four of the toasted bread slices. Add a patty, season the burgers with salt and pepper, then top with the remaining toasted bread.

NOTE Crisp fried onion flakes and chilli garlic sauce are available from Asian grocery stores.

INGREDIENTS

Basil aïoli
1 garlic clove
15 g (¼ cup) torn basil leaves
1 egg yolk
125 ml (½ cup) olive oil
2 teaspoons lemon juice

2 large red capsicums (peppers), quartered, core and seeds removed
1 eggplant (aubergine), cut in 5 mm (¼ inch) thick rounds
1 orange sweet potato (kumera), peeled and cut on the diagonal into 5 mm (¼ inch) thick rounds
3 zucchini (courgettes), sliced lengthways into 5 mm (¼ inch) thick slices
2 red onions, cut into 1 cm (½ inch) thick rounds
80 ml (⅓ cup) olive oil
1 loaf Turkish bread, split and cut into 4 equal pieces

1 To make the basil aïoli, put the garlic, basil and egg yolk in a food processor and blend until smooth. With the motor running, gradually add the oil in a thin stream until the mixture thickens. Stir in the lemon juice and season to taste. Cover and refrigerate until you are ready to dish up.

2 Preheat a barbecue chargrill plate to medium direct heat. Put the capsicum, skin-side down, around the cool edge of the grill and cook it for 8–10 minutes or until the skin has softened and is blistering.

3 Meanwhile, brush the eggplant, sweet potato, zucchini and onion slices on both sides with olive oil and season them lightly. Cook the vegetables in batches on the middle of the chargrill for 5–8 minutes, or until they are cooked through but still firm. As the vegetable pieces cook, put them on a tray in a single layer to prevent them from steaming, then grill the Turkish bread on both sides until it is lightly marked and toasted.

4 Spread both cut sides of the bread with 1 tablespoon of basil aïoli and pile on some of the chargrilled vegetables. Top with the remaining toast and serve immediately.

SERVES 4

SESAME CHICKEN KEBABS

3 tablespoons oil
2 tablespoons soy sauce
2 tablespoons honey
1 tablespoon grated fresh ginger
1 tablespoon sesame oil
4 large chicken breast fillets, cubed
8 spring onions, cut into short lengths
1 tablespoon toasted sesame seeds

1 Soak 12 wooden skewers in water to prevent scorching. To make the marinade, whisk together the oil, soy sauce, honey, ginger and sesame oil. Thread the chicken and spring onion onto the skewers and put in a non-metallic dish. Add the marinade, cover and refrigerate for at least 2 hours.

2 Place the skewers on a hot, lightly oiled barbecue flatplate or grill and baste with the remaining marinade. Cook for 4 minutes on each side, or until the chicken is cooked through. Sprinkle with the sesame seeds.

SERVES 4

2 teaspoons ground cardamom
$^1/_2$ teaspoon ground turmeric
1 teaspoon ground allspice
4 cloves garlic, crushed
3 tablespoons lemon juice
3 tablespoons olive oil
4 large chicken thigh fillets, excess fat removed
lemon wedges, to serve
plain yoghurt, to serve

1 Soak 8 wooden skewers in water to prevent scorching. To make the marinade, whisk together the cardamom, turmeric, allspice, garlic, lemon juice and oil. Season with salt and ground black pepper.

2 Cut each chicken thigh fillet into 3–4 cm (1–1$^1/_2$ inch) cubes. Toss the cubes in the spice marinade. Thread the chicken onto skewers and place on a tray. Cover and refrigerate overnight.

3 Cook the skewers on a hot, lightly oiled barbecue grill or flatplate for 4 minutes on each side, or until the chicken is cooked through. Serve with lemon wedges and plain yoghurt.

PERSIAN CHICKEN SKEWERS

SERVES 4

MEDITERRANEAN CHICKEN SKEWERS

32 chicken tenderloins
24 cherry tomatoes
6 cap mushrooms, cut into quarters
2 cloves garlic, crushed
rind of 1 lemon, grated
2 tablespoons lemon juice
2 tablespoons olive oil
1 tablespoon fresh oregano leaves, chopped

1 Soak 8 wooden skewers in water to prevent scorching. Thread a piece of chicken onto each skewer, followed by a tomato, then a piece of mushroom. Repeat three times for each skewer. Put the skewers in a shallow, non-metallic dish.

2 Combine the garlic, lemon rind, lemon juice, olive oil and chopped oregano, pour over the skewers and toss well. Marinate for at least 2 hours, or overnight if time permits.

3 Cook the skewers on a hot, lightly oiled barbecue grill or flatplate for 4 minutes on each side, basting occasionally, until the chicken is cooked and the tomatoes have shrivelled slightly.

MAKES 8 skewers

INGREDIENTS

100 g (3^1/$_2$ oz) butter, softened
50 g (^{1}/$_3$ cup) semi-dried (sun-blushed) tomatoes, finely chopped
2 tablespoons baby capers in brine, drained and crushed
1^1/$_2$ tablespoons shredded basil leaves
4 garlic cloves, crushed
60 ml (^{1}/$_4$ cup) extra virgin olive oil
300 g (10^1/$_2$ oz) slender asparagus spears, trimmed
4 swordfish steaks

1 Put the butter in a bowl with the tomato, capers, basil and two cloves of crushed garlic, and mash it all together. Shape the flavoured butter into a log, then wrap it in baking paper and twist the ends to close them off. Refrigerate until the butter is firm, then cut it into 1 cm (^{1}/$_2$ inch) slices and leave it, covered, at room temperature until needed.

2 Mix 2 tablespoons of the oil and the remaining garlic in a small bowl. Toss the asparagus spears with the oil until they are well coated, season them with salt and pepper, and leave for 30 minutes.

3 Preheat a ridged barbecue grill plate to high direct heat. Brush the swordfish steaks with the remaining oil and cook them for 2–3 minutes on each side or until they are just cooked through. Don't overcook the fish as residual heat will continue to coo the meat after it has been removed from the barbecue. Put a piece of the tomato butter on top of each steak as soon as it comes off the barbecue and season to taste. Cook the asparagus on the chargrill plate, turning it regularly, for 2–3 minutes, or until it is just tender. Serve the asparagus immediately with the fish.

SWORDFISH WITH TOMATO BUTTER AND GRILLED ASPARAGUS

SERVES 4

693

GREEK PEPPER LAMB SALAD

INGREDIENTS

300 g lamb backstraps or fillets
$1^{1}/_{2}$ tablespoons black pepper
3 vine-ripened tomatoes, cut into 8 wedges
2 Lebanese cucumbers, sliced
150 g (5 oz) lemon and garlic marinated Kalamata olives, drained (reserving $1^{1}/_{2}$ tablespoons oil)
100 g ($3^{1}/_{2}$ oz) Greek feta cheese, cubed
$^{3}/_{4}$ teaspoon dried oregano
1 tablespoon lemon juice
1 tablespoon extra virgin olive oil

1   Roll the backstraps in the pepper, pressing the pepper on with your fingers. Cover and refrigerate for 15 minutes.

2   Place the tomato, cucumber, olives, feta and $^{1}/_{2}$ teaspoon of the dried oregano in a bowl.

3   Heat a chargrill pan or barbecue plate, brush with oil and when very hot, cook the lamb for 2–3 minutes on each side, or until cooked to your liking. Keep warm.

4   Whisk the lemon juice, extra virgin olive oil, reserved Kalamata oil and the remaining dried oregano together well. Season. Pour half the dressing over the salad, toss together and arrange on a serving platter.

5   Cut the lamb on the diagonal into 1 cm thick slices and arrange on top of the salad. Pour the remaining dressing on top and serve.

SERVES 4

INGREDIENTS

Salsa verde
1 clove garlic
2 cups (60 g/2 oz) firmly packed fresh flat-leaf parsley
$^1/_3$ cup (80 ml/2$^3/_4$ fl oz) extra virgin olive oil
3 tablespoons chopped fresh dill
1$^1/_2$ tablespoons Dijon mustard
1 tablespoon sherry vinegar
1 tablespoon baby capers, drained

6 large chicken breast fillets

1   Place all the ingredients for the salsa verde in a food processor or blender and process until almost smooth.

2   Cook the chicken fillets on a very hot, lightly oiled barbecue grill or flatplate for 4–5 minutes each side, or until cooked through.

3   Cut each chicken fillet into three on the diagonal and arrange on serving plates. Top with a spoonful of salsa verde and season to taste.

CHICKEN WITH SALSA VERDE

SERVES 6

TANDOORI CHICKEN

INGREDIENTS

$^1/_2$ cup (125 g/4 oz) Greek-style plain yoghurt
2 tablespoons tandoori paste
2 cloves garlic, crushed
2 tablespoons lime juice
$1^1/_2$ teaspoons garam masala
2 tablespoons finely chopped fresh coriander (cilantro) leaves
6 chicken thigh fillets

1 Combine the yoghurt, tandoori paste, garlic, lime juice, garam masala and coriander in a bowl and mix well.

2 Add the chicken, coat well, cover and refrigerate for at least 1 hour.

3 Cook the chicken on a hot, lightly oiled barbecue grill or flatplate for 5 minutes on each side, basting with the remaining marinade, until golden and cooked through. Serve with cucumber raita and naan bread.

SERVES 4

INGREDIENTS

6 pork butterfly steaks
250 ml (1 cup) ginger wine
150 g ($^1/_2$ cup) orange marmalade
2 tablespoons oil
1 tablespoon grated fresh ginger

1 Trim the pork steak of excess fat and sinew. Mix together the wine, marmalade, oil and ginger. Place the steaks in a shallow non-metallic dish and add the marinade. Store, covered with plastic wrap, in the fridge for at least 3 hours, turning occasionally. Drain, reserving the marinade.

2 Cook the pork on a hot, lightly oiled barbecue flat plate or grill for 5 minutes each side or until tender, turning once.

3 While the meat is cooking, place the reserved marinade in a small pan. Bring to the boil, reduce the heat and simmer for 5 minutes, or until the marinade has reduced and thickened slightly. Pour over the pork.

GINGER-ORANGE PORK

SERVES 6

INGREDIENTS

Marinade
$^1/_2$ cup (125 ml/4 fl oz) olive oil
$^1/_3$ cup (80 ml/2$^3/_4$ fl oz) lemon juice
2 tablespoons wholegrain mustard
2 tablespoons honey
2 tablespoons chopped fresh dill

16–20 raw king prawns (jumbo shrimp)

Dill Mayonnaise
$^3/_4$ cup (185 g/6 oz) mayonnaise
2 tablespoons chopped fresh dill
1$^1/_2$ tablespoons lemon juice
1 gherkin, finely chopped
1 teaspoon chopped capers
1 clove garlic, crushed

1 To make the marinade, combine the olive oil, lemon juice, mustard, honey and dill, pour over the unpeeled prawns and coat well. Cover and refrigerate for at least 2 hours, turning occasionally.

2 To make the dill mayonnaise, whisk together the mayonnaise, dill, lemon juice, gherkin, capers and garlic. Cover and refrigerate.

3 Cook the drained prawns on a hot, lightly oiled barbecue grill or flatplate in batches for 4 minutes, turning frequently until pink and cooked through. Serve with the mayonnaise.

SERVES 4

INGREDIENTS

4 garlic cloves, crushed
1 tablespoon grated ginger
1 teaspoon oil
1 teaspoon sambal oelek
2 teaspoons ground coriander (cilantro)
2 teaspoons ground cumin
2 tablespoons soy sauce
2 teaspoons sesame oil
2 tablespoons sweet chilli sauce
2 tablespoons lemon juice
12 lamb cutlets

1 Combine the garlic, ginger, oil, sambal oelek, coriander, cumin, soy sauce, sesame oil, sweet chilli sauce and lemon juice in a bowl. Season with salt and cracked black pepper.

2 Place the cutlets in a non-metallic dish and pour on the marinade, coating all sides. Leave to marinate for 20 minutes.

3 Cook the cutlets on a very hot chargrill pan (griddle) or barbecue for 3 minutes each side, or until cooked to your liking. Serve with steamed rice.

CHILLI LAMB CUTLETS

SERVES 4

CAJUN PRAWNS WITH SALSA

Cajun spice mix

1 tablespoon garlic powder

1 tablespoon onion powder

2 teaspoons dried thyme

2 teaspoons ground white pepper

1½ teaspoons cayenne pepper

½ teaspoon dried oregano

Tomato salsa

4 Roma (plum) tomatoes, seeded and chopped

1 Lebanese (short) cucumber, peeled, seeded, chopped

2 tablespoons finely diced red onion

2 tablespoons chopped coriander (cilantro)

1 tablespoon chopped flat-leaf (Italian) parsley

1 garlic clove, crushed

2 tablespoons olive oil

1 tablespoon lime juice

1.25 kg (2 lb 12 oz) large raw prawns (shrimp)

100 g (3½ oz) butter, melted

60 g (2¼ oz) watercress, washed and picked over

4 spring onions (scallions), chopped

lemon wedges, to serve

1 Combine all the ingredients for the Cajun spice mix with 2 teaspoons cracked black pepper.

2 To make the tomato salsa, combine the tomato, cucumber, onion, coriander and parsley in a bowl. Mix the garlic, oil and lime juice together and season well. Add to the bowl and toss together.

3 Peel and devein the prawns, leaving the tails intact. Brush the prawns with the butter and sprinkle generously with the spice mix. Cook on a barbecue hotplate or under a hot grill (broiler), turning once, for 2–3 minutes each side, or until a crust forms and the prawns are pink and cooked.

4 Lay some watercress on serving plates, then spoon the salsa over the leaves. Arrange the prawns on top and sprinkle with some chopped spring onion. Serve with lemon wedges on the side.

SERVES 4-6

INGREDIENTS

1 kg (2 lb) calamari (squid)
1 cup (250 ml/8 fl oz) olive oil
2 tablespoons lemon juice
2 cloves garlic, crushed
2 tablespoons chopped fresh oregano
2 tablespoons chopped fresh flat-leaf parsley
lemon wedges, to serve

Salsa verde
2 anchovy fillets, drained
1 tablespoon capers
1 clove garlic, crushed
2 tablespoons chopped fresh flat-leaf parsley
2 tablespoons olive oil

1   To clean the calamari, hold onto the hood and gently pull the tentacles away from the
     head. Cut out the beak and discard with any intestines still attached to the tentacles.
     Rinse the tentacles in cold running water, pat dry and cut into 5 cm (2 inch) lengths.
     Place in a bowl. Clean out the hood cavity and remove the transparent backbone. Under
     cold running water, pull away the skin, rinse and dry well. Cut into rings and place in the
     bowl with the tentacles. Add the oil, lemon juice, garlic and oregano and toss to coat.
     Refrigerate for 30 minutes.

2   To make the salsa verde, crush the anchovy fillets in a mortar and pestle. Rinse and chop
     the capers very finely and mix with the anchovies. Add the garlic and parsley, then slowly
     stir in the olive oil. Season and mix well.

3   Drain the calamari and cook on a hot, lightly oiled barbecue grill or flatplate in batches for
     1–2 minutes each side, basting with the marinade. To serve, sprinkle the calamari with
     salt, pepper and fresh parsley, and serve with the salsa verde and lemon wedges.

CALAMARI RINGS WITH SALSA VERDE

SERVES 4

INGREDIENTS

20 large scallops with corals
250 g (8 oz) angel hair pasta
150 ml (5 fl oz) extra virgin olive oil
2 cloves garlic, finely chopped
$^1/_4$ cup (60 ml/2 fl oz) white wine
1 tablespoon lemon juice
100 g ($3^1/_2$ oz) baby rocket leaves
30 g (1 oz) chopped fresh coriander (cilantro)

1 Pull or trim any veins, membrane or hard white muscle from the scallops. Pat dry with paper towels. Cook the pasta in boiling water until al dente. Drain and toss with 1 tablespoon oil to keep it from sticking.

2 Meanwhile, heat 1 tablespoon oil in a frying pan, add the garlic and cook for a few seconds. Add the combined wine and lemon juice and remove from the heat.

3 Season the scallops with salt and pepper and cook on a hot, lightly oiled barbecue grill or flatplate for 1 minute each side, or until just cooked. Gently reheat the garlic mixture, add the rocket and stir over medium heat for 1–2 minutes, or until wilted. Toss through the pasta with the remaining oil, coriander and scallops.

INGREDIENTS

8 (800 g) large raw king prawns (jumbo shrimp)
$^{1}/_{3}$ cup (80 ml/2$^{3}/_{4}$ fl oz) olive oil
3 cloves garlic, crushed
1 tablespoon sweet chilli sauce
2 tablespoons lime juice
$^{1}/_{4}$ cup (60 ml/2 fl oz) olive oil, extra
2 tablespoons lime juice, extra

1 Remove the heads from the prawns and, using a sharp knife, cut through the centre of the prawns lengthways to form two halves, leaving the tails and shells intact.

2 Place the olive oil, 2 crushed garlic cloves, sweet chilli sauce and lime juice in a shallow, non-metallic dish and mix together well. Add the prawns, toss to coat and marinate for 30 minutes. Meanwhile, combine the extra oil and lime juice and remaining garlic to make a dressing.

3 Drain the prawns and cook on a hot barbecue grill or flatplate, cut-side-down first, for 1–2 minutes each side, brushing with the leftover marinade. Serve the prawns with the dressing spooned over the top of them.

SERVES 4

INGREDIENTS

800 g (1 lb 12 oz) lamb loin
60 ml (¹/₄ cup) hoisin sauce
2 tablespoons soy sauce
2 garlic cloves, bruised
1 tablespoon grated fresh ginger
2 teaspoons olive oil
16 spring onions (scallions), trimmed to 18 cm (7 inches) long
40 g (¹/₄ cup) chopped toasted peanuts

1 Trim the lamb of any excess fat and sinew. Combine the hoisin sauce, soy sauce, garlic, ginger and 1 teaspoon of the oil in a shallow dish, add the lamb and turn it so that it is well coated in the marinade. Cover the dish and refrigerate for 4 hours or overnight.

2 Toss the trimmed spring onions with the remaining oil and season them well. Remove the lamb from the marinade, season the meat and pour the marinade into a small saucepan. Simmer the marinade for 5 minutes, or until it is slightly reduced. Preheat a chargrill plate to medium direct heat. Cook the lamb for 5–6 minutes on each side, or until it is cooked to your liking, brushing it frequently with the reduced marinade, then let it rest, covered, for 3 minutes. Grill the spring onions for 1–2 minutes, or until they are tender, but still firm.

3 Cut the lamb across the grain into 2 cm (³/₄ inch) thick slices, and arrange it on a serving plate. Drizzle any juices that have been released during resting over the lamb and sprinkle it with the toasted peanuts. Serve with the spring onions.

SERVES 4

PASTA

INGREDIENTS

1 kg (2 lb 4 oz) baby clams (vongole)
375 g (13 oz) spaghetti
125 ml ($^1/_2$ cup) virgin olive oil
40 g (1$^1/_2$ oz) butter
1 small onion, very finely chopped
6 large garlic cloves, finely chopped
125 ml ($^1/_2$ cup) dry white wine
1 small red chilli, seeded and finely chopped
15 g ($^1/_2$ cup) chopped flat-leaf (Italian) parsley

1 Scrub the clams with a small stiff brush to remove any grit, discarding any that are open or cracked. Then soak and rinse the clams in several changes of water over an hour or so until the water is clean and free of grit. Drain and set aside.

2 Cook the pasta in a saucepan of boiling salted water until al dente.

3 Heat the oil and 1 tablespoon of the butter in a large saucepan over medium heat. Add the onion and half the garlic and cook for 10 minutes, or until lightly golden — ensure the garlic doesn't start to burn. Add the wine and cook for 2 minutes. Then add the clams, chilli and the remaining butter and garlic and cook, covered, for 8 minutes, shaking regularly, until the clams pop open — discard any that are still closed.

4 Stir in the parsley and season. Add the hot pasta and toss well.

SERVES 4

GENOVESE PESTO SAUCE

Pesto

2 garlic cloves
50 g (1³/₄ oz) pine nuts
120 g (4¹/₂ oz) basil, stems removed
150–180 ml (5–6 fl oz) extra virgin olive oil
50 g (1³/₄ oz) Parmesan cheese, finely grated,
 plus extra to serve

500 g (1 lb 2 oz) trenette
175 g (6 oz) green beans, trimmed
175 g (6 oz) small potatoes, very thinly sliced

1 Put the garlic and pine nuts in a mortar and pestle or food processor and pound or process until finely ground. Add the basil and then drizzle in the olive oil a little at a time while pounding or processing. When you have a thick purée stop adding the oil. Season and mix in the Parmesan.

2 Bring a large saucepan of salted water to the boil. Add the pasta, green beans and potatoes, stirring well to prevent the pasta from sticking together. Cook until the pasta is al dente (the vegetables should be cooked by this time), then drain, reserving a little of the water.

3 Return the pasta and vegetables to the saucepan, add the pesto, and mix well. If necessary, add some of the reserved water to loosen the pasta. Season and serve immediately with the extra Parmesan.

SERVES 4

INGREDIENTS

200 g (6½ oz) spiral pasta
425 g (14 oz) can cream of mushroom or broccoli soup
1 cup (250 g/8 oz) sour cream
1 teaspoon curry powder
1 barbecued chicken
250 g (8 oz) broccoli, cut into small pieces
1 cup (80 g/2¾ oz) fresh breadcrumbs
1½ cups (185 g/6 oz) grated Cheddar

1 Preheat the oven to moderate 180°C (350°F/Gas 4). Bring a saucepan of salted water to the boil, add the pasta and cook for 10–12 minutes, or until al dente. Drain.

2 Combine the soup, sour cream and curry powder, and season with freshly ground black pepper.

3 Remove the meat from the chicken. Discard the carcass and roughly chop the chicken. Combine the chicken with the cooked pasta, broccoli and soup mixture. Spoon the mixture into four lightly greased 2 cup (500 ml/16 fl oz) ovenproof dishes, and sprinkle with the combined breadcrumbs and grated cheese. Bake for 25–30 minutes, or until the cheese melts.

INDIVIDUAL CHICKEN AND PASTA CASSEROLES

SERVES 4

INGREDIENTS

Pesto
2 cloves garlic, crushed
1 teaspoon salt
¼ cup (40 g/1¼ oz) pine nuts, toasted
2 cups (60 g/2 oz) fresh basil
½ cup (60 g/2 oz) grated Parmesan
¼ cup (60 ml/2 fl oz) extra virgin olive oil

500 g (1 lb) pasta
150 g (5 oz) jar capers in brine
3 tablespoons olive oil
2 tablespoons extra virgin olive oil
2 cloves garlic, chopped
2 tomatoes, seeded and diced
150 g (5 oz) thin asparagus, trimmed, halved and blanched
2 tablespoons balsamic vinegar
150 g (5 oz) rocket
20 cooked prawns, peeled, tails intact
shaved Parmesan, to garnish

1 For the pesto, blend the garlic, salt, pine nuts, fresh basil leaves and grated Parmesan in a food processor or blender until thoroughly combined. With the motor running, add the oil in a thin steady stream and process until the pesto is smooth.

2 Cook the pasta in a large pan of rapidly boiling salted water until al dente. Drain well, transfer to a large bowl and toss the pesto through.

3 Pat the drained capers dry with paper towels, then heat the olive oil in a frying pan and fry the capers for 4–5 minutes, stirring occasionally, until crisp. Drain on paper towels.

4 Heat the extra virgin olive oil in a deep frying pan over medium heat and add the garlic, tomatoes and asparagus. Toss continuously for 1–2 minutes, or until warmed through. Stir in the balsamic vinegar.

5 When the pasta is just warm, not hot (or it will wilt the rocket), toss the tomato mixture, rocket and prawns with the pasta and season with salt and pepper, to taste. Serve sprinkled with capers and shaved Parmesan.

SERVES 4

INGREDIENTS

200 g (6¹/₂ oz) dried borlotti beans
¹/₄ cup (60 ml/2 fl oz) olive oil
90 g (3 oz) piece pancetta, finely diced
1 onion, finely chopped
2 cloves garlic, crushed
1 celery stick, thinly sliced
1 carrot, diced
1 bay leaf
1 sprig fresh rosemary
1 sprig fresh flat-leaf parsley
400 g (13 oz) can diced tomatoes, drained
1.6 litres vegetable stock
2 tablespoons finely chopped fresh flat-leaf parsley
150 g (5 oz) ditalini or other small dried pasta
extra virgin olive oil, to serve
grated fresh Parmesan, to serve

1 Place the beans in a large bowl, cover with cold water and leave to soak overnight. Drain and rinse.

2 Heat the oil in a large saucepan, add the pancetta, onion, garlic, celery and carrot, and cook over medium heat for 5 minutes, or until golden. Season with pepper. Add the bay leaf, rosemary, parsley, tomato, stock and beans, and bring to the boil. Reduce the heat and simmer for 1¹/₂ hours, or until the beans are tender. Add more boiling water if necessary to maintain the liquid level.

3 Discard the bay leaf, rosemary and parsley sprigs. Scoop out 1 cup (250 ml/8 fl oz) of the bean mixture and purée in a food processor or blender. Return to the pan, season with salt and ground black pepper, and add the parsley and pasta. Simmer for 6 minutes, or until the pasta is al dente. Remove from the heat and set aside for 10 minutes. Serve drizzled with extra virgin olive oil and sprinkled with Parmesan.

NOTE If you prefer, you can use three 400 g (13 oz) cans drained borlotti beans. Simmer with the other vegetables for 30 minutes.

PASTA AND BEAN SOUP

SERVES 4

INGREDIENTS

500 g (1 lb) orange sweet potato, cut into large pieces
1/4 cup (60 ml/2 fl oz) olive oil
150 g (5 oz) ricotta cheese
1 tablespoon chopped fresh basil
1 clove garlic, crushed
2 tablespoons grated Parmesan
2 x 250 g (8 oz) packets egg won ton wrappers
60 g (2 oz) butter
4 spring onions, sliced on the diagonal
2 cloves garlic, crushed, extra
300 ml (10 fl oz) cream
baby basil leaves, to serve

1 Preheat the oven to hot 220°C (425°F/Gas 7). Place the sweet potato on a baking tray and drizzle with oil. Bake for 40 minutes, or until tender.

2 Transfer the sweet potato to a bowl with the ricotta, basil, garlic and Parmesan and mash until smooth.

3 Cover the won ton wrappers with a damp tea towel. Place 2 level teaspoons of the sweet potato mixture into the centre of one wrapper and brush the edges with a little water. Top with another wrapper. Place onto a baking tray lined with baking paper and cover with a tea towel. Repeat with the remaining ingredients to make 60 ravioli, placing a sheet of baking paper between each layer.

4 Melt the butter in a frying pan. Add the spring onion and garlic and cook over medium heat for 1 minute. Add the cream, bring to the boil, then reduce the heat and simmer for 4–5 minutes, or until the cream has reduced and thickened. Keep warm.

5 Bring a large saucepan of water to the boil. Cook the ravioli in batches for 2–4 minutes, or until just tender. Drain well. Ladle the hot sauce over the top of the ravioli, garnish with the basil leaves and serve immediately.

SERVES 6

INGREDIENTS

1.5 kg (3 lb) vine-ripened tomatoes
2 cloves garlic, crushed
1 teaspoon sugar
$^1/_3$ cup (80 ml/2$^3/_4$ fl oz) olive oil
3 tablespoons chopped fresh flat-leaf parsley
6 fresh lasagne sheets
400 g (13 oz) smoked salmon
100 g (3$^1/_2$ oz) baby rocket leaves
extra virgin olive oil, for drizzling

1 Score a cross in the base of each tomato and place in a bowl of boiling water for 1 minute. Plunge into cold water and peel the skin away from the cross. Remove the core, then transfer to a food processor or blender and, using the pulse button, process until roughly chopped. Transfer to a saucepan with the garlic and sugar, bring to the boil, then reduce the heat and simmer for 5 minutes, or until reduced slightly. Remove from the heat and gradually whisk in the oil. Stir in the parsley and season. Keep warm.

2 Cut the lasagne sheets in half widthways to give 12 pieces, each about 12 cm (5 inches) squares. Cook the pasta in a large saucepan of boiling water in two batches until al dente. Remove from the water and lay out flat to prevent sticking.

3 Place a pasta sheet on each of four plates. Set aside $^1/_3$ cup of the tomato mix. Spoon half the remaining tomato mixture over the pasta sheets, then half the smoked salmon and rocket leaves. Repeat to give two layers. Finish with a third sheet of pasta.

4 Top each pasta stack with a tablespoon of the tomato sauce, drizzle with a little extra virgin olive oil and serve immediately.

SERVES 4

WARM PASTA AND SMOKED SALMON STACK

INGREDIENTS

250 g (8 oz) chicken breast fillet
1¹/₂ cups (375 ml/12 fl oz) chicken stock
350 g (11 oz) fusilli pasta
155 g (5 oz) asparagus, cut into short lengths
150 g (5 oz) Gruyère cheese, grated
2 spring onions, thinly sliced

Dressing
¹/₄ cup (60 ml/2 fl oz) olive oil
¹/₄ cup (60 ml/2 fl oz) lemon juice
¹/₂ teaspoon sugar

1   Put the chicken and stock in a frying pan. Bring to the boil, then reduce the heat and poach gently, turning regularly, for 8 minutes, or until tender. Remove the chicken, cool and slice thinly.

2   Cook the pasta in a large pan of boiling salted water for 10–12 minutes, or until al dente. Drain and cool.

3   Cook the asparagus in boiling water for 2 minutes. Drain and place in a bowl of iced water. Drain again. Combine with the chicken, pasta and cheese in a large bowl.

4   To make the dressing, whisk the ingredients together. Season with salt and pepper. Add to the salad and toss well. Transfer to a serving bowl and scatter with the spring onion.

SERVES 4

INGREDIENTS

375 g tagliatelle
140 ml extra virgin olive oil
1 small fresh red chilli, seeded and finely chopped
$^1/_4$ cup (50 g) drained capers
$1^1/_2$ tablespoons fresh lemon thyme leaf tips
500 g tuna steaks, trimmed and cut into 3 cm cubes
$^1/_4$ cup (60 ml) lemon juice
1 tablespoon grated lemon zest
$^1/_2$ cup (30 g) chopped fresh flat-leaf parsley

1   Cook the tagliatelle in a large saucepan of rapidly boiling salted water until al dente. Drain, then return to the pan.

2   Meanwhile, heat 1 tablespoon of the oil in a large frying pan. Add the chilli and capers and cook, stirring, for 1 minute, or until the capers are crisp. Add the thyme and cook for another minute. Transfer to a bowl.

3   Heat another tablespoon of oil in the pan. Add the tuna cubes and toss for 2–3 minutes, or until evenly browned on the outside but still pink in the centre—check with the point of a sharp knife. Remove from the heat.

4   Add the tuna to the caper mixture along with the lemon juice, lemon rind, parsley and the remaining oil, stirring gently until combined. Toss through the pasta, season with freshly ground black pepper and serve immediately.

SERVES 4

PROSCIUTTO AND SWEET POTATO PENNE

INGREDIENTS

500 g (1 lb) penne
500 g (1 lb) orange sweet potato, diced
2 tablespoons extra virgin olive oil
5 spring onions, sliced
2 small cloves garlic, crushed
8 thin slices prosciutto, chopped
125 g (4 oz) sun-dried tomatoes in oil, drained and sliced
¼ cup (15 g/½ oz) shredded fresh basil leaves

1 Cook the penne in a large pan of rapidly boiling salted water until al dente. Drain well and return to the pan to keep warm.

2 Meanwhile, steam the sweet potato for 5 minutes, or until tender. Heat the oil in a saucepan, add the spring onion, garlic and sweet potato and stir over medium heat for 2–3 minutes, or until the spring onion is soft. Add the prosciutto and tomato and cook for a further 1 minute.

3 Add the sweet potato mixture to the penne and toss over low heat until heated through. Add the basil and season with black pepper. Serve immediately with crusty bread.

NOTE Orange sweet potato is also known as kumera.

SERVES 4

INGREDIENTS

Meatballs
500 g (1 lb) beef mince
½ cup (40 g/1¼ oz) fresh breadcrumbs
1 onion, finely chopped
2 cloves garlic, crushed
2 teaspoons Worcestershire sauce
1 teaspoon dried oregano
¼ cup (30 g/1 oz) plain flour
2 tablespoons olive oil

Sauce
2 x 400 g (13 oz) cans chopped tomatoes
1 tablespoon olive oil
1 onion, finely chopped
2 cloves garlic, crushed
2 tablespoons tomato paste
½ cup (125 ml/4 fl oz) beef stock
2 teaspoons sugar

500 g (1 lb) spaghetti
grated Parmesan, to serve

1   Combine the mince, breadcrumbs, onion, garlic, Worcestershire sauce and oregano and
    season to taste. Use your hands to mix the ingredients well. Roll level tablespoons of the
    mixture into balls, dust lightly with the flour and shake off the excess. Heat the oil in a
    deep frying pan and cook the meatballs in batches, turning often, until browned all over.
    Drain well.

2   To make the sauce, purée the tomatoes in a food processor or blender. Heat the oil in the
    cleaned frying pan. Add the onion and cook over medium heat for a few minutes until soft
    and lightly golden. Add the garlic and cook for 1 minute more. Add the puréed tomatoes,
    tomato paste, stock and sugar to the pan and stir to combine. Bring the mixture to the
    boil, and add the meatballs. Reduce the heat and simmer for 15 minutes, turning the
    meatballs once. Season with salt and pepper.

3   Meanwhile, cook the spaghetti in a large pan of boiling water until just tender. Drain, divide
    among serving plates and top with the meatballs and sauce. Serve with grated Parmesan.

SPAGHETTI WITH MEATBALLS

SERVES 4

SPAGHETTI NIÇOISE

350 g spaghetti
8 quail eggs (or 4 hen eggs)
3 x 185 g cans tuna in oil
$1/3$ cup (50 g) pitted and halved Kalamata olives
100 g semi-dried tomatoes, halved lengthways
4 anchovy fillets, chopped into small pieces
1 teaspoon finely grated lemon zest
2 tablespoons lemon juice
3 tablespoons baby capers, drained
3 tablespoons chopped fresh flat-leaf parsley

1   Cook the pasta in a large saucepan of rapidly boiling salted water until al dente. Meanwhile, place the eggs in a saucepan of cold water, bring to the boil and cook for 4 minutes (10 minutes for hen eggs). Drain, cool under cold water, then peel. Cut the quail eggs into halves or the hen eggs into quarters.

2   Empty the tuna and its oil into a large bowl. Add the olives, tomato halves, anchovies, lemon rind and juice, capers and 2 tablespoons of the parsley. Drain the pasta and rinse in a little cold water, then toss gently through the tuna mixture. Divide among serving bowls, garnish with egg and the remaining chopped fresh parsley, and serve.

     SERVES 4-6

INGREDIENTS

2 tablespoons olive oil
1 teaspoon dried oregano
2 cloves garlic, finely chopped
6 Roma tomatoes, halved
500 g (1 lb) spaghetti
4 slices prosciutto
16 Kalamata olives
200 g (6$^1/_2$ oz) feta, cut into bite-size cubes
1 tablespoon balsamic vinegar
5 tablespoons olive oil, extra
3 cloves garlic, thinly sliced, extra
60 g (2 oz) rocket leaves, trimmed

1 Preheat the oven to slow 150°C (300°F/Gas 2). Combine the olive oil, oregano, garlic and 1 teaspoon salt in a bowl. Add the tomato and toss to combine, rubbing the mixture onto the cut halves of the tomato. Place the tomato cut-side-up on a lined baking tray and cook in the oven for 1 hour.

2 Meanwhile, cook the pasta in a large pan of rapidly boiling salted water until al dente. Drain well and return to the pan to keep warm. Place the prosciutto on a grill tray and cook under a hot grill, turning once, for 3–4 minutes, or until crispy. Break into pieces.

3 Toss the tomato, olives, feta, spaghetti and balsamic vinegar in a bowl and keep warm.

4 Heat the extra olive oil in a small saucepan and cook the extra garlic over low heat, without burning, for 1–2 minutes, or until the garlic has infused the oil.

5 Pour the garlic and oil over the spaghetti mixture, add the rocket leaves and toss well. Sprinkle with the prosciutto pieces and season well. Serve immediately.

MEDITERRANEAN PASTA

SERVES 4

INGREDIENTS

150 g (5 oz) spiral pasta
4 thick beef sausages
2 tablespoons olive oil
1 large red onion, cut into wedges
1 cup (250 g/8 oz) tomato pasta sauce
4 small ripe tomatoes, peeled, seeded and chopped
2 tablespoons chopped fresh flat-leaf parsley

1 Cook the pasta in a large pan of rapidly boiling salted water until al dente. Drain well and return to the pan to keep warm, reserving $1/4$ cup (60 ml/2 fl oz) of the cooking water.

2 Meanwhile, prick the sausages all over with a fork. Heat a non-stick frying pan and cook the sausages over medium heat, turning often, for 5 minutes, or until cooked. Cut into thick diagonal slices and set aside.

3 Clean the frying pan and heat the oil. Cook the onion wedges over medium heat for 3 minutes, or until soft. Add the tomato pasta sauce and the tomato. Cook for 5 minutes, or until the tomato has softened. Add the sliced sausage and heat through for 1 minute.

4 Toss the pasta through the sauce, adding a little of the reserved pasta water, if necessary. Sprinkle with parsley and serve.

SERVES 4

INGREDIENTS

500 g (1 lb) fresh tomato fettucine
600 g (1¹/₄ lb) chicken tenderloins
40 g (1¹/₄ oz) butter
3 eggs
300 ml (10 fl oz) cream
¹/₂ cup (50 g/1¹/₂ oz) grated Parmesan
shaved Parmesan and fresh basil leaves, to garnish

1   Cook the pasta in a large pan of rapidly boiling salted water until al dente. Drain and return to the pan to keep warm.

2   Trim and slice the tenderloins in half on the diagonal. Melt the butter in a frying pan and cook the chicken for 4–5 minutes, or until browned. Lightly beat the eggs and cream together and stir in the grated Parmesan. Season with salt to taste and stir through the chicken.

3   Combine the chicken and cream mixture with the fettucine in the frying pan. Reduce the heat and cook, stirring constantly, for 10–15 seconds, or until the sauce is slightly thickened. Do not keep on the heat too long or the eggs will set and scramble. Season with black pepper and serve, garnished with the extra Parmesan and basil leaves.

SERVES 4

INGREDIENTS

500 g (1 lb) pasta shells or gnocchi
2 tablespoons olive oil
400 g (13 oz) thin Italian sausages
1 red onion, finely chopped
2 cloves garlic, finely chopped
2 x 415 g (13 oz) cans chopped tomatoes
1 teaspoon caster sugar
35 g (1 oz) fresh basil, torn
$^{1}/_{2}$ cup (45 g/1$^{1}/_{2}$ oz) grated pecorino cheese

1   Cook the pasta in a large pan of rapidly boiling salted water until al dente. Drain and return to the pan to keep warm. Meanwhile, heat 2 teaspoons of the oil in a large frying pan. Add the sausages and cook, turning, for 5 minutes, or until well browned and cooked through. Drain on paper towels, then slice when cooled enough to hold. Keep warm.

2   Wipe clean the frying pan and heat the remaining oil. Add the onion and garlic and cook over medium heat for 2 minutes, or until the onion has softened. Add the tomato, sugar and 1 cup (250 ml/8 fl oz) water and season well. Reduce the heat and simmer for 12 minutes, or until thickened and reduced a little.

3   Pour the sauce over the pasta and stir through the sausage, basil and half the cheese. Serve hot, sprinkled with the remaining cheese.

SERVES 4-6

4 cloves garlic, unpeeled
⅓ cup (80 ml/2¾ fl oz) olive oil
250 g (8 oz) cherry tomatoes
300 g (10 oz) short cut bacon (see note)
350 g (11 oz) fresh fettucine
1 tablespoon white wine vinegar
2 tablespoons roughly chopped fresh basil
2 ripe avocados, diced
whole fresh basil leaves, to garnish

1 Preheat the oven to moderately hot 200°C (400°F/Gas 6). Place the garlic at one end of a roasting tin and drizzle with 2 tablespoons of the olive oil. Place the tomatoes at the other end and season well. Bake for 10 minutes, then remove the garlic. Return the tomatoes to the oven for a further 5–10 minutes, or until soft.

2 Cook the bacon under a hot grill for 4–5 minutes each side, or until crisp and golden. Roughly chop. Meanwhile, cook the pasta in a large saucepan of boiling water until al dente. Drain well and transfer to a large bowl. Drizzle 1 tablespoon of the olive oil over the pasta and toss well. Season to taste with salt and freshly ground black pepper and keep warm.

3 Slit the skin of each garlic clove and squeeze the garlic out. Place in a screw-top jar with the vinegar, chopped basil and remaining oil and shake well to combine. Add the tomatoes and their juices, bacon and avocado to the fettucine, pour on the dressing and toss well. Garnish with the basil leaves and serve with a green salad and crusty bread.

NOTE Short cut bacon is the meaty end of the bacon rasher and is also sold as eye bacon.

FETTUCINE WITH CHERRY TOMATOES, AVOCADO AND BACON

SERVES 4

PENNE WITH PUMPKIN, BAKED RICOTTA AND PROSCIUTTO

500 g (1 lb) penne
460 g (15 oz) butternut pumpkin, cut into small cubes
$^1/_4$ cup (60 ml/2 fl oz) extra virgin olive oil
2 cloves garlic, crushed
100 g ($3^1/_2$ oz) semi-dried tomatoes, chopped
4 slices prosciutto, chopped
250 g (8 oz) baked ricotta, cut into small cubes
3 tablespoons shredded fresh basil

1 Cook the pasta in a large pan of rapidly boiling salted water until al dente. Drain well. Meanwhile, cook the pumpkin in a saucepan of boiling water for 10–12 minutes, or until just tender, then drain.

2 Heat the oil in a large saucepan, add the garlic and cook over medium heat for 30 seconds. Add the tomato, prosciutto, pumpkin and penne and toss gently over low heat for 1–2 minutes, or until heated through.

3 Add the baked ricotta and the basil, season with salt and cracked black pepper and serve immediately.

SERVES 4

INGREDIENTS

400 g (13 oz) farfalle
2 tablespoons extra virgin olive oil
250 g (8 oz) bacon, chopped
1 red onion, finely chopped
250 g (8 oz) baby spinach leaves
1–2 tablespoons sweet chilli sauce
1/4 cup (30 g/1 oz) crumbled feta cheese

1   Cook the pasta in a large pan of rapidly boiling salted water until al dente. Drain and return to the pan to keep warm.

2   Meanwhile, heat the oil in a frying pan, add the bacon and cook over medium heat for 3 minutes, or until golden. Add the onion and cook for a further 4 minutes, or until softened. Toss the spinach leaves through the onion and bacon mixture for 30 seconds, or until just wilted.

3   Add the bacon and spinach mixture to the drained pasta, then stir in the sweet chilli sauce. Season to taste with salt and cracked black pepper and toss well. Spoon into warm pasta bowls and scatter with the crumbled feta. Serve immediately.

FARFALLE WITH SPINACH AND BACON

SERVES 4

CREAMY PASTA GNOCCHI WITH PEAS AND PROSCIUTTO

INGREDIENTS

100 g (3½ oz) thinly sliced prosciutto
3 teaspoons oil
2 eggs
1 cup (250 ml/8 fl oz) cream
⅓ cup (35 g/1¼ oz) finely grated Parmesan
2 tablespoons chopped fresh flat-leaf parsley
1 tablespoon chopped fresh chives
250 g (8 oz) fresh or frozen peas
500 g (1 lb) pasta gnocchi

1 Cut the prosciutto into 5 mm (¼ inch) wide strips. Heat the oil in a frying pan over medium heat, add the prosciutto and cook for 2 minutes, or until crisp. Drain on paper towels. Place the eggs, cream, Parmesan and herbs in a bowl and whisk well.

2 Bring a large saucepan of salted water to the boil. Add the peas and cook for 5 minutes, or until just tender. Leaving the pan on the heat, use a slotted spoon and transfer the peas to the bowl of cream mixture, and then add ¼ cup (60 ml/2 fl oz) of the cooking liquid to the same bowl. Using a potato masher or the back of a fork, roughly mash the peas.

3 Add the gnocchi to the boiling water and cook until al dente. Drain well, then return to the pan. Add the cream mixture, then warm through over low heat, gently stirring for about 30 seconds until the gnocchi is coated in the sauce. Season to taste with salt and cracked black pepper. Divide among warmed plates, top with the prosciutto and serve immediately.

NOTE Be careful not to overheat or cook for too long as the egg will begin to set and the result will look like a scrambled egg sauce.

SERVES 4

INGREDIENTS

2 onions, sliced
2 bay leaves, crushed
1.5 kg (3 lb) veal shin, cut into osso buco pieces (see note)
1 cup (250 ml/8 fl oz) red wine
2 x 400 g (13 oz) cans crushed tomatoes
1$\frac{1}{2}$ cups (375 ml/12 fl oz) beef stock
2 teaspoons chopped fresh rosemary
400 g (13 oz) penne
1 cup (150 g/5 oz) frozen peas

1 Preheat the oven to hot 220°C (425°F/Gas 7). Scatter the onion over the bottom of a large roasting tin, lightly spray with oil and place the bay leaves and veal pieces on top. Season with salt and pepper. Roast for 10–15 minutes, or until the veal is browned. Take care that the onion doesn't burn.

2 Pour the wine over the veal and return to the oven for a further 5 minutes. Reduce the heat to moderate 180°C (350°F/Gas 4), remove the tin from the oven and pour on the tomato, stock and 1 teaspoon of the rosemary. Cover with foil and return to the oven. Cook for 2 hours, or until the veal is starting to fall from the bone. Remove the foil and cook for a further 15 minutes, or until the meat loosens away from the bone and the liquid has evaporated slightly.

3 Cook the pasta in a large pan of rapidly boiling salted water until al dente. Drain and return to the pan to keep warm. Meanwhile, remove the veal from the oven and cool slightly. Add the peas and remaining rosemary and place over a hotplate. Cook over medium heat for 5 minutes, or until the peas are cooked. Serve the pasta topped with the ragout.

NOTE Most butchers sell veal shin cut into osso buco pieces. If sold in a whole piece, ask the butcher to cut it for you (the pieces are about 3–4 cm thick). It is also available at some supermarkets. You can either remove the meat from the bone before serving, or leave it on.

PENNE WITH VEAL RAGOUT

SERVES 4

PASTA WITH CREAMY TOMATO AND BACON SAUCE

INGREDIENTS

400 g (13 oz) pasta
1 tablespoon olive oil
180 g (6 oz) streaky bacon, thinly sliced (see note)
500 g (1 lb) Roma tomatoes, roughly chopped
$1/2$ cup (125 ml/4 fl oz) thick cream
2 tablespoons sun-dried tomato pesto
2 tablespoons finely chopped fresh flat-leaf parsley
$1/2$ cup (50 g/$1^3/_4$ oz) finely grated Parmesan

1 Cook the pasta in a large pan of rapidly boiling salted water until al dente. Drain and return to the pan to keep warm. Meanwhile, heat the oil in a frying pan, add the bacon and cook over high heat for 2 minutes, or until starting to brown. Reduce the heat to medium, add the tomato and cook, stirring frequently, for 2 minutes, or until the tomato has softened but still holds its shape.

2 Add the cream and tomato pesto and stir until heated through. Remove from the heat, add the parsley, then toss the sauce through the pasta with the grated Parmesan.

NOTE Streaky bacon is the tail fatty ends of bacon rashers and adds flavour to the dish. You can use ordinary bacon rashers if you prefer.

SERVES 4

INGREDIENTS

450 g (14 oz) pork fillet
3–4 teaspoons cracked black peppercorns
90 g (3 oz) butter
250 g (8 oz) pasta
1 onion, halved and thinly sliced
2 large zucchini, thinly sliced
$^2/_3$ cup (20 g/$^3/_4$ oz) fresh basil, torn
$^3/_4$ cup (150 g/5 oz) baby black olives
$^1/_2$ cup (60 g/2 oz) grated Romano cheese

1   Cut the pork fillet in half widthways and roll in the cracked peppercorns and some salt. Heat half the butter in a large deep frying pan, add the pork and cook for 4 minutes each side, or until golden brown and just cooked through. Remove from the pan and cut into thin slices, then set aside and keep warm.

2   Cook the pasta in a large pan of rapidly boiling salted water until al dente. Drain and return to the pan to keep warm. Meanwhile, melt the remaining butter in the frying pan, add the onion and cook, stirring, over medium heat for about 3 minutes, or until soft. Add the zucchini and toss for 5 minutes, or until starting to soften. Add the basil, olives, sliced pork and any juices and toss well. Stir the pork mixture through the hot pasta, then season well. Serve immediately, topped with the cheese.

PEPPERED PORK AND ZUCCHINI PASTA

SERVES 4

INGREDIENTS

500 g (1 lb) good-quality Italian sausages
2 tablespoons olive oil
3 cloves garlic, chopped
1 teaspoon fennel seeds
$^1/_2$ teaspoon chilli flakes
2 x 425 g (14 oz) cans crushed tomatoes
500 g (1 lb) bucatini
1 teaspoon balsamic vinegar
$^1/_4$ cup (7 g/$^1/_4$ oz) loosely packed fresh basil, chopped

1   Heat a frying pan over high heat, add the sausages and cook, turning, for 8–10 minutes, or until well browned and cooked through. Remove, cool slightly and slice thinly on the diagonal.

2   Heat the oil in a saucepan, add the garlic and cook over medium heat for 1 minute. Add the fennel seeds and chilli flakes and cook for a further minute. Stir in the tomato and bring to the boil, then reduce the heat and simmer, covered, for 20 minutes. Meanwhile, cook the pasta in a large pan of rapidly boiling salted water until al dente. Drain and return to the pan to keep warm.

3   Add the sausages to the sauce and cook, uncovered, for 5 minutes to heat through. Stir in the balsamic vinegar and basil. Divide the pasta among four bowls, top with the sauce and serve.

SERVES 4

500 g (1 lb) fresh linguine
1 tablespoon butter
2 large cloves garlic, chopped
150 g (5 oz) marinated artichokes, drained and quartered
150 g (5 oz) sliced leg ham, cut into strips
300 ml (10 fl oz) cream
2 teaspoons roughly grated lemon rind
$^1/_2$ cup (15 g/$^1/_2$ oz) fresh basil, torn
$^1/_3$ cup (35 g/1 oz) grated Parmesan

1 Cook the pasta in a large pan of rapidly boiling salted water until al dente. Drain and return to the pan to keep warm. Meanwhile, melt the butter in a large frying pan, add the garlic and cook over medium heat for 1 minute, or until fragrant. Add the artichokes and ham and cook for a further 2 minutes.

2 Add the cream and lemon rind, reduce the heat and simmer for 5 minutes, gently breaking up the artichokes with a wooden spoon. Pour the sauce over the pasta, then add the basil and Parmesan and toss well until the pasta is evenly coated. Serve immediately.

LINGUINE WITH HAM, ARTICHOKE AND LEMON SAUCE

SERVES 4

PAPPARDELLE WITH SALAMI, LEEK AND PROVOLONE CHEESE

375 g (12 oz) pappardelle

2 tablespoons olive oil

2 leeks, thinly sliced (including some of the green section)

2 tablespoons white wine

2 x 400 g (13 oz) cans diced tomatoes

150 g (5 oz) sliced mild salami, cut into strips

$^1/_4$ cup (7 g/$^1/_4$ oz) fresh basil leaves, torn

125 g (4 oz) provolone cheese, sliced into strips

30 g (1 oz) grated Parmesan

1 Cook the pasta in a large pan of rapidly boiling salted water until al dente. Drain and return to the pan to keep warm. Meanwhile, heat the olive oil in a large deep frying pan, add the leek and cook over low heat for 4 minutes, or until soft but not browned. Increase the heat to medium, add the wine and stir until almost evaporated.

2 Add the tomato and salami, season with salt and cracked black pepper and simmer for 5 minutes, or until reduced slightly. Toss the tomato sauce mixture, basil and provolone lightly through the pasta. Sprinkle with Parmesan and serve.

SERVES 4

INGREDIENTS

250 g (8 oz) baby bok choy, leaves separated
600 g (1¹/₄ lb) fresh pappardelle
1 Chinese roast duck, skin removed (see note)
¹/₃ cup (80 ml/3³/₄ fl oz) peanut oil
3 cloves garlic, crushed
3 teaspoons grated fresh ginger
³/₄ cup (35 g/1 oz) chopped fresh coriander leaves
2 tablespoons hoisin sauce
2 tablespoons oyster sauce

1 Bring a large pan of water to the boil and blanch the bok choy for 1–2 minutes, or until tender but still crisp. Remove with a slotted spoon and keep warm. Cook the pasta in the water until al dente. Drain well and return to the pan to keep warm.

2 Remove and shred the duck meat. Heat the peanut oil in a small pan over high heat until smoking. Remove from the heat and cool for 1 minute, then swirl in the garlic and ginger to infuse the oil. Be careful not to allow the garlic to burn or it will turn bitter.

3 Pour the hot oil over the pasta and add the bok choy, duck, coriander, hoisin and oyster sauces. Toss well, season and serve immediately.

NOTE Chinese roast duck can be bought from Asian barbecue food shops or restaurants.

CHINESE ROAST DUCK WITH PAPPARDELLE

SERVES 4-6

SMOKED SALMON PASTA

500 g (1 lb) pasta
1 tablespoon olive oil
4 spring onions, finely chopped
180 g (6 oz) button mushrooms, sliced
1 cup (250 ml/8 fl oz) dry white wine
300 ml (10 fl oz) cream
1 tablespoon finely chopped fresh dill
1 tablespoon lemon juice
90 g (3 oz) Parmesan, grated
200 g (6$^{1}/_{2}$ oz) smoked salmon, cut into strips
shaved Parmesan and lemon wedges, to serve

1 Cook the pasta in a large pan of rapidly boiling salted water until al dente. Drain and return to the pan to keep warm.

2 Meanwhile, heat the oil in a small saucepan, add the spring onion and mushrooms and cook over medium heat for 1–2 minutes, or until soft. Add the wine and cream and bring to the boil, then reduce the heat and simmer for 1 minute.

3 Pour the mushroom sauce over the pasta and stir through the dill and lemon juice. Add the Parmesan and stir until warmed through. Remove from the heat and stir in the smoked salmon. Season with pepper and serve with Parmesan shavings and lemon wedges.

SERVES 4

INGREDIENTS

20 large scallops with roe
250 g (8 oz) angel hair pasta
150 ml (5 fl oz) extra virgin olive oil
2 cloves garlic, finely chopped
$^1/_4$ cup (60 ml/2 fl oz) white wine
1 tablespoon lemon juice
100 g (3$^1/_2$ oz) baby rocket leaves
$^1/_2$ cup (30 g/1 oz) chopped fresh coriander leaves

1 Pull or trim any veins, membrane or hard white muscle from the scallops. Pat the scallops dry with paper towels. Cook the pasta in a large pan of rapidly boiling salted water until al dente. Drain and transfer to a bowl. Toss with 1 tablespoon of the oil.

2 Meanwhile, heat 1 tablespoon oil in a frying pan, add the garlic and cook for a few seconds, or until fragrant. Do not brown. Add the wine and lemon juice, and remove from the heat.

3 Heat a chargrill pan or barbecue grill plate over high heat and brush with a little oil. Season the scallops with salt and pepper and cook for 1 minute each side, or until just cooked. Gently reheat the garlic mixture, add the rocket and stir over medium heat for 1–2 minutes, or until wilted. Toss through the pasta and mix together well. Add the remaining oil and half the coriander and mix well. Divide the pasta among four bowls, arrange the scallops over the top and garnish with the remaining coriander.

ANGEL HAIR PASTA WITH GARLIC, SCALLOPS AND ROCKET

SERVES 4

RICOTTA AGNOLOTTI WITH SALMON AND CAPERS

125 ml ($^1/_2$ cup) olive oil
100 g ($3^1/_2$ oz) capers, patted dry
500 g (1 lb 2 oz) salmon fillets, skinned
625 g (1 lb 6 oz) ricotta agnolotti
150 g ($5^1/_2$ oz) butter
$1^1/_2$ teaspoons grated lemon zest
2 tablespoons lemon juice
3 tablespoons chopped parsley

1   Heat half the oil in a small frying pan and cook the capers over high heat for 3–4 minutes, or until golden and crispy. Drain on paper towels.

2   Season the salmon on both sides with salt and pepper. Heat the remaining oil in a non-stick frying pan and cook the salmon for 2–3 minutes each side, or until just cooked through but still pink in the centre. Remove from the pan and keep warm. Gently break into flakes with your fingers, being careful to remove any bones.

3   Cook the pasta in a large saucepan of boiling salted water until al dente. Drain and return to the pan to keep warm. Heat the butter in a frying pan over low heat for 5 minutes, or until golden. Add the lemon zest, lemon juice and parsley. Top the pasta with the flaked salmon and pour on the brown butter. Scatter with the capers and serve immediately.

SERVES 4

INGREDIENTS

375 g (12 oz) spaghetti
$^1/_3$ cup (80 ml/2$^3/_4$ fl oz) olive oil
2 onions, finely chopped
3 cloves garlic, finely chopped
$^1/_2$ teaspoon chilli flakes
6 large ripe tomatoes, diced
4 tablespoons capers in brine, rinsed, drained
7–8 anchovies in oil, drained, minced
150 g (5 oz) Kalamata olives
3 tablespoons chopped fresh flat-leaf parsley

1   Cook the pasta in a large pan of rapidly boiling salted water until al dente. Drain and return to the pan to keep warm.

2   Meanwhile, heat the oil in a saucepan, add the onion and cook over medium heat for 5 minutes. Add the garlic and chilli flakes, and cook for 30 seconds, then add the tomato, capers and anchovies. Simmer over low heat for 5–10 minutes, or until thick and pulpy, then stir in the olives and parsley.

3   Stir the pasta through the sauce. Season and serve immediately with crusty bread.

SPAGHETTI WITH OLIVE, CAPER AND ANCHOVY SAUCE

SERVES 6

PASTA WITH CLAMS

2 tablespoons salt
2 tablespoons plain flour
1 kg (2 lb) clams or pipis
500 g (1 lb) shell pasta
1 tablespoon olive oil
2 cloves garlic, crushed
2 x 425 g (14 oz) cans crushed tomatoes
1/4 cup (60 ml/2 fl oz) red wine
2 tablespoons chopped fresh parsley
1 teaspoon sugar

1 Blend the salt and plain flour with enough water to make a paste. Add to a large pan of cold water and soak the shellfish overnight. This will draw out sand from inside the shells. Scrub the shells well. Rinse and drain.

2 Cook the pasta in a large pan of rapidly boiling salted water until al dente. Drain and return to the pan to keep warm. Meanwhile, heat the oil in a large pan. Add the garlic and cook over low heat for 30 seconds. Add the tomatoes, wine, parsley and sugar and season. Stir and bring to the boil. Reduce the heat and simmer, stirring occasionally, for 5 minutes.

3 Add the clams to the sauce and cook for 3–5 minutes, stirring occasionally, until opened. Discard any clams that do not open in the cooking time. Serve over the pasta.

SERVES 4

INGREDIENTS

¹/₂ cup (125 ml/4 fl oz) dry white wine
pinch of saffron threads
500 g (1 lb) fresh saffron or plain angel-hair pasta
1 tablespoon virgin olive oil
30 g (1 oz) butter
750 g (1¹/₂ lb) raw prawns, peeled and deveined
3 cloves garlic, crushed
100 g (3¹/₂ oz) butter, for pan-frying, extra
¹/₂ preserved lemon, rinsed, pith and flesh removed, cut into thin strips
1 tablespoon lemon juice
4 spring onions, thinly sliced
4 kaffir lime leaves, thinly shredded
¹/₂ cup (125 ml/4 fl oz) chicken stock
2 tablespoons snipped chives

1   Place the wine and saffron in a small saucepan and boil for 3 minutes, or until reduced by half. Remove from the heat.

2   Cook the pasta in a large pan of rapidly boiling salted water until al dente. Drain and return to the pan to keep warm.

3   Heat the oil and butter in a large frying pan and cook the prawns in batches over high heat for 3 minutes, or until pink and tender. Cut into thirds, then transfer to a plate and keep warm.

4   Add the garlic and extra butter to the same pan and cook over medium heat for 3 minutes, or until golden. Add the wine and stir to remove any sediment from the bottom of the pan. Add the preserved lemon, lemon juice, spring onion, lime leaves and stock and bring to the boil, then reduce the heat and simmer for 2 minutes.

5   Return the prawns to the frying pan and heat through. Serve the pasta topped with some of the prawns and sauce and sprinkle with chives.

SAFFRON PASTA WITH GARLIC PRAWNS AND PRESERVED LEMON

SERVES 4

CAJUN SCALLOPS WITH PASTA AND BUTTERY CORN SAUCE

350 g (11 oz) small pasta shells
20 large scallops, without roe
2 tablespoons Cajun spice mix
2 tablespoons corn oil
250 g (8 oz) butter
3 cloves garlic, crushed
400 g (13 oz) can corn kernels, drained
¼ cup (60 ml/2 fl oz) lime juice
4 tablespoons finely chopped fresh coriander leaves

1 Cook the pasta in a large pan of rapidly boiling salted water until al dente. Drain and return to the pan to keep warm. Meanwhile, pat the scallops dry with paper towel and lightly coat in the spice mix. Heat the oil in a large frying pan and cook the scallops for 1 minute each side over high heat (ensuring they are well spaced), then remove from the pan, cover and keep warm.

2 Reduce the heat to medium, add the butter and cook for 4 minutes, or until foaming and golden brown. Remove from the heat, add the garlic, corn and lime juice. Gently toss the corn mixture through the pasta with 2 tablespoons of the coriander and season well. Divide among four serving plates, top with the scallops, drizzle with any juices and sprinkle with the remaining coriander.

NOTE Scallops should not be crowded when they are cooked or they will release all their juices, causing them to stew and toughen.

SERVES 4

INGREDIENTS

600 g (1¹/₄ lb) broccoli, cut into florets
500 g (1 lb) orecchiette
1 tablespoon olive oil
4 cloves garlic, finely chopped
8 anchovy fillets, roughly chopped
1 cup (250 ml/8 fl oz) cream
1 cup (30 g/1 oz) fresh basil, torn
2 teaspoons finely grated lemon rind
100 g (3¹/₂ oz) Parmesan, grated

1 Blanch the broccoli in a large saucepan of boiling salted water for 3–4 minutes. Remove and plunge into chilled water. Drain well with a slotted spoon. Cook the pasta in a large pan of rapidly boiling salted water until al dente. Drain and return to the pan to keep warm, reserving 2 tablespoons of the cooking water.

2 Meanwhile, heat the oil in a frying pan over medium heat. Add the garlic and anchovies and cook for 1–2 minutes, or until the garlic begins to turn golden. Add the broccoli and cook for a further 5 minutes. Add the cream and half the basil and cook for 10 minutes, or until the cream has reduced and slightly thickened and the broccoli is very tender.

3 Purée half the mixture in a food processor until nearly smooth, then return to the pan with the lemon rind, half the Parmesan and 2 tablespoons of the reserved water. Stir together well, then season. Add the warm pasta and remaining basil, and toss until well combined. Sprinkle with the remaining Parmesan and serve immediately.

SERVES 4

INGREDIENTS

4 x 200 g (6$^1/_2$ oz) tuna steaks
$^2/_3$ cup (170 ml/5$^1/_2$ oz) balsamic vinegar
$^1/_2$ cup (125 ml/4 fl oz) good-quality olive oil
1 lemon
1 clove garlic, finely chopped
1 red onion, finely chopped
2 tablespoons capers, rinsed and dried
$^1/_2$ cup (15 g/$^1/_2$ oz) fresh flat-leaf parsley, finely chopped
500 g (1 lb) fresh fettucine

1 Place the tuna steaks in a non-metallic dish and cover with the balsamic vinegar. Turn to coat evenly and marinate for 10 minutes. Heat 2 tablespoons of the oil in a large frying pan over medium heat and cook the tuna for 2–3 minutes each side. Remove from the pan, cut into small cubes and transfer to a bowl.

2 Finely grate the rind from the lemon to give $^1/_2$ teaspoon rind, then squeeze the lemon to give $^1/_4$ cup (60 ml/2 fl oz) juice. Wipe the frying pan clean, and heat 2 tablespoons of the olive oil over medium heat, then add the garlic and cook for 30 seconds. Stir in the chopped onion and cook for 2 minutes. Add the lemon rind and capers and cook for 1 minute, then stir in the parsley and cook for 1 minute. Add the lemon juice and remaining oil and gently toss together. Season to taste.

3 Cook the pasta in a large pan of rapidly boiling salted water until al dente. Drain, return to the pan and toss with the caper mixture. Divide the pasta among serving bowls and arrange the tuna pieces over the top.

SERVES 6

800 g (1 lb 10 oz) vine-ripened tomatoes
375 g (12 oz) spaghetti
3 x 125 g (4 oz) cans smoked tuna slices in oil
1 red onion, chopped
2 cloves garlic, crushed
1 teaspoon sugar
150 g (5 oz) black olives
2 tablespoons chopped fresh basil
75 g (2¹/₂ oz) feta cheese, crumbled

1 Score a cross in the base of each tomato. Place the tomatoes in a bowl of boiling water for 1 minute, then plunge into cold water and peel the skin away from the cross. Cut in half and remove the seeds with a teaspoon. Roughly chop the flesh. Cook the pasta in a large pan of rapidly boiling salted water until al dente. Drain and return to the pan to keep warm.

2 Drain the oil from the tuna slices, reserving 1 tablespoon. Heat the reserved oil in a large saucepan, add the onion and cook over low heat for 3–4 minutes, or until soft but not brown. Add the garlic and cook for another minute, then add the chopped tomatoes and sugar. Cook over medium heat for 8–10 minutes, or until pulpy.

3 Add the tuna slices, olives and chopped basil, stir well and cook for 2 minutes, or until warmed through. Toss through the spaghetti and season with salt and cracked black pepper. Sprinkle with crumbled feta and serve.

SPAGHETTI WITH SMOKED TUNA AND OLIVES

SERVES 4

ANGEL HAIR PASTA WITH CREAMY GARLIC PRAWNS

2 tablespoons olive oil
16 raw prawns, peeled and deveined
1 leek, chopped
6 cloves garlic, crushed
$^{1}/_{2}$ teaspoon dried chilli flakes
$^{1}/_{2}$ cup (125 ml/4 fl oz) dry white wine
200 ml ($6^{1}/_{2}$ fl oz) cream
250 g (8 oz) angel hair pasta
3 tablespoons chopped fresh flat-leaf parsley

1 Heat half the oil in a frying pan, season the prawns with salt and pepper, add to the pan and cook over high heat for 2–3 minutes, or until cooked through. Remove from the pan, cover and keep warm.

2 Heat the remaining oil in the same pan, add the leek and cook, stirring, over medium heat for 2–3 minutes, or until softened. Add the garlic and chilli flakes and stir for 1 minute. Pour in the wine, reduce the heat and simmer for 4 minutes, or until reduced. Add the cream and simmer for 3 minutes, or until just thickened.

3 Meanwhile, cook the pasta in a large pan of rapidly boiling salted water until al dente. Drain and return to the pan to keep warm. Stir the parsley into the sauce and season well. Add to the pasta and stir to coat. Divide the pasta among bowls and top with the prawns.

SERVES 4

INGREDIENTS

500 g (1 lb) mussels
1 kg (2 lb) clams
400 g (13 oz) spaghetti
2 tablespoons olive oil
4 French shallots, finely chopped
2 cloves garlic, crushed
1 cup (250 ml/8 fl oz) dry white wine
3 tablespoons chopped fresh flat-leaf parsley

1   Scrub the mussels with a stiff brush and remove any barnacles with a knife. Pull away the beards. Discard any mussels or clams that are broken or open ones that do not close when tapped on the work surface. Wash them both thoroughly under cold running water. Cook the pasta in a large pan of rapidly boiling salted water until al dente. Drain and return to the pan to keep warm.

2   Meanwhile, heat the oil in a large saucepan over medium heat and cook the shallots for 4 minutes, or until softened. Add the garlic and cook for a further 1 minute. Pour in the wine, bring to the boil and cook for 2 minutes, or until reduced slightly. Add the clams and mussels, tossing to coat them in the liquid, then cover the pan. Cook, shaking the pan regularly, for about 3 minutes, or until the shells have opened. Discard any clams or mussels that do not open in the cooking time. Toss the clam mixture through the spaghetti, scatter with parsley and transfer to a warmed serving dish. Season and serve with salad and bread.

SPAGHETTI WITH SHELLFISH AND WHITE WINE SAUCE

SERVES 4

PASTA IN CHAMPAGNE SAUCE WITH SMOKED SALMON

375 g (12 oz) pappardelle
1 tablespoon olive oil
2 large cloves garlic, crushed
$^1/_2$ cup (125 ml/4 fl oz) Champagne
1 cup (250 ml/8 fl oz) thick cream
200 g (6$^1/_2$ oz) smoked salmon, cut into thin strips
2 tablespoons small capers in brine, rinsed and dried
2 tablespoons chopped fresh chives
2 tablespoons chopped fresh dill

1 Cook the pasta in a large pan of rapidly boiling salted water until al dente. Drain and keep warm. Heat the oil in a frying pan; cook the garlic over medium heat for 30 seconds. Pour in the Champagne and cook for 2–3 minutes, or until reduced slightly. Add the cream and cook for 3–4 minutes, or until thickened.

2 Toss the sauce and remaining ingredients with the pasta and serve.

SERVES 4

INGREDIENTS

400 g (13 oz) pappardelle
60 g (2 oz) butter
4 large cloves garlic, crushed
250 g (8 oz) Swiss brown mushrooms, sliced
500 g (1 lb) fresh or frozen lobster tail meat or raw bug tails
$^1/_2$ cup (125 ml/4 fl oz) white wine
$^1/_2$ teaspoon saffron threads
700 ml (23 fl oz) thick cream
2 egg yolks

1 Cook the pasta in a large pan of rapidly boiling salted water until al dente. Drain and return to the pan to keep warm. Meanwhile, melt the butter in a large deep frying pan, add the garlic and mushrooms and cook over medium heat for 2–3 minutes, or until soft. Add the lobster and cook for 4–5 minutes, or until just cooked through. Remove from the pan.

2 Add the wine and saffron to the pan, scraping the bottom to collect any bits. Bring to the boil and cook for 2–3 minutes, or until reduced. Add the cream, reduce the heat and simmer for 5 minutes. Whisk through the egg yolks until thickened. Return the lobster mixture to the pan and stir until warmed through. Drain the pasta and divide among serving dishes. Spoon on the lobster sauce and season to taste. Serve immediately.

PAPPARDELLE WITH LOBSTER AND SAFFRON CREAM SAUCE

SERVES 4-6

SEAFOOD LASAGNE

INGREDIENTS

250 g (8 oz) fresh lasagne sheets
1 tablespoon olive oil
30 g (1 oz) butter
1 onion, finely chopped
2 cloves garlic, crushed
400 g (13 oz) raw medium prawns, peeled and deveined
500 g (1 lb) skinless firm white fish fillets, cut into 2 cm (¾ inch) pieces
250 g (8 oz) scallops with roe, membrane removed
750 g (1½ lb) bottled tomato pasta sauce
1 tablespoon tomato paste
1 teaspoon soft brown sugar
½ cup (60 g/2 oz) grated Cheddar
¼ cup (25 g/¾ oz) grated Parmesan

Cheese Sauce
120 g (4 oz) butter
⅔ cup (85 g/3 oz) plain flour
1.5 litres milk
2 cups (250 g/8 oz) grated Cheddar
1 cup (100 g/3½ oz) grated Parmesan

1 Preheat the oven to moderate 180°C (350°F/Gas 4). Lightly grease a 27 cm x 21 cm (10¾ inch x 8½ inch), 2.5 litre ovenproof dish and line with the lasagne sheets.

2 Heat the oil and butter in a large saucepan. Add the onion and cook for 2–3 minutes, or until softened. Add the garlic and cook for 30 seconds. Cook the prawns and fish pieces for 2 minutes, then add the scallops and cook for 1 minute. Stir in the pasta sauce, tomato paste and sugar and simmer for 5 minutes.

3 For the cheese sauce, melt the butter over low heat in a saucepan, stir in the flour and cook for 1 minute, or until pale and foaming. Remove from the heat and gradually stir in the milk. Return to the heat and stir until the sauce boils and thickens. Reduce the heat, simmer for 2 minutes, then stir in the cheeses. Season, to taste.

4 Spoon one-third of the seafood sauce over the lasagne sheets. Top with one-third of the cheese sauce. Arrange lasagne sheets over the top. Repeat to make three layers. Sprinkle with the combined cheeses and bake for 30 minutes or until golden. Leave for 10 minutes before slicing.

SERVES 4

INGREDIENTS

1 tablespoon olive oil
2 cloves garlic, crushed
1 onion, chopped
1 carrot, grated
1 celery stalk, diced
125 g (4 oz) mushrooms, chopped
600 g (1¼ lb) minced beef
2½ cups (600 ml/20 fl oz) Italian tomato passata
1 teaspoon dried oregano leaves
300 g (10 oz) instant lasagne sheets
1 cup (100 g/3½ oz) grated Parmesan

Cheese Sauce

60 g (2 oz) butter
⅓ cup (40 g/1¼ oz) plain flour
1 litre milk
½ teaspoon ground nutmeg
1 cup (125 g/4 oz) grated Cheddar

1 Heat the oil in a large heavy-based pan. Add the garlic, onion, carrot, celery and mushroom. Cook, stirring, over medium heat for 2–3 minutes, or until the onion has softened. Increase the heat, add the mince and stir for a further 3–4 minutes, or until the mince has browned and is well broken up.

2 Add the tomato passata, oregano and 2 cups (500 ml/16 fl oz) water. Bring to the boil, stirring, then lower the heat and simmer for 1 hour, or until the mixture has thickened. Stir occasionally.

3 To make the cheese sauce, melt the butter in a heavy-based pan. Add the flour and cook, stirring, for 1 minute until pale and foaming. Remove from the heat, gradually add the milk and stir until smooth. Return to the heat and stir continuously for 3–4 minutes, or until the sauce boils and thickens. Cook over low heat for 1 minute. Stir in the nutmeg and Cheddar. Season.

4 To assemble, preheat the oven to moderate 180°C (350°F/Gas 4). Grease a 2.5 litre baking dish. Arrange four lasagne sheets over the base of the baking dish. Spread one-third of the meat mixture over the sheets, then pour over about ¾ cup (185 ml/6 fl oz) of the cheese sauce. Repeat with two more layers of each. Top with the four remaining lasagne sheets, then with the remaining sauce and finish with the Parmesan. Bake for 45 minutes, or until golden. Leave to stand for 5 minutes before serving.

SERVES 8

PASTICCIO

¼ cup (60 ml/2 fl oz) olive oil

1 onion, finely chopped

2 cloves garlic, crushed

80 g (2¾ oz) pancetta, finely chopped

500 g (1 lb) beef mince

1 teaspoon chopped fresh oregano

60 g (2 oz) small button mushrooms, sliced

115 g (4 oz) chicken livers, trimmed and finely chopped

¼ teaspoon ground nutmeg

pinch cayenne pepper

¼ cup (60 ml/2 fl oz) dry white wine

2 tablespoons tomato paste

1½ cups (375 ml/12 fl oz) beef stock

2 tablespoons grated Parmesan

1 egg, beaten

150 g (5 oz) macaroni

100 g (3½ oz) ricotta cheese

2 tablespoons milk

pinch cayenne pepper, extra

pinch ground nutmeg, extra

1 egg, beaten, extra

1 cup (100 g/3½ oz) grated Parmesan, extra

Bechamel sauce

40 g (1¼ oz) butter

1½ tablespoons plain flour

pinch ground nutmeg

300 ml (10 fl oz) milk

1 small bay leaf

1 Preheat the oven to moderate 180°C (350°F/Gas 4). Lightly grease a 1.5 litre ovenproof dish. Heat the oil in a large frying pan over medium heat and cook the onion, garlic and pancetta, stirring, for 5 minutes, or until the onion is golden. Add the beef, increase the heat and stir for 5 minutes, or until browned.

2 Add the oregano, mushrooms, chicken livers, nutmeg and cayenne, season and cook for 2 minutes, or until the livers change colour. Add the wine and cook over high heat for 1 minute, or until evaporated. Stir in tomato paste and stock. Reduce heat and simmer for 45 minutes, or until thickened. Beat the Parmesan and egg together, and quickly stir into sauce.

3 Cook the macaroni in lightly salted boiling water until al dente. Blend the ricotta, milk, extra cayenne, extra nutmeg, extra egg and ¼ cup (25 g/¾ oz) extra Parmesan. Season. Drain the macaroni, add to the ricotta mixture and mix well.

4 To make the Béchamel sauce, melt the butter in a small saucepan. Stir in the flour and cook over low heat until beginning to turn golden, then stir in the nutmeg. Remove from the heat and gradually stir in the milk. Add the bay leaf and season. Return to low heat and simmer, stirring, until thickened. Discard the bay leaf.

5 Spread half the meat sauce in the dish, layer half the pasta over the top and sprinkle with half the remaining Parmesan. Layer with remaining meat sauce and pasta. Press down firmly with the back of a spoon. Spread the Béchamel sauce over the top and sprinkle with remaining Parmesan. Bake for 45–50 minutes, or until golden. Rest for 15 minutes before serving.

SERVES 4-6

INGREDIENTS

200 g (7 oz) short curly pasta such as cotelli or fusilli

4 eggs, hard-boiled and roughly chopped

4 spring onions (scallions), finely chopped

1 tablespoon chopped dill

1 tablespoon lemon juice

115 g (4 oz) butter

3 teaspoons madras curry powder

50 g ($^1/_3$ cup) plain (all-purpose) flour

375 ml (1$^1/_2$ cups) milk

375 ml (1$^1/_2$ cups) cream

175 g (6 oz) whole-egg mayonnaise

3 x 210 g (7$^1/_2$ oz) cans tuna, drained

160 g (2 cups) fresh white breadcrumbs

1 garlic clove, crushed

1 tablespoon finely chopped flat-leaf (Italian) parsley

2 tablespoons grated Parmesan cheese

1 Preheat the oven to 180°C (350°F/Gas 4). Cook the pasta in a large saucepan of rapidly boiling salted water until al dente. Drain well. Lightly grease a 2 litre (8 cup) ovenproof dish. Combine the egg, spring onion, dill and lemon juice and season.

2 Melt 60 g (2$^1/_4$ oz) of the butter in a saucepan, add the curry powder and cook for 30 seconds. Stir in the flour and cook for 1 minute, or until foaming. Remove from the heat, gradually stir in the milk and cream, then return to low heat and stir constantly until the sauce boils and thickens. Reduce to a simmer for 2 minutes, then stir in the mayonnaise. Combine the sauce, cooked pasta, tuna and egg mixture and spoon into the prepared dish.

3 Melt the remaining butter in a frying pan, add the breadcrumbs and garlic and cook, stirring, for 1 minute, or until the breadcrumbs are golden and coated in butter. Stir in the parsley and grated Parmesan and then sprinkle over the tuna mixture. Bake for 15–20 minutes, or until golden and heated through.

SERVES 6

CREAMY TOMATO AND PRAWN PASTA

400 g (14 oz) dried egg tagliatelle
1 tablespoon olive oil
3 garlic cloves, finely chopped
20 medium raw prawns (shrimp), peeled and deveined, with tails intact
550 g (1 lb 4 oz) Roma (plum) tomatoes, diced
2 tablespoons thinly sliced basil
125 ml ($^1/_2$ cup) white wine
80 ml ($^1/_3$ cup) cream
basil leaves, to garnish

1 Cook the pasta in a large saucepan of boiling salted water until al dente. Drain and keep warm, reserving 2 tablespoons of the cooking water.

2 Meanwhile, heat the oil and garlic in a large frying pan over low heat for 1–2 minutes. Increase the heat to medium, add the prawns and cook for 3–5 minutes, stirring frequently until cooked. Remove the prawns and keep warm.

3 Add the tomato and sliced basil and stir for 3 minutes, or until the tomato is soft. Pour in the wine and cream, bring to the boil and simmer for 2 minutes.

4 Purée the sauce in a blender, return to the pan, then add the reserved pasta water and bring to a simmer. Stir in the prawns until heated through. Toss through the pasta and serve garnished with the basil leaves.

SERVES 4

PASTA CARBONARA

400 g (14 oz) penne
1 tablespoon olive oil
200 g (7 oz) piece pancetta or bacon, cut into long thin strips
6 egg yolks
185 ml (³/₄ cup) thick (double/heavy) cream
75 g (³/₄ cup) grated Parmesan cheese

1 Cook the pasta in a saucepan of boiling salted water until al dente.

2 Meanwhile, heat the oil in a frying pan and cook the pancetta over high heat for 6 minutes, or until crisp and golden. Remove with a slotted spoon and drain on paper towels.

3 Beat the egg yolks, cream and the Parmesan together in a bowl and season generously. Return the freshly cooked and drained pasta to its saucepan and pour the egg mixture over the pasta, tossing gently. Add the pancetta, then return the pan to very low heat and cook for 30–60 seconds, or until the sauce thickens and coats the pasta. Season with pepper and serve immediately.

NOTE Be careful not to cook the pasta over high heat once you have added the egg mixture, or the sauce risks being scrambled by the heat.

400 g (14 oz) spaghettini (thin spaghetti)
125 ml ($^1/_2$ cup) olive oil
4 garlic cloves, finely chopped
10 anchovy fillets, chopped
1 tablespoon baby capers, rinsed and squeezed dry
1 teaspoon chilli flakes
2 tablespoons lemon juice
2 teaspoons finely grated lemon zest
3 tablespoons chopped parsley
3 tablespoons chopped basil leaves
3 tablespoons chopped mint
50 g ($^1/_2$ cup) coarsely grated Parmesan cheese, plus extra, to serve
extra virgin olive oil, to drizzle

1 Cook the pasta in a saucepan of boiling salted water until al dente.

2 Heat the oil in a frying pan and cook the garlic over medium heat for 2–3 minutes, or until starting to brown. Add the anchovies, capers and chilli and cook for 1 minute.

3 Add the hot pasta to the pan with the lemon juice, zest, parsley, basil, mint and Parmesan. Season with salt and pepper and toss together well.

4 To serve, drizzle with a little extra oil and sprinkle with Parmesan.

SPAGHETTI WITH ANCHOVIES, CAPERS AND CHILLI

SERVES 4

INGREDIENTS

Meatballs
2 slices white bread, crusts removed
60 ml ($^1/_4$ cup) milk
500 g (1 lb 2 oz) minced (ground) pork and veal (see note)
1 small onion, finely chopped
2 garlic cloves, finely chopped
3 tablespoons finely chopped flat-leaf (Italian) parsley
2 teaspoons finely grated lemon zest
1 egg, lightly beaten
50 g ($^1/_2$ cup) grated Parmesan cheese
plain (all-purpose) flour, to coat
2 tablespoons olive oil

125 ml ($^1/_2$ cup) white wine
2 x 400 g (14 oz) cans chopped tomatoes
1 tablespoon tomato paste (purée)
1 teaspoon caster (superfine) sugar
$^1/_2$ teaspoon dried oregano
500 g (1 lb 2 oz) penne rigate (penne with ridges)
oregano leaves, to garnish

1 To make the meatballs, soak the bread in the milk for 5 minutes, then squeeze out any moisture. Put the bread, mince, onion, garlic, parsley, zest, egg and Parmesan in a bowl, season and mix well with your hands.

2 Shape into walnut-size balls using damp hands, and roll lightly in the flour. Heat the oil in a large deep frying pan and cook the meatballs in batches over medium heat, turning frequently, for 10 minutes, or until brown all over. Remove with a slotted spoon and drain on paper towels.

3 Pour the wine into the same frying pan and boil over medium heat for 2–3 minutes, or until it evaporates a little. Add the tomato, tomato paste, sugar and dried oregano. Reduce the heat, then simmer for 20 minutes to thicken the sauce. Add the meatballs and simmer for 10 minutes. Meanwhile, cook the pasta in a saucepan of boiling salted water until al dente.

4 To serve, divide the hot pasta among six serving plates and spoon some meatballs and sauce over the top of each. Garnish with the oregano.

NOTE Use minced beef instead of the pork and veal, if you prefer.

SERVES 6

INGREDIENTS

500 g (1 lb 2 oz) spaghetti
1 tablespoon olive oil
1 onion, finely chopped
3 garlic cloves, finely chopped
2 x 400 g (14 oz) cans chopped tomatoes
2 tablespoons tomato paste (purée)
170 ml ($^2/_3$ cup) dry white wine
2 teaspoons soft brown sugar
1 teaspoon finely grated lemon zest
2 tablespoons torn basil leaves, plus extra, to garnish
2 tablespoons finely chopped flat-leaf (Italian) parsley
12 medium raw prawns (shrimp), peeled and deveined, with tails intact
8 black mussels, scrubbed and beards removed
8 large white scallops, without roe
2 small squid tubes, cleaned and cut into 1 cm ($^1/_2$ inch) rings

1   Cook the pasta in a saucepan of boiling salted water until al dente.

2   Meanwhile, heat the oil in a large saucepan, add the onion and cook over medium heat for
5–8 minutes, or until golden. Add the garlic, tomato, tomato paste, wine, sugar, lemon zest,
1 tablespoon of the basil, parsley and 250 ml (1 cup) water. Cook, stirring occasionally, for
1 hour, or until the sauce is reduced and thickened. Season.

3   Add the prawns and mussels and cook for 1 minute, then add the scallops and cook for
2 minutes. Stir in the squid and cook for 1 minute more, or until all the seafood is cooked
through and tender.

4   Add the hot pasta to the sauce with the remaining basil and toss together until well
combined. Serve.

SERVES 4

RAVIOLI WITH PRAWNS AND CREAMY LIME SAUCE

50 g (1³/₄ oz) butter

4 garlic cloves, crushed

750 g (1 lb 10 oz) medium raw prawns (shrimp), peeled and deveined

1¹/₂ tablespoons plain (all-purpose) flour

375 ml (1¹/₂ cups) fish stock

500 ml (2 cups) cream

5 makrut (kaffir) lime leaves, shredded

650 g (1 lb 7 oz) seafood ravioli (see note)

3 teaspoons fish sauce

1 Melt the butter in a large deep frying pan and cook the garlic over medium heat for 1 minute. Add the prawns and cook for 3–4 minutes, or until they turn pink and are cooked through. Remove from the pan, leaving any juices in the pan. Add the flour and stir for 1 minute, or until lightly golden. Gradually stir in the stock, then add the cream and lime leaves. Reduce the heat and simmer for 10 minutes, or until slightly thickened.

2 Meanwhile, cook the pasta in a large saucepan of boiling salted water until al dente. Drain.

3 Stir the fish sauce through the cream sauce, add the prawns and stir until warmed through. Divide the pasta among four warm serving plates and spoon on the prawns and sauce. Season with salt and cracked black pepper and serve.

NOTE Seafood ravioli is available from speciality pasta shops, but if it is unavailable you can use ricotta ravioli instead — the flavours work well.

SERVES 4

INGREDIENTS

500 g (1 lb 2 oz) ham and cheese tortellini
60 g (2¹/₄ oz) butter
100 g (1 cup) walnuts, chopped
100 g (²/₃ cup) pine nuts
2 tablespoons finely chopped flat-leaf (Italian) parsley
2 teaspoons chopped thyme
60 g (¹/₄ cup) ricotta cheese
60 ml (¹/₄ cup) thick (double/heavy) cream

1   Cook the pasta in a large saucepan of boiling water until al dente. Drain and return
    to the pan.

2   Meanwhile, heat the butter in a frying pan over medium heat until foaming. Add the
    walnuts and pine nuts and stir for 5 minutes, or until golden brown. Add the parsley and
    thyme and season to taste.

3   Beat the ricotta and cream together. Add the nutty sauce to the pasta and toss. Divide
    among serving bowls and top with the ricotta cream.

SERVES 4-6

TAGLIATELLE WITH PRAWNS AND LEEK IN SAFFRON CREAM

40 g (1¹/₂ oz) butter
1 small leek, julienned
4 garlic cloves, finely chopped
pinch of saffron threads
125 ml (¹/₂ cup) dry vermouth
250 ml (1 cup) fish stock
300 ml (10¹/₂ fl oz) thick (double/heavy) cream
400 g (14 oz) fresh tagliatelle or any long, flat pasta
24 medium raw prawns (shrimp), peeled and deveined, with tails intact
1 tablespoon lemon juice
1 tablespoon finely chopped chervil, plus extra, to garnish

1 Melt the butter in a saucepan over medium heat, add the leek and garlic and cook for 5 minutes, or until the leek is soft and translucent. Add the saffron, vermouth and fish stock and bring to the boil, skimming off any scum that rises to the surface. Reduce the heat to low and simmer for 10 minutes, or until the sauce has reduced by half. Pour in the cream and simmer for 15 minutes, or until the sauce has thickened and reduced by about a third.

2 Meanwhile, cook the pasta in a saucepan of boiling salted water until al dente.

3 Add the prawns to the sauce and simmer for 2–3 minutes, or until cooked through. Remove from the heat and stir in the lemon juice and chervil. Season well, then toss through the hot pasta. Serve immediately, garnished with a little extra chervil, if desired.

NOTE This creamy pasta is very rich and more suitable as a starter than a main course.

SERVES 4-6

VEAL TORTELLINI WITH BAKED PUMPKIN AND BASIL BUTTER

1 kg (2 lb 4 oz) jap pumpkin, cut into 2 cm (³/₄ inch) cubes
600 g (1 lb 5 oz) veal tortellini
100 g (3¹/₂ oz) butter
3 garlic cloves, crushed
80 g (¹/₂ cup) pine nuts
45 g (³/₄ cup) firmly packed shredded basil
200 g (7 oz) feta cheese, crumbled

1 Preheat the oven to 220°C (425°F/Gas 7). Line a baking tray with baking paper. Place the pumpkin on the prepared tray and season well with salt and cracked black pepper. Bake for 30 minutes, or until tender.

2 Meanwhile, cook the pasta in a large saucepan of boiling salted water until al dente. Drain and return to the pan.

3 Heat the butter over medium heat in a small frying pan until foaming. Add the garlic and pine nuts and cook for 3–5 minutes, or until the nuts are starting to turn golden. Remove from the heat and add the basil. Toss the basil butter, pumpkin and feta through the cooked pasta and serve.

SERVES 4

INGREDIENTS

30 g (1 oz) butter
4 rashers bacon, diced
2 garlic cloves, finely chopped
300 g (10^1/$_2$ oz) Swiss brown or button mushrooms, sliced
60 ml (^{1}/$_4$ cup) dry white wine
375 ml (1^1/$_2$ cups) cream
1 teaspoon chopped thyme
500 g (1 lb 2 oz) veal tortellini
50 g (^{1}/$_2$ cup) grated Parmesan cheese
1 tablespoon chopped flat-leaf (Italian) parsley

1 Melt the butter in a large frying pan, add the bacon and cook over medium heat for 5 minutes, or until crisp. Add the garlic and cook for 2 minutes, then add the mushrooms, cooking for a further 8 minutes, or until softened.

2 Stir in the wine and cream and add the thyme and bring to the boil. Reduce the heat to low and simmer for 10 minutes, or until the sauce has thickened. Meanwhile, cook the pasta in a large saucepan of boiling salted water until al dente

3 Combine the sauce with the hot pasta, Parmesan and parsley. Season to taste and serve immediately.

PASTA BOSCAIOLA

SERVES 4-6

SPAGHETTINI WITH SQUID IN BLACK INK

1 kg (2 lb 4 oz) medium squid

2 tablespoons olive oil

1 onion, finely chopped

6 garlic cloves, finely chopped

1 bay leaf

1 small red chilli, seeded and thinly sliced

80 ml ($\frac{1}{3}$ cup) white wine

80 ml ($\frac{1}{3}$ cup) dry vermouth

250 ml (1 cup) fish stock

60 g ($\frac{1}{4}$ cup) tomato paste (purée)

500 ml (2 cups) tomato passata

15 g ($\frac{1}{2}$ oz) squid ink

500 g (1 lb 2 oz) spaghettini

$\frac{1}{2}$ teaspoon Pernod (optional)

4 tablespoons chopped flat-leaf (Italian) parsley

1 garlic clove, extra, crushed

1 To clean the squid, pull the tentacles away from the hood (the intestines should come away at the same time). Remove the intestines by cutting under the eyes, and remove the beak by using your fingers to push up the centre. Pull out the transparent quill from inside the body. Remove any white membrane. Cut the squid into thin slices.

2 Heat the oil in a saucepan over medium heat. Add the onion and cook until lightly golden. Add the garlic, bay leaf and chilli and cook for 2 minutes, or until the garlic is lightly golden. Stir in the wine, vermouth, stock, tomato paste, passata and 250 ml (1 cup) water, then increase the heat to high and bring to the boil. Reduce to a simmer and cook for 45 minutes, or until the liquid has reduced by half. Add the squid ink and cook for 2 minutes, or until the sauce is evenly black and glossy. Meanwhile, cook the pasta in a large saucepan of boiling salted water until al dente.

3 Add the squid rings and Pernod, stir well, then cook for 4–5 minutes, or until they turn opaque and are cooked through. Stir in the parsley and the extra garlic and season. Toss through the hot pasta and serve immediately.

SERVES 4-6

INGREDIENTS

2 tablespoons olive oil
2 garlic cloves, finely chopped
1 large onion, finely chopped
1 carrot, finely chopped
1 celery stalk, finely chopped
50 g (1³/₄ oz) pancetta or bacon, finely chopped
500 g (1 lb 2 oz) minced (ground) beef
500 ml (2 cups) beef stock
375 ml (1¹/₂ cups) red wine
2 x 400 g (14 oz) cans chopped tomatoes
2 tablespoons tomato paste (purée)
1 teaspoon sugar
500 g (1 lb 2 oz) fresh tagliatelle (see note)
shaved Parmesan cheese, to serve

1   Heat the oil in a large deep saucepan. Add the garlic, onion, carrot, celery and pancetta and cook, stirring, over medium heat for about 5 minutes, or until softened.

2   Add the mince and break up any lumps with the back of a spoon, stirring until just browned. Add the stock, red wine, tomatoes, tomato paste and sugar. Bring to the boil, then reduce the heat to very low and simmer, covered, stirring occasionally, for 1¹/₂ hours. Remove the lid and simmer, stirring occasionally, for a further 1¹/₂ hours. Season to taste with salt and freshly ground pepper. While the meat is cooking, cook the pasta in a saucepan of boiling salted water until al dente.

3   To serve, spoon the sauce over the hot pasta and sprinkle with some of the shaved Parmesan.

NOTE   Traditionally, bolognese was served with tagliatelle, but now we tend to serve it with spaghetti.

SERVES 4-6

SPAGHETTI PUTTANESCA

400 g (14 oz) spaghetti
2 tablespoons olive oil
1 onion, finely chopped
2 garlic cloves, finely sliced
1 small red chilli, cored, seeded and sliced
6 anchovy fillets, finely chopped
400 g (14 oz) canned chopped tomatoes
1 tablespoon fresh oregano, finely chopped
16 black olives, halved and pitted
2 tablespoons baby capers
a handful basil leaves

1 Cook the spaghetti in a large saucepan of boiling salted water until al dente, stirring once or twice to make sure the pieces are not stuck together. The cooking time will vary depending on the brand of spaghetti. Check the pasta occasionally as it cooks because the time given on packet instructions is often too long by a minute or two.

2 Heat the olive oil in a large saucepan and add the onion, garlic and chilli. Gently fry for about 8 minutes, or until the onion is soft. Add the anchovies and cook for another minute. Add the tomato, oregano, olive halves and capers and bring to the boil. Reduce the heat, season with salt and pepper, and leave the sauce to simmer for 3 minutes.

3 Drain the spaghetti and add it to the sauce. Toss together well so that the pasta is coated in the sauce. Scatter the basil over the top and serve.

SERVES 4

INGREDIENTS

24 conchiglione (large pasta shells)
200 g (6^1/$_2$ oz) prosciutto, roughly chopped
2 tablespoons chopped chives
1 cup (60 g/2 oz) chopped fresh basil
90 g (3 oz) butter
500 g (1 lb) ricotta
1 cup (150 g/5 oz) chopped sun-dried capsicum
1 cup (100 g/3^1/$_2$ oz) grated Parmesan
3 cups (750 g/1^1/$_2$ lb) bottled tomato pasta sauce

1 Preheat the oven to moderate 180°C (350°F/Gas 4). Cook the pasta in a large pan of rapidly boiling salted water until al dente. Drain well and return to the pan to keep warm. Place the prosciutto, chives and basil in a food processor or blender and pulse until chopped.

2 Melt the butter in a large frying pan over medium heat. Add the prosciutto mixture and cook for about 5 minutes, or until the prosciutto is golden and crisp. Transfer the mixture to a bowl, add the ricotta, capsicum and a quarter of the Parmesan. Stir well and season to taste.

3 Pour the pasta sauce into a 3-litre ovenproof dish. Spoon the ricotta mixture into the pasta shells and place in the dish. Sprinkle the remaining Parmesan over the shells and bake for 25–30 minutes, or until golden. Spoon the sauce over the shells and serve.

SERVES 4-6

BAKED SHELLS WITH RICOTTA AND PROSCIUTTO

VEGETARIAN

INGREDIENTS

2 corn cobs
3 tablespoons chopped fresh coriander (cilantro) leaves
6 spring onions, finely chopped
1 small red chilli, seeded and finely chopped
1 large egg
2 teaspoons ground cumin
$1/2$ teaspoon ground coriander (cilantro)
1 cup (125 g) plain flour
oil, for deep-frying
sweet chilli sauce, to serve

1 Cut down the side of the corn with a sharp knife to release the kernels. Roughly chop the kernels, then place them in a large bowl. Holding the cobs over the bowl, scrape down the sides of the cobs with a knife to release any corn juice from the cob into the bowl.

2 Add the fresh coriander, spring onion, chilli, egg, cumin, ground coriander, 1 teaspoon salt and some cracked black pepper to the bowl and stir well. Add the flour and mix well. The texture of the batter will vary depending on the juiciness of the corn. If the mixture is too dry, add 1 tablespoon water, but no more than that as the batter should be quite dry. Stand for 10 minutes.

3 Fill a large heavy-based saucepan or deep-fryer one-third full of oil and heat to 180°C (350°F), or until a cube of bread dropped in the oil browns in 15 seconds. Drop slightly heaped teaspoons of the corn batter into the oil and cook for about $1^1/_2$ minutes, or until puffed and golden. Drain on crumpled paper towels and serve immediately with a bowl of the sweet chilli sauce to dip the puffs into.

SPICY CORN PUFFS

MAKES 36

INGREDIENTS

500 g (1 lb) orange sweet potato (kumera), peeled and cut into chunks
1 red or yellow capsicum (pepper), cut into chunks
2 zucchini (courgette), sliced
350 g (12 oz) eggplant (aubergine), cut into chunks
2 tomatoes, cut into chunks
8 spring onions, cut into lengths
1 tablespoon extra virgin olive oil
1 teaspoon sea salt
1 teaspoon grated lemon zest
2 tablespoons lemon juice

1   Preheat the oven to hot 220°C (425°F/Gas 7). Place the vegetables in a large baking dish, drizzle with oil, sprinkle with sea salt and roast for 45 minutes, or until soft.

2   Transfer the vegetables to a food processor, add the lemon zest and the lemon juice. Blend until smooth. Spoon into a serving dish and cool to room temperature.

MAKES 4 cups

INGREDIENTS

2 kg (4 lb) round ricotta cheese
olive oil
2 cloves garlic, crushed
1 preserved lemon, rinsed, pith and flesh removed, cut into thin strips
150 g (5 oz) semi-dried (sun-blushed) tomatoes, roughly chopped
1 cup (30 g/1 oz) finely chopped fresh flat-leaf parsley
1 cup (50 g/1³/₄ oz) chopped fresh coriander (cilantro) leaves
¹/₃ cup (80 ml/2³/₄ fl oz) extra virgin olive oil
3 tablespoons lemon juice

1 Preheat the oven to very hot 250°C (500°F/Gas 10). Place the ricotta on a baking tray lined with baking paper, brush lightly with the olive oil and bake for 20–30 minutes, or until golden brown. Leave for 10 minutes then, using egg flips, transfer to a large platter. (If possible, have someone help you move the ricotta.)

2 Meanwhile, place the garlic, preserved lemon, semi-dried tomato, parsley, coriander, oil and lemon juice in a bowl and mix together well.

3 Spoon the dressing over the baked ricotta and serve with crusty bread. It is delicious hot or cold.

BAKED RICOTTA WITH PRESERVED LEMON AND SEMI-DRIED TOMATOES

SERVES 8-10

SPINACH PÂTÉ

400 g English spinach
30 g (1 oz) butter
$1/2$ teaspoon ground coriander (cilantro)
pinch cayenne pepper
2 spring onions, roughly chopped
1 clove garlic
$1/3$ cup (50 g/$1^3/4$ oz) blanched almonds
2 teaspoons white wine vinegar
$1/2$ cup (125 g/$4^1/2$ oz) sour cream

1   Remove the stems from the spinach. Wash the leaves and place wet in a pan. Cover and cook for 2 minutes, or until wilted, then drain, reserving $1/4$ cup (60 ml) of the cooking liquid. Cool the spinach then squeeze dry.

2   Melt the butter in a small pan. Add the coriander, cayenne pepper, spring onion, garlic and almonds, and cook until the onion is tender. Cool.

3   Place in a food processor and process until finely chopped. Add the spinach and process, gradually adding the reserved cooking liquid and vinegar.

4   Stir in the sour cream and season well with salt and pepper.

INGREDIENTS

1¾ cups (215 g/7 oz) plain (all-purpose) flour

120 g (4 oz) chilled butter, cubed

¼ cup (60 ml/2 fl oz) cream

1–2 tablespoons chilled water

1 large (250 g/8 oz) Desiree potato, cut into 2 cm (1 inch) cubes

1 tablespoon olive oil

2 cloves garlic, crushed

1 red capsicum (pepper), cut into cubes

1 red onion, sliced into rings

2 zucchini (courgettes), sliced

2 tablespoons chopped fresh dill

1 tablespoon chopped fresh thyme

1 tablespoon drained baby capers

150 g (5 oz) marinated quartered artichoke hearts, drained

⅔ cup (30 g/1 oz) baby English spinach leaves

Salsa verde

1 clove garlic

2 cups (40 g/1¼ oz) fresh flat-leaf parsley

⅓ cup (80 ml/2¾ fl oz) extra virgin olive oil

3 tablespoons chopped fresh dill

1½ tablespoons Dijon mustard

1 tablespoon red wine vinegar

1 tablespoon drained baby capers

1 Sift the flour and ½ teaspoon salt into a large bowl. Add the butter and rub it into the flour with your fingertips until it resembles fine breadcrumbs. Add the cream and water and mix with a flat-bladed knife until the mixture comes together in beads. Gather together and lift onto a lightly floured work surface. Press into a ball, then flatten into a disc, wrap in plastic wrap and refrigerate for 30 minutes.

2 Preheat the oven to moderately hot 200°C (400°F/Gas 6). Grease a 27 cm (11 inch) loose-bottomed flan tin. Roll the dough out between two sheets of baking paper large enough to line the tin. Remove the paper and invert the pastry into the tin. Use a small pastry ball to press the pastry into the tin, allowing any excess to hang over the side. Roll a rolling pin over the tin, cutting off any excess. Cover the pastry with a piece of crumpled baking paper, then add baking beads. Place the tin on a baking tray and bake for 15–20 minutes. Remove the paper and beads, reduce the heat to moderate 180°C (350°F/Gas 4) and bake for 20 minutes, or until golden.

3 To make the salsa verde, combine all the ingredients in a food processor and process until almost smooth.

4 Boil the potato until just tender. Drain. Heat the oil in a large frying pan and cook the garlic, capsicum and onion over medium heat for 3 minutes, stirring frequently. Add the zucchini, dill, thyme and capers and cook for 3 minutes. Reduce the heat to low, add the potato and artichokes, and heat through. Season to taste.

5 To assemble, spread 3 tablespoons of the salsa over the pastry. Spoon the vegetable mixture into the case and drizzle with half the remaining salsa. Pile the spinach in the centre and drizzle with the remaining salsa.

VEGETABLE TART WITH SALSA VERDE

SERVES 6

ASPARAGUS AND MUSHROOM SALAD

155 g (5 oz) asparagus spears
1 tablespoon wholegrain mustard
¼ cup (60 ml/2 fl oz) orange juice
2 tablespoons lemon juice
1 tablespoon lime juice
1 tablespoon orange zest
2 teaspoons lemon zest
2 teaspoons lime zest
2 cloves garlic, crushed
¼ cup (90 g/3 oz) honey
400 g (13 oz) button mushrooms, halved
150 g (5 oz) rocket
1 red capsicum (pepper), cut into strips

1 Snap the woody ends from the asparagus spears and cut in half on the diagonal. Cook in boiling water for 1 minute, or until just tender. Drain, plunge into cold water and set aside.

2 Place the mustard, citrus juice and zest, garlic and honey in a large saucepan and season with pepper. Bring to the boil, then reduce the heat and add the mushrooms, tossing for 2 minutes. Cool.

3 Remove the mushrooms from the sauce with a slotted spoon. Return the sauce to the heat, bring to the boil, then reduce the heat and simmer for 3–5 minutes, or until reduced and syrupy. Cool slightly.

4 Toss the mushrooms, rocket leaves, capsicum and asparagus. Put on a plate and drizzle with the sauce.

SERVES 4

INGREDIENTS

Tomato salsa
2 ripe tomatoes
1 cup (150 g/5 oz) frozen broad beans
2 tablespoons chopped fresh basil
1 small Lebanese cucumber, diced
2 small cloves garlic, crushed
$1^1/_2$ tablespoons balsamic vinegar
1 tablespoon extra virgin olive oil

Corn and polenta pancakes
$^3/_4$ cup (90 g/3 oz) self-raising flour
$^3/_4$ cup (110 g/$3^1/_2$ oz) fine polenta
1 cup (250 ml/8 fl oz) milk
310 g (10 oz) can corn kernels
olive oil, for frying

1   To make the salsa, score a cross in the base of each tomato, then place in a bowl of boiling water for 30 seconds. Plunge into cold water and peel the skin away from the cross. Dice. Pour boiling water over the broad beans and leave for 2–3 minutes. Drain and rinse under cold water. Remove the skins. Put the beans in a bowl and stir in the tomato, basil, cucumber, garlic, vinegar and extra virgin olive oil.

2   To make the pancakes, sift the flour into a bowl and stir in the polenta. Add the milk and corn and stir until just combined, adding more milk if the batter is too dry. Season.

3   Heat the oil in a large frying pan and spoon half the batter into the pan, making four 9 cm ($3^1/_2$ inch) pancakes. Cook for 2 minutes each side, or until golden and cooked through. Repeat with the remaining batter, adding more oil if necessary. Drain well and serve with the salsa.

CORN AND POLENTA PANCAKES WITH TOMATO SALSA

SERVES 4

CHANNA MASALA

1 cup (220 g/7 oz) dried chickpeas
2 tablespoons oil
2 onions, finely chopped
2 large ripe tomatoes, chopped
$^{1}/_{2}$ teaspoon ground coriander (cilantro)
1 teaspoon ground cumin
1 teaspoon chilli powder
$^{1}/_{4}$ teaspoon ground turmeric
1 tablespoon channa (chole) masala (see note)
20 g ($^{3}/_{4}$ oz) ghee or butter
1 small white onion, sliced
fresh mint and coriander (cilantro) leaves, to garnish

1 Place the chickpeas in a bowl, cover with water and leave to soak overnight. Drain, rinse and place in a large saucepan. Cover with plenty of water and bring to the boil, then reduce the heat and simmer for 40 minutes, or until soft. Drain.

2 Heat the oil in a large saucepan, add the onion and cook over medium heat for 15 minutes, or until golden brown. Add the tomato, ground coriander and cumin, chilli powder, turmeric, channa (chole) masala and 2 cups (500 ml/16 fl oz) cold water, and cook for 10 minutes, or until the tomato is soft. Add the chickpeas, season well with salt and cook for 7–10 minutes, or until the sauce thickens. Transfer to a serving dish. Place the ghee or butter on top and allow to melt before serving. Garnish with sliced onion and fresh mint and coriander leaves.

NOTE Channa (chole) masala is a spice blend specifically used in this dish. It is available at Indian grocery stores. Garam masala can be used as a substitute, but this will alter the final flavour.

SERVES 6

INGREDIENTS

½ cup (125 ml/4 fl oz) oil
2 zucchini (courgettes), sliced on the diagonal
500 g (1 lb) eggplant (aubergine), sliced
1 small fennel bulb, sliced
1 red onion, sliced
300 g (10 oz) ricotta cheese
60 g (2 oz) Parmesan, grated
1 tablespoon chopped fresh flat-leaf parsley
1 tablespoon chopped fresh chives
1 red capsicum (pepper), grilled, peeled and cut into large
    pieces
1 yellow capsicum (pepper), grilled, peeled and cut into
    large pieces

Spicy tomato sauce
1 tablespoon oil
1 onion, finely chopped
2 cloves garlic, crushed
1 red chilli, seeded and chopped
425 g (14 oz) can chopped tomatoes
2 tablespoons tomato paste (purée)

1 Heat 1 tablespoon of the oil in a large frying pan. Cook the vegetables in separate batches over high heat for 5 minutes, or until golden, adding the remaining oil as needed. Drain each vegetable separately on paper towels.

2 Preheat the oven to moderately hot 200°C (400°F/Gas 6). Place the cheeses and herbs in a small bowl and mix together well. Season to taste.

3 Lightly grease four 1¼ cup (315 ml/10 fl oz) ramekins and line with baking paper. Using half the eggplant, put a layer in the base of each dish. Layer the zucchini, capsicum, cheese mixture, fennel and onion over the eggplant. Cover with the remaining eggplant and press down firmly. Bake for 10–15 minutes, or until hot. Leave for 5 minutes before turning out.

4 To make the sauce, heat the oil in a saucepan and cook the onion and garlic for 2–3 minutes, or until soft. Add the chilli, tomato and tomato paste and simmer for 5 minutes, or until thick and pulpy. Purée in a food processor. Return to the saucepan and keep warm. Spoon over the terrines.

INDIVIDUAL VEGETABLE TERRINES WITH A SPICY TOMATO SAUCE

SERVES 4 (as starter)

SOYA BEAN MOUSSAKA

2 eggplants (aubergine)
1 tablespoon oil
1 onion, finely chopped
2 cloves garlic, crushed
2 ripe tomatoes, peeled, seeded and chopped
2 teaspoons tomato paste (purée)
½ teaspoon dried oregano
½ cup (125 ml/4 fl oz) dry white wine
300 g (10 oz) can soya beans, rinsed and drained
3 tablespoons chopped fresh flat-leaf parsley
30 g (1 oz) butter
2 tablespoons plain (all-purpose) flour
pinch of ground nutmeg
1¼ cups (315 ml/10 fl oz) milk
⅓ cup (40 g/1¼ oz) grated Cheddar

1 Preheat the oven to moderate 180°C (350°F/Gas 4). Cut the eggplants in half lengthways. Spoon out the flesh, leaving a narrow border and place on a large baking tray, cut-side-up. Use crumpled foil around the sides of the eggplant to help support it.

2 Heat the oil in a large frying pan. Cook the onion and garlic over medium heat for 3 minutes, or until soft. Add the tomato, tomato paste, oregano and wine. Boil for 3 minutes, or until the liquid is reduced and the tomato is soft. Stir in the soya beans and parsley.

3 To make the sauce, melt the butter in a saucepan. Stir in the flour and cook over medium heat for 1 minute, or until pale and foamy. Remove from the heat and gradually stir in the nutmeg and milk. Return to the heat and stir constantly until the sauce boils and thickens. Pour one third of the white sauce into the tomato mixture and stir well.

4 Spoon the mixture into the eggplant shells. Smooth the surface before spreading the remaining sauce evenly over the top and sprinkling with cheese. Bake for 50 minutes, or until cooked through. Serve hot.

SERVES 4

INGREDIENTS

Hollandaise sauce
175 g (6 oz) butter
4 egg yolks
1 tablespoon lemon juice

4 eggs, at room temperature
310 g (10 oz) asparagus spears, trimmed
Parmesan shavings, to serve

1 To make the hollandaise, melt the butter in a small saucepan and skim off any froth. Remove from the heat and cool. Mix the egg yolks and 2 tablespoons water in another small saucepan for 30 seconds, or until pale and foamy. Place the saucepan over very low heat and whisk for 2–3 minutes, or until thick and foamy—do not overheat or it will scramble. Remove from the heat. Gradually add the butter, whisking well after each addition (avoid using the whey at the bottom). Stir in the lemon juice and season. If the sauce is runny, return to the heat and whisk until thick—do not scramble.

2 Place the eggs in a saucepan half filled with water. Bring to the boil and cook for 6–7 minutes, stirring occasionally to centre the yolks. Drain and cover with cold water until cooled a little, then peel off the shells.

3 Plunge the asparagus into a large saucepan of boiling water and cook for 3 minutes, or until just tender. Drain and pat dry. Divide among four plates. Spoon on the hollandaise. Cut the eggs in half and arrange two halves on each plate. Sprinkle with Parmesan shavings to serve.

WARM ASPARAGUS AND EGG SALAD WITH HOLLANDAISE

SERVES 4

FRESH BEETROOT AND GOAT'S CHEESE SALAD

1 kg (2 lb) (4 bulbs with leaves) fresh beetroot
200 g (6½ oz) green beans
1 tablespoon red wine vinegar
2 tablespoons extra virgin olive oil
1 clove garlic, crushed
1 tablespoon drained capers, coarsely chopped
100 g (31/2 oz) goat's cheese

1 Trim the leaves from the beetroot. Scrub the bulbs and wash the leaves well. Add the whole bulbs to a large saucepan of boiling water, reduce the heat and simmer, covered, for 30 minutes, or until tender when pierced with the point of a knife. (The cooking time may vary depending on the size of the bulbs.)

2 Meanwhile, bring a saucepan of water to the boil, add the beans and cook for 3 minutes, or until just tender. Remove with a slotted spoon and plunge into a bowl of cold water. Drain well. Add the beetroot leaves to the same saucepan of boiling water and cook for 3–5 minutes, or until the leaves and stems are tender. Drain, plunge into a bowl of cold water, then drain again well.

3 Drain and cool the beetroots, then peel the skins off and cut the bulbs into thin wedges.

4 To make the dressing, put the red wine vinegar, oil, garlic, capers, ½ teaspoon salt and ½ teaspoon pepper in a screw-top jar and shake.

5 To serve, divide the beans, beetroot leaves and bulbs among four serving plates. Crumble goat's cheese over the top and drizzle with the dressing.

SERVES 4

INGREDIENTS

500 g (1 lb) new potatoes, unpeeled, halved

6 parsnips, peeled and quartered lengthways

500 g (1 lb) orange sweet potato (kumera), cut into large
pieces

335 g (11 oz) baby carrots, with stalks

6 pickling onions, halved

⅓ cup (80 ml/2¾ fl oz) oil

2 tablespoons poppy seeds

200 g (6½ oz) Brie cheese, thinly sliced

Orange Dressing

½ cup (125 ml/4 fl oz) orange juice

2 cloves garlic, crushed

1 tablespoon Dijon mustard

1 teaspoon white wine vinegar

1 teaspoon sesame oil

1 Preheat the oven to moderately hot 200°C (400°F/Gas 6). Place all the vegetables and the oil in a large deep baking dish. Toss the vegetables to coat with the oil. Bake for 50 minutes, or until the vegetables are crisp and tender, tossing every 15 minutes. Sprinkle with the poppy seeds.

2 Whisk together all the dressing ingredients.

3 Pour the dressing over the warm vegetables and toss to coat. Transfer to a large bowl, top with the Brie and serve immediately, while still warm.

SERVES 6-8

ORANGE POPPY SEED ROASTED VEGETABLES

INGREDIENTS

200 g (6½ oz) haloumi cheese
¼ cup (60 ml/2 fl oz) olive oil
2 cloves garlic, crushed
1 tablespoon chopped fresh oregano
1 tablespoon chopped fresh marjoram
8 egg (Roma) tomatoes, halved
1 small red onion, cut into 8 wedges with base intact
¼ cup (60 ml/2 fl oz) olive oil, extra
2 tablespoons balsamic vinegar
150 g (5 oz) baby English spinach leaves

1 Cut the haloumi into 1 cm (½ inch) slices lengthways and put in a shallow dish. Mix together the oil, garlic and herbs and pour over the haloumi. Marinate, covered, for 1–2 hours.

2 Preheat the oven to moderately hot 200°C (400°F/Gas 6). Place the tomato and onion in a single layer in a roasting tin, drizzle with 2 tablespoons of the extra olive oil and 1 tablespoon of the vinegar and sprinkle with salt and cracked black pepper. Bake for 50–60 minutes, or until golden.

3 Meanwhile, heat a non-stick frying pan over medium heat. Drain the haloumi and cook for 1 minute each side, or until golden brown.

4 Divide the spinach leaves among four serving plates and top with the tomato and onion. Whisk together the remaining olive oil and balsamic vinegar in a small bowl and drizzle over the salad. Top with the haloumi.

SERVES 4

INGREDIENTS

2 teaspoons yellow mustard seeds

2 teaspoons black mustard seeds

1 teaspoon ground turmeric

1 teaspoon tamarind purée

2–3 tablespoons mustard oil or oil

2 garlic cloves, finely chopped

$^1/_2$ onion, finely chopped

600 g (1 lb 5 oz) cauliflower, broken into small florets

3 mild green chillies, seeded and finely chopped

2 teaspoons kalonji (nigella) seeds

1 Grind the yellow and black mustard seeds together to a fine powder in a spice grinder or mortar and pestle. Mix with the turmeric, tamarind purée and 100 ml (3$^1/_2$ fl oz) water to form a smooth, quite liquid paste.

2 Heat 2 tablespoons of the oil in a large heavy-based saucepan over medium heat until almost smoking. Reduce the heat to low, add the garlic and onion and fry until golden. Cook the cauliflower in batches, adding more oil if necessary, and fry until lightly browned, then remove. Add the chilli and fry for 1 minute, or until tinged with brown around the edges.

3 Return all the cauliflower to the pan, sprinkle it with the mustard mixture and kalonji and stir well. Increase the heat to medium and bring to the boil, even though there's not much sauce. Reduce the heat to low, cover and cook until the cauliflower is nearly tender and the seasoning is dry. Sprinkle a little water on the cauliflower as it cooks to stop it sticking to the pan. If there is still excess liquid when the cauliflower is cooked, simmer with the lid off until it dries out. Season with salt, and remove from the heat. Serve with rice or Indian bread, or as an accompaniment to meat dishes.

CAULIFLOWER WITH MUSTARD

SERVES 4

VEGETABLE BAKE

4 large unpeeled potatoes, halved
600 g (1lb 5 oz) unpeeled orange sweet potatoes (kumera), halved
20 g ($^3/_4$ oz) butter
1 tablespoon olive oil
2 large leeks, thinly sliced
3 garlic cloves, crushed
6 zucchini (courgettes), thinly sliced on the diagonal
300 ml (10$^1/_2$ fl oz) cream
130 g (1 cup) grated Parmesan cheese
1 tablespoon finely chopped thyme
1 tablespoon chopped flat-leaf (Italian) parsley
130 g (1 cup) grated Cheddar cheese

1 Preheat the oven to 180°C (350°F/ Gas 4) and grease a deep 2.5 litre (10 cup) ovenproof dish. Boil the potato and sweet potato for 10 minutes.

2 Meanwhile, heat the butter and oil in a frying pan. Add the leek and cook over low heat for 4–5 minutes, or until softened. Add 1 garlic clove and the zucchini and cook for 3–4 minutes, or until the zucchini starts to soften. Combine the cream, Parmesan, herbs and remaining garlic and season.

3 When the potatoes and sweet potatoes are cool, peel off the skins and thinly slice. Layer half the potato slices in the base of the dish. Season. Spread with a quarter of the cream mixture, then cover with the zucchini mixture, patting down well. Top with another quarter of the cream mixture. Use all the sweet potato slices to make another layer, and cover with half of the remaining cream mixture. Top with the remaining potato slices, then the last of the cream mixture. Season and top with the Cheddar.

4 Bake for 1$^1/_4$ hours, or until the vegetables are cooked. Cover with a tented sheet of foil towards the end if the top starts over-browning. Stand for 10 minutes before cutting.

SERVES 6

INGREDIENTS

2 large (600 g/1 lb 5 oz) eggplants (aubergines)
1 red onion, chopped
1 garlic clove, chopped
2.5 cm (1 inch) piece of ginger, chopped
1 green chilli, chopped
100 ml (3^1/$_2$ fl oz) oil
^{1}/$_4$ teaspoon chilli powder
^{1}/$_2$ teaspoon garam masala
2 teaspoons ground cumin
2 teaspoons ground coriander (cilantro)
2 teaspoons salt
^{1}/$_2$ teaspoon ground black pepper
2 ripe tomatoes, chopped
3–4 tablespoons coriander (cilantro) leaves, finely chopped

1 Using a pair of tongs, scorch the eggplants by holding them over a medium gas flame. Alternatively, heat them under a grill (broiler) or on an electric hotplate. Keep turning them until the skin is blackened on all sides. Set aside until cool, then peel off the charred skin. Roughly chop the flesh. Don't worry if black specks remain on the flesh because they add to the smoky flavour.

2 Combine the onion, garlic, ginger and chilli in a blender and process until chopped together but not a paste. Alternatively, chop finely with a knife and mix in a bowl.

3 Heat the oil in a deep heavy-based frying pan over medium heat, add the onion mixture and cook until slightly browned. Add all the spices and the salt and pepper and stir for 1 minute. Add the tomato and simmer until the liquid has reduced.

4 Put the eggplants in the pan and mash them with a wooden spoon, stirring around with the spices. Simmer for 10 minutes, or until soft. Stir in the coriander leaves and season with salt. Serve with bread as a light meal, or as a cold relish with a main meal, such as an Indian curry.

SMOKY SPICED EGGPLANT

SERVES 4

SPANISH CRISP POTATOES IN SPICY TOMATO SAUCE

olive oil, for deep-frying

1 kg (2 lb 4 oz) desiree potatoes, peeled and cut into 2 cm ($^3/_4$ inch) cubes, then rinsed and patted completely dry

500 g (1 lb 2 oz) ripe Roma (plum) tomatoes

2 tablespoons olive oil, extra

$^1/_4$ red onion, finely chopped

2 garlic cloves, crushed

3 teaspoons paprika

$^1/_4$ teaspoon cayenne pepper

1 bay leaf

1 teaspoon sugar

1 tablespoon chopped flat-leaf (Italian) parsley

1 Fill a deep-fryer or large heavy-based saucepan one-third full of oil and heat to 180°C (350°F), or until a cube of bread dropped in the oil browns in 15 seconds. Cook the potato in batches for 10 minutes, or until golden. Drain on crumpled paper towels. Do not discard the oil.

2 Score a cross in the base of each tomato. Place in a bowl of boiling water for 1 minute, then plunge into cold water and peel the skin away from the cross. Chop the flesh.

3 Heat the extra olive oil in a saucepan, add the onion and cook over medium heat for 3 minutes, or until soft and golden. Add the garlic, paprika and cayenne and cook for 1–2 minutes. Add the tomato, bay leaf, sugar and 100 ml (3$^1/_2$ fl oz) water and cook, stirring occasionally, for 20 minutes. Cool slightly, remove the bay leaf, then process in a food processor until smooth, adding a little water if needed. Prior to serving, reheat the sauce over low heat. Season well.

4 Reheat the oil to 180°C (350°F). Recook the potato in batches for 2 minutes, or until crisp. Drain. Place the potatoes on a platter and pour over the sauce. Garnish with parsley.

SERVES 6

INGREDIENTS

500 g (2¼ cups) chickpeas
2 tablespoons oil or ghee
2 large red onions, thinly sliced
2 cm (¾ inch) piece of ginger, finely chopped
2 teaspoons sugar
2 teaspoons ground coriander (cilantro)
2 teaspoons ground cumin
pinch of chilli powder (optional)
1 teaspoon garam masala
3 tablespoons tamarind purée (see note)
4 ripe tomatoes, chopped
4 tablespoons coriander (cilantro) or mint leaves, finely chopped

1 Soak the chickpeas overnight in 2 litres (8 cups) water. Drain, then put the chickpeas in a large saucepan with 2 litres (8 cups) water. Bring to the boil, spooning off any scum from the surface. Cover and simmer over low heat for 1−1½ hours until soft. It is important they are soft at this stage as they won't soften any more once the sauce has been added. Drain.

2 Heat the oil in a heavy-based frying pan. Fry the onion until soft and brown, then stir in the ginger. Add the chickpeas, sugar, coriander, cumin, chilli powder, garam masala and a pinch of salt. Stir, then add the tamarind and tomato and simmer for 2−3 minutes. Add 500 ml (2 cups) water, bring to the boil and cook until the sauce has thickened. Stir in the coriander leaves. Serve with Indian bread such as rotis or naan.

NOTE Tamarind is a souring agent made from the pods of the tamarind tree. It is sold as a block of pulp (including husks and seeds), as cleaned pulp, or as ready-prepared tamarind purée or concentrate.

SERVES 6

915

INGREDIENTS

2 tablespoons oil
2 onions, chopped
1 teaspoon ground ginger
2 teaspoons ground paprika
2 teaspoons ground cumin
1 cinnamon stick
pinch of saffron threads
1.5 kg (3 lb) vegetables, peeled and cut into large chunks (carrot, eggplant, orange sweet potato, parsnip, potato, pumpkin)
½ preserved lemon, rinsed, pith and flesh removed, thinly sliced
400 g (13 oz) can peeled tomatoes
1 cup (250 ml/8 fl oz) vegetable stock
100 g (3½ oz) dried pears, halved
60 g (2 oz) pitted prunes
2 zucchini (courgettes), cut into large chunks
300 g (10 oz) instant couscous
1 tablespoon olive oil
3 tablespoons chopped fresh flat-leaf parsley
⅓ cup (50 g/1¾ oz) almonds

1 Preheat the oven to moderate 180°C (350°F/Gas 4). Heat the oil in a large saucepan or ovenproof dish, add the onion and cook over medium heat for 5 minutes, or until soft. Add the spices and cook for 3 minutes.

2 Add the vegetables and cook, stirring, until coated with the spices and the outside begins to soften. Add the lemon, tomatoes, stock, pears and prunes. Cover, transfer to the oven and cook for 30 minutes. Add the zucchini and cook for 15–20 minutes, or until the vegetables are tender.

3 Cover the couscous with the olive oil and 2 cups (500 ml/16 fl oz) boiling water and leave until all the water has been absorbed. Flake with a fork.

4 Remove the cinnamon stick from the vegetables, then stir in the parsley. Serve on a large platter with the couscous formed into a ring and the vegetable tagine in the centre, sprinkled with the almonds.

SERVES 4-6

INGREDIENTS

600 g (1 lb 5 oz) peeled and seeded pumpkin, cut into 3 cm (1¼ inch) cubes

2 tablespoons oil

1 tablespoon ready-made red curry paste

400 ml (14 fl oz) coconut cream

200 g (7 oz) green beans, cut into 3 cm (1¼ inch) lengths

2 kaffir lime (makrut) leaves, crushed

1 tablespoon grated light palm sugar or soft brown sugar

1 tablespoon fish sauce

30 g (1 cup) Thai basil leaves, plus extra, to garnish

1 tablespoon lime juice

1 Preheat the oven to 200°C (400°F/Gas 6). Place the pumpkin in a baking dish with 1 tablespoon of the oil and toss to coat. Bake for 20 minutes, or until tender.

2 Heat the remaining oil in a saucepan, add the curry paste and cook, stirring constantly, breaking up with a fork, over medium heat for 1–2 minutes. Add the coconut cream 125 ml (½ cup) at a time, stirring well with a wooden spoon between each addition for a creamy consistency. Add the pumpkin and any roasting juices, the beans and lime leaves. Reduce the heat to low and cook for 5 minutes.

3 Stir in the palm sugar, fish sauce, basil and lime juice. Garnish with extra basil leaves. Serve with rice.

RED CURRY OF ROAST PUMPKIN, BEANS AND BASIL

SERVES 4

DUM ALU

Curry paste
4 cardamom pods
1 teaspoon grated fresh ginger
2 cloves garlic
6 small fresh red chillies
1 teaspoon cumin seeds
1/4 cup (40 g/1 1/4 oz) raw cashew nut pieces
1 tablespoon white poppy seeds (khus) (see note)
1 cinnamon stick
6 cloves

1 kg (2 lb) potatoes, cubed
2 onions, roughly chopped
2 tablespoons oil
1/2 teaspoon ground turmeric
1 teaspoon besan (chickpea flour)
1 cup (250 g/8 oz) plain yoghurt
fresh coriander (cilantro) leaves, to garnish

1 To make the curry paste, lightly crush the cardamom pods with the flat side of a heavy knife. Remove the seeds, discarding the pods. Place the seeds and the remaining curry paste ingredients in a food processor, and process to a smooth paste.

2 Bring a large saucepan of lightly salted water to the boil. Add the potato and cook for 5–6 minutes, or until just tender. Drain.

3 Place the onion in a food processor and process in short bursts until it is finely ground but not puréed. Heat the oil in a large saucepan, add the ground onion and cook over low heat for 5 minutes. Add the curry paste and cook, stirring, for a further 5 minutes, or until fragrant. Stir in the potato, turmeric, salt to taste and 1 cup (250 ml/8 fl oz) water.

4 Reduce the heat and simmer, tightly covered, for 10 minutes, or until the potato is cooked but not breaking up and the sauce has thickened slightly.

5 Combine the besan with the yoghurt, add to the potato mixture and cook, stirring, over low heat for 5 minutes, or until thickened again. Garnish with the coriander leaves.

NOTE White poppy seeds (khus) should not be mistaken for black and do not yield opium. They are off-white, odourless and flavourless until roasted when they have a slight sesame aroma and flavour. If they are not available, replace the poppy seeds with sesame seeds.

SERVES 6

INGREDIENTS

Curry paste
10 small fresh green chillies
50 g (1¾ oz) red Asian shallots, peeled
2 cloves garlic
1 cup (50 g/1¾ oz) finely chopped coriander (cilantro)
   stems and roots
1 stem lemon grass (white part only), chopped
2 tablespoons grated fresh galangal
1 tablespoon ground coriander (cilantro)
1 teaspoon ground cumin
1 teaspoon black peppercorns
1/2 teaspoon ground turmeric
1 tablespoon lime juice

2 tablespoons oil
1 onion, sliced
400 ml (13 fl oz) can coconut cream
4–5 kaffir lime (makrut) leaves, torn
500 g (1 lb) firm tofu, cut into 2 cm (¾ inch) cubes
1 tablespoon lime juice
1 tablespoon shredded fresh Thai basil

1 To make the curry paste, place all the ingredients in a food processor and process until smooth.

2 Heat the oil in a frying pan, add the onion and cook for 5 minutes, or until soft. Add 4 tablespoons curry paste (or more for a stronger flavour) and cook, stirring, for 2 minutes. Stir in the coconut cream and 1 cup (250 ml/8 fl oz) water, and season with salt. Bring to the boil and add the lime leaves and tofu. Reduce the heat and simmer for 8 minutes, stirring often. Stir in the lime juice and Thai basil, and serve.

NOTE The recipe for the curry paste makes 1 cup, but you will only need ⅓ cup. Freeze the remaining paste in two portions to use at a later date.

SERVES 6

INDONESIAN VEGETABLE AND COCONUT CURRY

INGREDIENTS

Curry paste
5 candlenuts
75 g (2¹/₂ oz) red Asian shallots
2 cloves garlic
2 teaspoons sambal oelek
¹/₄ teaspoon ground turmeric
1 teaspoon grated fresh galangal
1 tablespoon peanut butter

2 tablespoons oil
1 onion, sliced
400 ml (13 fl oz) can coconut cream
200 g (6¹/₂ oz) carrots, julienned
200 g (6¹/₂ oz) snake beans, cut into 7 cm (2³/₄ inch) lengths
300 g (10 oz) Chinese cabbage, roughly shredded
100 g (3¹/₂ oz) fresh shiitake mushrooms
¹/₄ teaspoon sugar

1   To make the curry paste, place the candlenuts, red Asian shallots, garlic, sambal oelek, turmeric, galangal and peanut butter in a food processor, and process to a smooth paste.

2   Heat the oil in a large saucepan over low heat. Cook the curry paste, stirring, for 5 minutes, or until fragrant. Add the onion and cook for 5 minutes. Stir in ¹/₄ cup (60 ml/2 fl oz) coconut cream and cook, stirring constantly, for 2 minutes, or until thickened. Add the carrot and snake beans, and cook over high heat for 3 minutes. Stir in the Chinese cabbage, mushrooms and 1 cup (250 ml/8 fl oz) water. Cook over high heat for 8–10 minutes, or until the vegetables are nearly cooked.

3   Stir in the remaining coconut cream and the sugar, and season to taste with salt. Bring to the boil, stirring constantly, then reduce the heat and simmer for 8–10 minutes to allow the flavours to develop. Serve hot.

SERVES 6

INGREDIENTS

Curry paste

1 tablespoon oil
1 teaspoon coriander (cilantro) seeds
1 teaspoon cumin seeds
8 cloves
1/2 teaspoon fennel seeds
seeds from 4 cardamom pods
6 red Asian shallots, chopped
3 cloves garlic, chopped
1 teaspoon finely chopped lemon grass (white part only)
1 teaspoon finely chopped fresh galangal
4 large dried red chillies
1 teaspoon ground nutmeg
1 teaspoon white pepper

1 tablespoon oil
250 g (8 oz) baby onions
500 g (1 lb) small new potatoes
300 g (10 oz) carrots, cut into 3 cm (1 1/4 inch) pieces
225 g (7 oz) can whole champignons, drained
1 cinnamon stick
1 kaffir lime (makrut) leaf
1 bay leaf
1 cup (250 ml/8 fl oz) coconut cream
1 tablespoon lime juice
3 teaspoons grated palm sugar or soft brown sugar
1 tablespoon shredded fresh Thai basil leaves
1 tablespoon crushed roasted peanuts
fresh Thai basil leaves, extra, to garnish

1   To make the curry paste, heat the oil in a frying pan over low heat, add the coriander, cumin, cloves, fennel seeds and cardamom seeds, and cook for 1–2 minutes, or until fragrant. Place in a food processor and add the shallots, garlic, lemon grass, galangal, chillies, nutmeg and white pepper. Process until smooth, adding a little water as necessary.

2   Heat the oil in a large saucepan, add the curry paste and cook, stirring, over medium heat for 2 minutes, or until fragrant. Add the vegetables, cinnamon stick, kaffir lime leaf and bay leaf, and season with salt. Add enough water to cover—about 2 cups (500 ml/16 fl oz)— and bring to the boil. Reduce the heat and simmer, covered, stirring frequently, for 30–35 minutes, or until the vegetables are cooked. Stir in the coconut cream and cook, uncovered, for 4 minutes, stirring frequently, until thickened slightly. Stir in the lime juice, palm sugar and shredded Thai basil. Add a little water if the sauce is too dry. Garnish with the peanuts and Thai basil leaves.

SERVES 4-6

INGREDIENTS

250 g (8 oz) potatoes, diced
250 g (8 oz) pumpkin, diced
200 g (6½ oz) cauliflower, broken into florets
150 g (5 oz) yellow squash, cut into quarters
1 tablespoon oil
2 onions, chopped
3 tablespoons curry powder
400 g (13 oz) can crushed tomatoes
1 cup (250 ml/8 fl oz) vegetable stock
150 g (5 oz) green beans, cut into short lengths
⅓ cup (90 g/3 oz) natural yoghurt
¼ cup (30 g/1 oz) sultanas

1 Bring a saucepan of water to the boil, add the potato and pumpkin, and cook for 6 minutes, then remove. Add the cauliflower and squash, cook for 4 minutes, then remove.

2 Heat the oil in a large saucepan, add the onion and cook, stirring, over medium heat for 8 minutes, or until starting to brown.

3 Add the curry powder and stir for 1 minute, or until fragrant. Stir in the crushed tomato and vegetable stock.

4 Add the parboiled potato, pumpkin, cauliflower and squash and cook for 5 minutes, then add the green beans and cook for a further 2–3 minutes, or until the vegetables are just tender.

5 Add the yoghurt and sultanas, and stir to combine. Simmer for 3 minutes, or until thickened slightly. Season to taste and serve with lemon wedges.

SERVES 6

YELLOW VEGETABLE CURRY

¹/₄ cup (60 ml/2 fl oz) oil
1 onion, finely chopped
2 tablespoons yellow curry paste
250 g (8 oz) potato, diced
200 g (6¹/₂ oz) zucchini (courgette), diced
150 g (5 oz) red capsicum (pepper), diced
100 g (3¹/₂ oz) beans, trimmed
50 g (1³/₄ oz) bamboo shoots, sliced
1 cup (250 ml/8 fl oz) vegetable stock
400 ml (13 fl oz) can coconut cream
fresh Thai basil leaves, to garnish

1 Heat the oil in a large saucepan, add the onion and cook over medium heat for 4–5 minutes, or until softened and just turning golden. Add the yellow curry paste and cook, stirring, for 2 minutes, or until fragrant.

2 Add all the vegetables and cook, stirring, over high heat for 2 minutes. Pour in the vegetable stock, reduce the heat to medium and cook, covered, for 15–20 minutes, or until the vegetables are tender. Cook, uncovered, over high heat for 5–10 minutes, or until the sauce has reduced slightly.

3 Stir in the coconut cream, and season with salt. Bring to the boil, stirring frequently, then reduce the heat and simmer for 5 minutes. Garnish with the Thai basil leaves.

SERVES 6

INGREDIENTS

1 cup (185 g/6 oz) couscous
4 tablespoons oil
1 eggplant (aubergine), finely diced
1 onion, finely chopped
1 clove garlic, crushed
2 teaspoons ground cumin
2 teaspoons ground coriander (cilantro)
1 red capsicum (pepper), finely diced
2 tablespoons chopped fresh coriander (cilantro)
2 teaspoons grated lemon rind
2 teaspoons lemon juice
5 tablespoons natural yoghurt
1 egg, lightly beaten
oil, for shallow-frying

1 Place the couscous in a bowl. Add 1 cup (250 ml/8 fl oz) of boiling water and leave for 10 minutes, or until all the water has been absorbed. Fluff up the grains with a fork.

2 Heat 2 tablespoons of the oil in a large frying pan and fry the eggplant until soft and golden, then place in a bowl. Heat 1 tablespoon of the oil in the pan. Add the onion, garlic, cumin and ground coriander. Cook over medium heat for 3–4 minutes, or until soft, then add to the bowl. Heat the remaining oil and cook the capsicum for 5 minutes, or until soft. Place in the bowl and stir well.

3 Add the vegetable mixture to the couscous with the fresh coriander, lemon rind, lemon juice, yoghurt and egg. Season to taste and mix well.

4 Using damp hands, divide the mixture into four portions and form into large patties—they should be about 2 cm (¾ inch) thick. Cover and refrigerate for 15 minutes. Shallow-fry the patties over medium heat for 5 minutes on each side, or until golden. Drain the patties well and serve with yoghurt.

SERVES 4

EGGPLANT WITH BUCKWHEAT NOODLES

10 g ($^{1}/_{4}$ oz) dried shiitake mushrooms
350 g (12 oz) buckwheat (soba) noodles
2 teaspoons sesame oil
3 tablespoons tahini
1 tablespoon light soy sauce
1 tablespoon dark soy sauce
1 tablespoon honey
2 tablespoons lemon juice
3 tablespoons peanut oil
2 long, thin eggplants (aubergines), cut into very thin strips
2 carrots, julienned
10 spring onions (scallions), cut on the diagonal
6 fresh shiitake mushrooms, thinly sliced
50 g (1 cup) roughly chopped coriander (cilantro) leaves

1   Soak the dried shiitake mushrooms in 125 ml ($^{1}/_{2}$ cup) hot water for 10 minutes. Drain, reserving the liquid. Discard the woody stems and finely slice the caps.

2   Cook the noodles in a saucepan of boiling water for 5 minutes, or until tender. Drain. Refresh under cold water, then toss with 1 teaspoon of the sesame oil.

3   Combine the tahini, light and dark soy sauces, honey, lemon juice, 2 tablespoons of the reserved mushroom liquid and the remaining teaspoon of sesame oil in a food processor until smooth.

4   Heat 2 tablespoons of the peanut oil over high heat. Add the eggplant and cook, turning often, for 4–5 minutes, or until soft and golden. Drain on paper towels.

5   Heat the remaining oil. Add the carrot, spring onion and fresh and dried mushrooms. Cook, stirring constantly, for 1–2 minutes, or until just softened. Remove from the heat and toss with the noodles, eggplant and dressing. Garnish with the coriander.

SERVES 4-6

INGREDIENTS

500 g (1 lb 2 oz) ready-made potato gnocchi
walnuts, to garnish
375 ml (1½ cups) cream
200 g (7 oz) mild gorgonzola cheese, crumbled
2 tablespoons grated Parmesan cheese
40 g (1½ oz) butter
pinch of grated nutmeg

1 Cook the gnocchi in a large saucepan of boiling salted water until al dente.

2 Spread the walnuts on a baking tray and toast in a 180°C (350°F/Gas 4) oven for 5–8 minutes, or until lightly coloured. Alternatively, place them on a tray under a hot grill (broiler). Once they start to brown, nuts burn very quickly, so watch them carefully. Cool, then roughly chop.

3 Put the cream, gorgonzola, Parmesan and butter in a saucepan and heat over low heat, stirring occasionally, for 3 minutes, or until the cheeses have melted into a smooth sauce.

4 Stir in the nutmeg and serve immediately over the hot pasta. Garnish with the walnuts.

NOTE This dish is very rich and is recommended as a starter rather than a main course.

GNOCCHI WITH GORGONZOLA CREAM

SERVES 4-6

LENTIL AND CAULIFLOWER CURRY STACKS

60 g (2 oz) ghee or butter
2 onions, thinly sliced
2 tablespoons Madras curry paste
2 cloves garlic, crushed
180 g (6 oz) button mushrooms, sliced
1 litre (32 fl oz) vegetable stock
300 g (10 oz) brown or green lentils
400 g (13 oz) can chopped tomatoes
2 cinnamon sticks
300 g (10 oz) cauliflower, cut into small florets
oil, for deep-frying
18 small (8 cm/3 inch) pappadums
plain yoghurt and coriander (cilantro), to serve

1 Heat the ghee in a large pan over medium heat and cook the onion for 2–3 minutes, or until soft. Add the curry paste, garlic and mushrooms and cook for 2 minutes, or until soft.

2 Add the stock, lentils, tomato and cinnamon and mix well. Bring to the boil and cook for 40 minutes, or until the lentils are tender. Add the cauliflower in the last 10 minutes and cover. If the curry is too wet, continue to cook, uncovered, until the excess liquid has evaporated. Season to taste with salt and cracked black pepper. Remove the cinnamon.

3 Meanwhile, fill a deep heavy-based saucepan one third full of oil and heat until a cube of bread dropped into the oil browns in 15 seconds. Cook the pappadums in batches for 10 seconds, or until golden brown and puffed all over. Drain on crumpled paper towels and season with salt.

4 To assemble, place a pappadum on each serving plate and spoon on a little of the curry. Place a second pappadum on top and spoon on some more curry. Cover with the remaining pappadum and top with a spoonful of yoghurt. Garnish with coriander sprigs and serve immediately (the pappadums will become soggy if left to stand for too long.)

SERVES 6

ITALIAN ZUCCHINI PIE

600 g (1 lb 5 oz) zucchini (courgettes), grated and mixed with $\frac{1}{4}$ teaspoon salt
150 g (5$\frac{1}{2}$ oz) provolone cheese, grated
120 g (4$\frac{1}{2}$ oz) ricotta cheese
3 eggs
2 garlic cloves, crushed
2 teaspoons finely chopped basil
pinch ground nutmeg
2 sheets ready-rolled shortcrust pastry
1 egg (extra), lightly beaten

1 Preheat the oven to 200°C (400°F/ Gas 6) and heat a baking tray. Grease a 23 cm (9 inch) (top) pie dish. Drain the zucchini in a colander for 30 minutes, then squeeze out any excess liquid. Place in a bowl with the cheeses, eggs, garlic, basil and nutmeg. Season and mix well.

2 Using two-thirds of the pastry, line the base and sides of the dish. Spoon the filling into the pastry shell and level the surface. Brush the exposed rim of the pastry with egg. Use two-thirds of the remaining pastry to make a lid. Cover the filling with it, pressing the edges together firmly. Trim the edges and reserve the scraps. Crimp the rim. Prick the top all over with a skewer and brush with egg.

3 From the remaining pastry, cut a strip about 30 cm x 10 cm (12 inches x 4 inches). Cut this into nine lengths 1 cm ($\frac{1}{2}$ inch) wide. Press three ropes together at one end and press onto the workbench. Plait the ropes. Make two more plaits, trim the ends and space the plaits parallel across the centre of the pie. Brush with egg. Bake on the hot tray for 50 minutes, or until golden.

INGREDIENTS

185 ml (³/₄ cup) olive oil
1 onion, finely chopped
2 garlic cloves, finely chopped
2 x 400 g (14 oz) cans chopped tomatoes
400 g (14 oz) bucatini or spaghetti
1 large eggplant (aubergine), about 500 g (1 lb 2 oz)
30 g (¹/₂ cup) basil leaves, torn, plus extra, to garnish
60 g (¹/₂ cup) ricotta salata (see note), crumbled
45 g (¹/₂ cup) grated pecorino or Parmesan cheese
1 tablespoon extra virgin olive oil, to drizzle

1 Heat 2 tablespoons of the oil in a frying pan and cook the onion over medium heat for 5 minutes, or until softened. Stir in the garlic and cook for 30 seconds. Add the tomato and season. Reduce the heat to low and cook for 20–25 minutes, or until the sauce has thickened and reduced.

2 Cook the pasta in a saucepan of boiling salted water until al dente. Meanwhile, cut the eggplant lengthways into 5 mm (¹/₄ inch) thick slices. Heat the remaining olive oil in a large frying pan. When the oil is hot but not smoking, add the eggplant slices a few at a time and cook for 3–5 minutes, or until lightly browned on both sides. Remove from the pan and drain on crumpled paper towels.

3 Add the eggplant to the sauce with the basil, stirring over very low heat.

4 Add the hot pasta to the sauce with half each of the ricotta and pecorino and toss together well. Serve immediately, sprinkled with the remaining cheeses and extra basil and drizzled with oil.

NOTE Ricotta salata is a lightly salted, pressed ricotta cheese. If unavailable, use a mild feta cheese.

SERVES 4-6

PASTA WITH PUMPKIN AND FETA

1 kg (2 lb 4 oz) butternut pumpkin (squash), peeled and cut into 2 cm ($^3/_4$ inch) chunks
1 red onion, thinly sliced
8 garlic cloves, unpeeled
1 tablespoon rosemary leaves
80 ml ($^1/_3$ cup) olive oil
400 g (14 oz) casserechi pasta, or macaroni, gemelli or other short pasta
200 g (7 oz) marinated feta cheese, crumbled
2 tablespoons grated Parmesan cheese
2 tablespoons finely chopped parsley

1 Preheat the oven to 200°C (400°F/Gas 6). Put the pumpkin, onion, garlic and rosemary in a roasting tin, then drizzle with 1 tablespoon of the oil. Season. Using your hands, rub the oil over all the ingredients until well coated. Roast for 30 minutes, or until the pumpkin is soft and starting to caramelize.

2 Cook the pasta in a saucepan of boiling salted water until al dente.

3 Squeeze the roasted garlic out of its skin and place it in a bowl with the remaining oil. Mash with a fork.

4 Add the garlic oil to the hot pasta, then the remaining ingredients. Toss well and season.

　　　SERVES 4

INGREDIENTS

30 g (1 oz) dried porcini mushrooms
1 litre (4 cups) chicken or vegetable stock
100 g (3½ oz) butter
1 onion, finely chopped
250 g (9 oz) mushrooms, sliced
2 garlic cloves, crushed
385 g (1¾ cups) risotto rice (arborio, vialone nano or carnaroli)
pinch of ground nutmeg
1 tablespoon finely chopped parsley
45 g (1½ oz) Parmesan cheese, grated

1 Put the porcini in a bowl, cover with 500 ml (2 cups) hot water and leave to soak for 15 minutes. Squeeze them dry, reserving the soaking liquid. If the porcini are large, roughly chop them. Strain the soaking liquid into a saucepan and add enough stock to make up to 1 litre (4 cups). Heat up and maintain at a low simmer.

2 Melt the butter in a deep heavy-based frying pan and gently cook the onion until soft but not browned. Add the mushrooms and porcini and fry for a few minutes. Add the garlic, stir briefly, then add the rice and reduce the heat to low. Season and stir to coat the grains of rice in the butter.

3 Increase the heat to medium and add a ladleful of the stock. Cook at a fast simmer, stirring constantly. When the stock has been absorbed, stir in another ladleful. Continue like this for about 20 minutes, or until the rice is creamy and al dente. Add a little more stock or water if you need to — every risotto will use a different amount.

4 Stir in the nutmeg, parsley and half the Parmesan, then serve with the rest of the Parmesan sprinkled over the top.

SERVES 4

PULAO WITH ONIONS AND SPICES

INGREDIENTS

200 g (1 cup) basmati rice
500 ml (2 cups) chicken stock
6 tablespoons ghee or oil
5 cardamom pods
5 cm (2 inch) piece of cinnamon stick
6 cloves
8 black peppercorns
4 Indian bay leaves (cassia leaves)
1 onion, finely sliced

1 Wash the rice in a sieve under cold running water until the water from the rice runs clear. Drain.

2 Heat the stock to near boiling point in a saucepan.

3 Meanwhile, heat 2 tablespoons of the ghee over medium heat in a large heavy-based saucepan. Add the cardamom, cinnamon, cloves, peppercorns and bay leaves and fry for 1 minute. Reduce the heat to low, add the rice and stir constantly for 1 minute. Add the heated stock and some salt to the rice and bring rapidly to a boil. Cover and simmer over low heat for 15 minutes. Allow the rice to rest for 10 minutes before uncovering. Lightly fluff up the rice before serving.

4 Meanwhile, heat the remaining ghee in a frying pan over low heat and fry the onion until soft. Increase the heat and fry until the onion is dark brown. Drain on paper towels, then use as a garnish. Serve with casseroles or Indian curries.

SERVES 4

INGREDIENTS

6 sheets ready-rolled puff pastry
1.2 kg pumpkin, cut into 6 cm pieces
6 tablespoons sour cream or cream cheese
sweet chilli sauce, to serve

1 Preheat the oven to moderately hot 200°C (400°F/Gas 6). Lightly grease six 10 cm pie dishes. Cut six 15 cm circles from the pastry, carefully place in the prepared dishes and pleat the pastry to fit. Prick the pastry with a fork. Place on a baking tray and bake for 15–20 minutes, or until lightly golden, pressing down any pastry that puffs up. Cool.

2 Meanwhile, steam the pumpkin pieces for about 15 minutes, or until just tender.

3 Place a tablespoon of sour cream in the middle of each pastry shell and pile the pumpkin pieces on top. Season with salt and black pepper and drizzle with sweet chilli sauce to taste. Return to the oven for 5 minutes to heat through. Remove from the tins and serve immediately.

PUMPKIN TARTS

SERVES 6

PUY LENTILS AND BEAN PUREE ON MUSHROOMS WITH RED WINE SAUCE

INGREDIENTS

4 large (10 cm/4 inch) field mushrooms
1 tablespoon olive oil
1 red onion, cut into thin wedges
1 clove garlic, crushed
1 cup (200 g/6½ oz) puy lentils
¾ cup (185 ml/6 fl oz) red wine
1¾ cups (440 ml/14 fl oz) vegetable stock
1 tablespoon finely chopped fresh flat-leaf parsley
30 g (1 oz) butter
2 cloves garlic, crushed, extra

Bean puree

1 large potato, cut into chunks
2 tablespoons extra virgin olive oil
400 g (13 oz) can cannellini beans, drained and rinsed
2 large cloves garlic, crushed
1 tablespoon vegetable stock

Red wine sauce

⅔ cup (170 ml/5½ fl oz) red wine
2 tablespoons tomato paste (purée)
1½ cups (375 ml/12 fl oz) vegetable stock
1 tablespoon soft brown sugar

1 Remove the stalks from the mushrooms and chop them. Heat the oil in a large saucepan and cook the onion over medium heat for 2–3 minutes, or until soft. Add the garlic and mushroom stalks and cook for a further 1 minute. Stir in the lentils, wine and stock and bring to the boil. Reduce the heat and simmer, covered, for 20–25 minutes, stirring occasionally, or until reduced and the lentils are cooked through. If the mixture is too wet, remove the lid and boil until slightly thick. Stir in the parsley and keep warm.

2 Meanwhile, to make the bean purée, bring a small saucepan of water to the boil over high heat and cook the potato for 10 minutes, or until tender. Drain and mash with a potato masher or fork until smooth. Stir in half the extra virgin olive oil. Combine the cannellini beans and garlic in a food processor bowl. Add the stock and the remaining oil and process until smooth. Transfer to a bowl and fold in the mashed potato. Keep warm.

3 Melt the butter in a deep frying pan. Add the mushrooms and extra garlic and cook in batches over medium heat for 4 minutes each side, or until tender. Remove and keep warm.

4 To make the red wine sauce, add the red wine to the same frying pan, then scrape the bottom to remove any sediment. Add the combined tomato paste, stock and sugar and bring to the boil. Cook for about 10 minutes, or until reduced and thickened.

5 To assemble, place the mushrooms onto serving plates and top with the bean purée. Spoon on the lentil mixture and drizzle with the red wine sauce. Season and serve immediately.

NOTE The mushrooms tend to shrivel if you keep them warm in the oven—either turn the oven off or find another warm place.

SERVES 4

INGREDIENTS

20 g (³/₄ oz) dried porcini mushrooms
1 litre (4 cups) vegetable or chicken stock
2 tablespoons olive oil
1 tablespoon butter
1 small onion, finely chopped
2 garlic cloves, crushed
385 g (1³/₄ cups) risotto rice (arborio, vialone nano or carnaroli)
250 g (9 oz) mushrooms, sliced
pinch of ground nutmeg
40 g (1¹/₂ oz) Parmesan cheese, grated
3 tablespoons finely chopped parsley

1 Soak the porcini in 500 ml (2 cups) boiling water for 30 minutes. Drain, reserving the liquid. Chop the porcini and pass the liquid through a fine sieve. Put the vegetable or chicken stock in a saucepan, bring to the boil and then maintain at a low simmer.

2 Heat the oil and butter in a large wide heavy-based saucepan. Cook the onion and garlic until softened but not browned. Add the rice and reduce the heat to low. Season and stir briefly to thoroughly coat the rice. Toss in the fresh mushrooms and nutmeg. Season and cook, stirring, for 1–2 minutes. Add the porcini and the reserved soaking liquid, increase the heat and cook until the liquid has been absorbed.

3 Stir in a ladleful of hot stock and cook over moderate heat, stirring continuously. When the stock has been absorbed, stir in another ladleful. Continue like this for about 20 minutes, until all the stock has been added and the rice is creamy and al dente. (You may not need to use all the stock, or you may need a little extra.) Remove the pan from the heat and stir in the Parmesan and parsley. Season and serve.

SERVES 4

TOFU PUFFS WITH MUSHROOMS AND ROUND RICE NOODLES

8 dried shiitake mushrooms
500 g (1 lb 2 oz) fresh round rice noodles
3 litres (12 cups) good-quality chicken stock
1 carrot, thinly sliced on the diagonal
100 g (3$^1/_2$ oz) fried tofu puffs, cut in half
800 g (1 lb 12 oz) bok choy (pak choi), trimmed and quartered
1–1$^1/_2$ tablespoons mushroom soy sauce
6 drops sesame oil
ground white pepper, to season
100 g (3$^1/_2$ oz) enoki mushrooms, ends trimmed

1 Place the shiitake mushrooms in a heatproof bowl, cover with boiling water and soak for 20 minutes. Drain and remove the stems, squeezing out any excess water.

2 Meanwhile, place the noodles in a heatproof bowl, cover with boiling water and soak briefly. Gently separate the noodles with your hands and drain well.

3 Place the chicken stock in a large saucepan, cover and slowly heat over low heat.

4 Add the noodles to the simmering stock along with the carrot, tofu puffs, shiitake mushrooms and bok choy. Cook for 1–2 minutes, or until the carrot and noodles are tender and the bok choy has wilted slightly. Stir in the soy sauce and sesame oil and season to taste with white pepper.

5 Divide the noodles, vegetables, tofu puffs and enoki mushrooms among four serving bowls, ladle the broth on top and serve immediately.

2 tablespoons oil

4 spring onions, cut into 3 cm lengths

3 cloves garlic, crushed

1 fresh red chilli, seeded and sliced

75 g button mushrooms, quartered

100 g Chinese cabbage, roughly chopped

2 tablespoons soy sauce

1 teaspoon fish sauce

1 tablespoon oyster sauce

$^1/_4$ cup (60 ml) vegetable stock

$^1/_2$ teaspoon grated palm sugar

150 g snow peas (mangetout)

150 g cauliflower, cut into small florets

150 g broccoli, cut into small florets

fresh coriander (cilantro) leaves, chopped, to garnish

1 Heat a wok until very hot, add the oil and swirl to coat. Add the spring onion, garlic and chilli. Stir-fry for 20 seconds. Add the mushrooms and cabbage and stir-fry for 1 minute.

2 Stir in the sauces, stock, palm sugar, snow peas, cauliflower and broccoli. Cook for 2 minutes, or until tender. Garnish with the coriander leaves.

STIR-FRIED MIXED VEGETABLES

SERVES 6

INGREDIENTS

50 ml (1³/₄ fl oz) extra virgin olive oil
1 red onion, cut into thin wedges
600 g (1 lb 5 oz) orange sweet potato (kumera), peeled and cut into 2 cm (³/₄ inch) cubes
440 g (2 cups) arborio rice
1.25 litres (5 cups) hot vegetable stock
75 g (³/₄ cup) shredded Parmesan cheese
3 tablespoons shredded sage
shaved Parmesan cheese, extra, to garnish

1 Heat 3 tablespoons oil in a large saucepan and cook the onion over medium heat for 2–3 minutes, or until softened. Add the sweet potato and rice and stir until well coated in the oil.

2 Add 125 ml (¹/₂ cup) hot stock, stirring constantly over medium heat until the liquid is absorbed. Continue adding more stock, 125 ml (¹/₂ cup) at a time, stirring constantly for 20–25 minutes, or until all the stock is absorbed, the sweet potato is cooked and the rice is tender and creamy.

3 Add the Parmesan and 2 tablespoons of the sage. Season well and stir to combine. Spoon into four bowls and drizzle with the remaining oil. Sprinkle the remaining sage over the top and garnish with shaved Parmesan.

SERVES 4

200 g (2 cups) shelled walnuts
20 g ($^1/_3$ cup) roughly chopped parsley
50 g (1$^3/_4$ oz) butter
200 ml (7 fl oz) extra virgin olive oil
1 garlic clove, crushed
30 g (1 oz) Parmesan cheese, grated
100 ml (3$^1/_2$ fl oz) thick (double/heavy) cream
400 g (14 oz) pasta, such as tagliatelle

1   Lightly toast the walnuts in a dry frying pan over moderately high heat for 2 minutes, or until browned. Set aside to cool for 5 minutes.

2   Put the walnuts in a food processor with the parsley and blend until finely chopped. Add the butter and mix together. Gradually pour in the olive oil in a steady stream with the motor running. Add the garlic, Parmesan and cream. Season with salt and black pepper.

3   Cook the pasta in a large saucepan of boiling salted water until al dente. Drain, then toss through the sauce to serve.

TAGLIATELLE WITH WALNUT SAUCE

SERVES 4

TOMATO AND RICOTTA ORECCHIETTE

400 g (14 oz) orecchiette, or conchiglie or cavatelli
450 g (1 lb) Roma (plum) tomatoes
310 g (1¼ cups) ricotta cheese
40 g (1½ oz) Parmesan cheese, grated, plus extra, to serve
8 basil leaves, torn into pieces

1   Cook the pasta in a large saucepan of boiling salted water until al dente.

2   Score a cross in the top of each tomato, plunge them into boiling water (you can use the pasta water) for 20 seconds, then drain and peel the skin away from the cross. Core and chop the tomatoes. Mash the ricotta, then add the Parmesan and season with salt and freshly ground black pepper.

3   Drain the pasta and return to the pan. Add the ricotta mixture, the tomato and basil. Season and toss. Serve at once with Parmesan.

SERVES 4

INGREDIENTS

500 g (1 lb 2 oz) toor dal (yellow lentils)
5 pieces of kokum, each 5 cm (2 inch) long (see note)
2 teaspoons coriander (cilantro) seeds
2 teaspoons cumin seeds
2 tablespoons oil
2 teaspoons black mustard seeds
10 curry leaves
7 cloves
10 cm (4 inch) piece of cinnamon stick
5 green chillies, finely chopped
$^1/_2$ teaspoon ground turmeric
400 g (14 oz) can chopped tomatoes
20 g ($^3/_4$ oz) jaggery or soft brown sugar, or 10 g ($^1/_4$ oz) molasses
coriander (cilantro) leaves

1 Soak the lentils in cold water for 2 hours. Rinse the kokum, remove any stones and put in a bowl with cold water for a few minutes to soften. Drain the lentils and place in a heavy-based pan with 1 litre (4 cups) water and the kokum. Bring slowly to the boil, then simmer for 40 minutes, or until the lentils feel soft when pressed.

2 Place a small frying pan over low heat and dry-roast the coriander seeds until aromatic. Remove and dry-roast the cumin seeds. Grind the roasted seeds to a fine powder using a spice grinder or mortar and pestle.

3 Heat the oil in a small pan over low heat. Add the mustard seeds and allow to pop. Add the curry leaves, cloves, cinnamon, chilli, turmeric and the roasted spice mix and cook for 1 minute. Add the tomato and cook for 2–3 minutes, or until the tomato is soft and can be broken up easily. Add the jaggery, then pour the spicy mixture into the simmering lentils and cook for 10 minutes. Season with salt. Garnish with coriander leaves.

NOTE Kokum is the sticky dried purple fruit of the gamboge tree. It imparts an acid fruity flavour to Indian cuisine. Sold in Indian food shops.

SERVES 8

INGREDIENTS

200 g (1 cup) dried haricot beans
$^1/_4$ teaspoon saffron threads
2 tablespoons olive oil
1 onion, diced
1 red capsicum (pepper), cut into 1 x 4 cm ($^1/_2$ x 1$^1/_2$ inch) strips
5 garlic cloves, crushed
275 g (1$^1/_4$ cups) paella or arborio rice
1 tablespoon sweet paprika
$^1/_2$ teaspoon mixed spice
750 ml (3 cups) vegetable stock
400 g (14 oz) can chopped tomatoes
1$^1/_2$ tablespoons tomato paste (purée)
150 g (5$^1/_2$ oz) fresh or frozen soya beans (see note)
100 g (3$^1/_2$ oz) silverbeet (Swiss chard) leaves (no stems), shredded
400 g (14 oz) can artichoke hearts, drained and quartered
4 tablespoons chopped coriander (cilantro) leaves

VEGETARIAN PAELLA

1   Put the haricot beans in a bowl, cover with cold water and soak overnight. Drain and rinse well. Place the saffron threads in a small frying pan over medium–low heat. Dry-fry, shaking the pan, for 1 minute, or until darkened. Remove from the heat and, when cool, crumble into a small bowl. Pour in 125 ml ($^1/_2$ cup) warm water and allow to steep.

2   Heat the oil in a large paella or frying pan. Add the onion and capsicum and cook over medium–high heat for 4–5 minutes, or until the onion is soft. Stir in the garlic and cook for 1 minute. Reduce the heat and add the beans, rice, paprika, mixed spice and $^1/_2$ teaspoon salt. Stir to coat. Add the saffron water, stock, tomato and tomato paste and bring to the boil. Cover, reduce the heat and simmer for 20 minutes.

3   Stir in the soya beans, silverbeet and artichoke hearts and cook, covered, for 8 minutes, or until all the liquid is absorbed and the rice and beans are tender. Turn off the heat and leave for 5 minutes. Stir in the coriander just before serving.

NOTE Fresh or frozen soya beans are available from Asian grocery stores.

INGREDIENTS

500 g (1 lb) cotelli
2 cups (300 g/10 oz) frozen peas
2 cups (300 g/10 oz) frozen broad beans
$\frac{1}{3}$ cup (80 ml/2$\frac{3}{4}$ fl oz) olive oil
6 spring onions, cut into short pieces
2 cloves garlic, finely chopped
1 cup (250 ml/8 fl oz) chicken stock
12 asparagus spears, chopped
1 lemon

1   Cook the pasta in a large pan of rapidly boiling salted water until al dente. Drain and return to the pan to keep warm.

2   Meanwhile, cook the peas in a saucepan of boiling water for 1–2 minutes, or until tender. Remove with a slotted spoon and plunge into cold water. Add the broad beans to the same saucepan of boiling water and cook for 1–2 minutes, then drain and plunge into cold water. Remove and slip out of their skins.

3   Heat 2 tablespoons of the oil in a frying pan. Add the spring onion and garlic and cook over medium heat for 2 minutes, or until softened. Pour in the stock and cook for 5 minutes, or until slightly reduced. Add the asparagus and cook for 3–4 minutes, or until bright green and just tender. Stir in the peas and broad beans and cook for 2–3 minutes to heat through.

4   Toss the remaining oil through the pasta, then add the vegetable mixture, $\frac{1}{2}$ teaspoon finely grated lemon rind and $\frac{1}{4}$ cup (60 ml/2 fl oz) lemon juice. Season and toss together well. Serve with Parmesan shavings.

SERVES 4

INGREDIENTS

½ butternut pumpkin (squash) (600 g/1¼ lb), peeled and
    seeded
2 tablespoons olive oil
3 teaspoons finely chopped fresh rosemary
1 teaspoon sea salt flakes
¼ cup (60 ml/2 fl oz) lime juice
¼ cup (60 ml/2 fl oz) white wine
¼ cup (60 ml/2 fl oz) vegetable stock
3 French shallots, finely chopped
1 clove garlic, crushed

¼ teaspoon white pepper
1 tablespoon cream
150 g (5 oz) butter, chilled and cut into small cubes
2 teaspoons finely diced mustard fruit (see note)
100 g (3½ oz) fresh lasagne sheets, cut into eight 8 cm
    (3 inch) squares
100 g (3½ oz) ricotta
1 amaretti cookie, crushed (optional) (see note)
small sprigs fresh rosemary, to garnish

1   Preheat the oven to moderately hot 200°C (400°F/Gas 6). Cut the piece of pumpkin in half, then each half into eight slices. Place half the oil, 2 teaspoons of the rosemary and the salt in a bowl and toss the pumpkin slices through the mixture.

2   Put the pumpkin in a single layer on a baking tray and bake for 25–30 minutes, or until cooked and slightly caramelised. Remove from the oven, cover and keep warm.

3   Meanwhile, combine the lime juice, wine, stock, shallots, garlic, white pepper and the remaining rosemary in a small saucepan and simmer for about 15–20 minutes, or until the liquid has reduced to about 2 tablespoons. Strain into a small clean saucepan, then add the cream and simmer for 2–3 minutes, or until thickened slightly. Whisk in the butter a few cubes at a time until all the butter is incorporated and the sauce is thickened, smooth and glossy. Remove from the heat and stir in the mustard fruit. Season with salt and pepper and leave covered.

4   Fill a large saucepan with water, add the remaining oil and bring to the boil, then reduce to a simmer. Add the lasagne squares in batches and cook, stirring, for 1–2 minutes, or until al dente. Drain well.

5   Gently reheat the pumpkin and the lime butter if necessary. To assemble, place one lasagne square on each plate. Place two slices of pumpkin onto each square, top with one quarter of the ricotta, then top with another two slices of pumpkin and finish with a final layer of lasagne. Give the lime butter a quick whisk, then spoon a little over the top and around the lasagne on the plate. Season with salt and pepper. Sprinkle the top of each lasagne with a little of the crushed amaretti and some fresh rosemary.

NOTE   Mustard fruit is a piquant fruit relish made from crystallised fruits preserved in white wine, honey and mustard. Buy it and amaretti from delicatessens and gourmet food stores.

SERVES 4

INGREDIENTS

350 g (12 oz) pasta
285 g (9 oz) jar marinated artichoke hearts, drained and chopped
2 tablespoons olive oil
1 cup (250 ml/8 fl oz) thick cream
2 tablespoons chopped fresh thyme
2 cloves garlic, crushed
$^3/_4$ cup (75 g/2$^1/_2$ oz) grated Parmesan
1$^2/_3$ cups (200 g/6$^1/_2$ oz) grated Cheddar
1 kg (2 lb) tomatoes, thinly sliced

1 Cook the pasta in a large pan of rapidly boiling salted water until al dente. Drain well. Grease a 23 x 30 cm (9 x 12 inch) ovenproof dish. Stir the artichokes, olive oil, cream, thyme, garlic, half the Parmesan and 1$^1/_4$ cups (150 g/5 oz) of the Cheddar through the hot pasta and season well. Spread evenly into the prepared dish.

2 Arrange the tomatoes over the top, overlapping. Season and sprinkle with the remaining Cheddar and Parmesan. Grill for 6 minutes to brown the top.

SERVES 4

INGREDIENTS

650 g (1 lb 5 oz) pumpkin
2 tablespoons olive oil
500 g (1 lb) ricotta
$^{1}/_{3}$ cup (60 g/2 oz) pine nuts, toasted
$^{3}/_{4}$ cup (35 g/1 oz) fresh basil
2 cloves garlic, crushed
$^{1}/_{3}$ cup (30 g/1 oz) grated Parmesan
125 g (4 oz) fresh lasagne sheets
$1^{1}/_{4}$ cups (185 g/6 oz) grated mozzarella

1 Preheat the oven to moderate 180°C (350°F/Gas 4). Lightly grease a baking tray. Cut the pumpkin into thin slices and arrange in a single layer on the tray. Brush with oil and cook for 1 hour, or until softened, turning halfway through cooking.

2 Mix together the ricotta, pine nuts, basil, garlic and Parmesan.

3 Brush a square 20 cm (8 inch) ovenproof dish with oil. Cook the pasta according to the packet instructions. Arrange one-third of the pasta sheets over the base of the dish. Spread with the ricotta mixture. Top with half the remaining lasagne sheets.

4 Arrange the pumpkin evenly over the pasta with as few gaps as possible. Season with salt and cracked black pepper and top with the final layer of pasta sheets. Sprinkle with mozzarella. Bake for 20–25 minutes, or until the cheese is golden. Leave for 10 minutes, then cut into squares.

NOTE If the pasta has no cooking instructions, blanch the sheets one at a time.

SERVES 4

PUMPKIN, BASIL AND RICOTTA LASAGNE

ROAST PUMPKIN SAUCE ON PAPPARDELLE

1.5 kg (3 lb) butternut pumpkin (squash), cut into small cubes
4 cloves garlic, crushed
3 teaspoons fresh thyme leaves
100 ml (3$\frac{1}{2}$ fl oz) olive oil
500 g (1 lb) pappardelle
2 tablespoons cream
$\frac{3}{4}$ cup (185 ml/6 fl oz) hot chicken stock
30 g (1 oz) shaved Parmesan

1 Preheat the oven to moderately hot 200°C (400°F/Gas 6). Place the pumpkin, garlic, thyme and $\frac{1}{4}$ cup (60 ml/2 fl oz) of the olive oil in a bowl and toss together. Season with salt, transfer to a baking tray and cook for 30 minutes, or until tender and golden. Meanwhile, cook the pasta in a large pan of rapidly boiling salted water until al dente. Drain and return to the pan. Toss through the remaining oil and keep warm.

2 Place the pumpkin and cream in a food processor or blender and process until smooth. Add the hot stock and process until smooth. Season with salt and cracked black pepper and gently toss through the pasta. Serve with Parmesan and extra thyme leaves.

SERVES 4

INGREDIENTS

2 orange sweet potatoes (about 800 g/1 lb 10 oz in total)
½ cup (90 g/3 oz) ditalini
30 g (1 oz) toasted pine nuts
2 cloves garlic, crushed
4 tablespoons finely chopped fresh basil
½ cup (50 g/1¾ oz) grated Parmesan
⅓ cup (35 g/1¼ oz) dry breadcrumbs
plain (all-purpose) flour, for dusting
olive oil, for shallow-frying

1   Preheat the oven to very hot 250°C (500°F/Gas 10). Pierce the sweet potatoes several
    times with a fork, then place in a roasting tin and roast for about 1 hour, or until soft.
    Remove from the oven and cool. Meanwhile, cook the pasta in a large saucepan of boiling
    water until al dente. Drain and rinse under running water.

2   Peel the sweet potato and mash the flesh with a potato masher or fork, then add the pine
    nuts, garlic, basil, Parmesan, breadcrumbs and the pasta and combine. Season.

3   Shape the mixture into eight even patties (about 1.5 cm/⅝ inch thick) with floured hands,
    then lightly dust the patties with flour. Heat the oil in a large frying pan and cook the
    patties in batches over medium heat for 2 minutes each side, or until golden and heated
    through. Drain on crumpled paper towels, sprinkle with salt and serve immediately. Great
    with a fresh green salad.

NOTE   To save time, drop spoonfuls of the mixture into the pan and flatten with an oiled spatula.

SERVES 4

ZUCCHINI PASTA BAKE

200 g (6½ oz) risoni
40 g (1¼ oz) butter
4 spring onions, thinly sliced
400 g (13 oz) zucchini (courgette), grated
4 eggs
1/2 cup (125 ml/4 fl oz) cream
100 g (3½ oz) ricotta (see note)
⅔ cup (100 g/3½ oz) grated mozzarella
¾ cup (75 g/2½ oz) grated Parmesan

1 Preheat the oven to moderate 180°C (350°F/Gas 4). Cook the pasta in a large saucepan of boiling water until al dente. Drain well. Meanwhile, heat the butter in a frying pan, add the spring onion and cook for 1 minute, then add the zucchini and cook for a further 4 minutes, or until soft. Cool slightly.

2 Place the eggs, cream, ricotta, mozzarella, risoni and half of the Parmesan in a bowl and mix together well. Stir in the zucchini mixture, then season with salt and pepper. Spoon the mixture into four 2 cup (500 ml/16 fl oz) greased ovenproof dishes, but do not fill to the brim. Sprinkle with the remaining Parmesan and cook for 25–30 minutes, or until firm and golden.

NOTE With such simple flavours, it is important to use good-quality fresh ricotta from the delicatessen or the deli section of your local supermarket.

INGREDIENTS

Pizza base
7 g (¹/₄ oz) sachet dry yeast
³/₄ cup (90 g/3 oz) plain (all-purpose) flour
³/₄ cup (110 g/3¹/₂ oz) wholemeal plain (all-purpose) flour
1 tablespoon olive oil

1 tablespoon oil
2 onions, sliced
2 teaspoons soft brown sugar
1–2 tablespoons olive paste
250 g (8 oz) cherry tomatoes, halved
200 g (6¹/₂ oz) feta cheese, crumbled
3 tablespoons shredded fresh basil

1 To make the dough, mix the yeast and flours in a large bowl. Make a well in the centre and add the olive oil and ¹/₂ cup (125 ml/4 fl oz) warm water. Mix well, adding a little more water if necessary, then gather together with your hands. Turn out and knead on a lightly floured surface for 5 minutes. Place in a lightly oiled bowl, cover with plastic wrap and leave in a draught-free place for 1 hour.

2 Meanwhile, heat the oil in a frying pan and cook the onion over medium–low heat for 20 minutes, stirring regularly. Add the sugar and cook, stirring, for 1–2 minutes, or until caramelized. Set aside to cool.

3 Preheat the oven to hot 220°C (425°F/Gas 7). Punch down the dough and knead for 1 minute. Roll out to a 30 cm (12 inches) round (it will shrink as you roll it), then tuck the edge of the dough under to create a rim. Sprinkle an oven tray lightly with polenta or brush with oil, and place the dough on the tray.

4 Spread the paste over the dough, leaving a narrow border, then top with the onion. Arrange the tomato halves over the onion, and sprinkle with feta and basil. Bake for 25 minutes.

SERVES 4-6

FETA, TOMATO AND OLIVE PIZZA

HIGH-TOP VEGETABLE PIE

INGREDIENTS

Pastry
1 cup (125 g/4 oz) plain (all-purpose) flour
60 g (2 oz) chilled butter, chopped
1 egg yolk
2 teaspoons poppy seeds
1–2 tablespoons iced water

30 g (1 oz) butter
2 tablespoons oil
1 onion, cut into thin wedges
1 leek, sliced
3 potatoes, cut into large chunks
300 g (10 oz) orange sweet potato (kumera), cut into large chunks
300 g (10 oz) pumpkin, cut into large chunks
200 g (6^1/$_2$ oz) swede, peeled and cut into large chunks
1 cup (250 ml/8 fl oz) vegetable stock
1 red capsicum (pepper), cut into large pieces
200 g (6^1/$_2$ oz) broccoli, cut into large florets
2 zucchini (courgette), cut into large pieces
1 cup (125 g/4 oz) grated vintage Cheddar

1   Preheat the oven to moderately hot 200°C (400°F/Gas 6). To make the pastry, sift the flour into a large bowl and add the butter. Rub the butter in with your fingertips until it resembles fine breadcrumbs. Make a well in the centre and add the egg yolk, poppy seeds and water and mix with a flat-bladed knife, using a cutting action, until the mixture comes together in beads. Gently gather the dough together and lift out onto a lightly floured work surface. Press the dough together into a ball and flatten it slightly into a disc, wrap in plastic wrap and refrigerate for 20 minutes.

2   Roll the dough out between two sheets of baking paper, then remove the top sheet and invert the pastry over a 23 cm (9 inch) pie plate. Use a small ball of pastry to help press the pastry into the plate then trim the edge. Prick the base with a fork and bake for 15–20 minutes, or until dry to the touch and golden.

3   To make the filling, heat the butter and oil in a large saucepan, add the onion and leek and cook over medium heat for 5 minutes, or until soft and golden. Add the potato, sweet potato, pumpkin and swede and cook, stirring occasionally, until the vegetables start to soften. Add the stock and simmer for 30 minutes.

4   Add the remaining vegetables, reduce the heat and simmer for 20 minutes, or until the vegetables are soft—some may break up slightly. The mixture should be just mushy. Season to taste with salt and pepper. Allow the mixture to cool a little.

5   Spoon the mixture into the shell, sprinkle with cheese and cook under a medium grill for 5–10 minutes, or until the cheese is golden brown.

SERVES 6

INGREDIENTS

Pastry

2 cups (250 g/8 oz) plain (all-purpose) flour

30 g (1 oz) chilled butter, chopped

¼ cup (60 ml) olive oil

Filling

500 g (1 lb) English spinach leaves

2 teaspoons olive oil

1 onion, finely chopped

3 spring onions, finely chopped

200 g (6½ oz) feta, crumbled

2 tablespoons chopped fresh flat-leaf parsley

1 tablespoon chopped fresh dill

2 tablespoons grated kefalotyri cheese

¼ cup (45 g/1½ oz) cooked white rice

¼ cup (40 g/1½ oz) pine nuts, toasted and roughly chopped

¼ teaspoon ground nutmeg

½ teaspoon ground cumin

3 eggs, lightly beaten

1 Lightly grease a shallow 17 x 26 cm (7 x 10 inch) tin. To make the pastry, sift the flour and ½ teaspoon salt into a large bowl. Rub in the butter until it resembles fine breadcrumbs. Make a well in the centre and add the oil. Using your hands, mix together. Add ½ cup (125 ml/4 fl oz) warm water and mix with a flat-bladed knife, in a cutting action, until the mixture comes together in beads. Gently gather the dough together and lift out onto a lightly floured surface. Press into a ball and flatten into a disc. Wrap in plastic wrap and refrigerate for 1 hour.

2 Trim and wash the spinach, then coarsely chop the leaves and stems. Wrap in a tea towel and squeeze out as much moisture as possible. Heat the oil in a frying pan, add the onion and spring onion and cook over low heat, without browning, for 5 minutes, or until softened. Place in a bowl with the spinach and the remaining filling ingredients and mix well. Season.

3 Preheat the oven to moderately hot 200°C (400°F/Gas 6). Roll out just over half the pastry between two sheets of baking paper, remove the top sheet and invert the pastry into the tin. Use a small ball of pastry to help press the pastry into the tin, allowing any excess to hang over the sides. Spoon the filling into the tin. Roll out the remaining pastry until large enough to cover the top. Place over the filling and press the two pastry edges firmly together to seal. Use a small sharp knife to trim away any extra pastry. Brush the top with a little oil, then score three strips lengthways, then on the diagonal to make a diamond pattern on the surface. Make two slits in the top to allow steam to escape.

4 Bake for 45–50 minutes, covering with foil if the surface becomes too brown. The pie is cooked when it slides when the tin is gently shaken. Turn out onto a rack for 10 minutes, then cut into pieces and serve.

SERVES 6

INDEX

All our recipes are thoroughly tested in a specially developed test kitchen. Standard metric measuring cups and spoons are used in the development of our recipes. All cup and spoon measurements are level. We have used 60 g (2 4 oz/Grade 3) eggs in all recipes. Sizes of cans vary from manufacturer to manufacturer and between countries – use the can size closest to the one suggested in the recipe.

CUP CONVERSIONS – DRY INGREDIENTS

1 cup almonds, slivered whole = 125 g (4½ oz)
1 cup cheese, lightly packed processed cheddar
    = 155 g (5½ oz)
1 cup wheat flour = 125 g (4½ oz)
1 cup wholemeal flour = 140 g (5 oz)
1 cup minced (ground) meat = 250 g (9 oz)
1 cup pasta shapes = 125 g (4½ oz)
1 cup raisins = 170 g (6 oz)
1 cup rice, short grain, raw = 200 g (7 oz)
1 cup sesame seeds = 160 g (6 oz)
1 cup split peas = 250 g (9 oz)

INTERNATIONAL GLOSSARY

capsicum	sweet bell pepper
chick pea	garbanzo bean
chilli	chile, chili pepper
cornflour	cornstarch
eggplant	aubergine
spring onion	scallion
zucchini	courgette
plain flour	all-purpose flour
prawns	shrimp
minced meat	ground meat

CONVERSION GUIDE

1 cup = 250 ml (9 fl oz)
1 teaspoon = 5 ml

1 Australian tablespoon = 20 ml (4 teaspoons)
1 UK/US tablespoon = 15 ml (3 teaspoons)

DRY MEASURES	LIQUID MEASURES	LINEAR MEASURES
30 g = 1 oz	30 ml = 1 fl oz	6 mm = ¼ inch
250 g = 9 oz	125 ml = 4 fl oz	1 cm = ½ inch
500 g = 1 lb 2 oz	250 ml = 9 fl oz	2.5 cm = 1 inch

Where temperature ran₭cated, the lower figure applies to gas ovens, the higher to electric ovens. This allows for t₭t the flame in gas ovens generates a drier heat, which effectively cooks food faster than t₭heat of an electric oven, even if the temperature setting is the same.

		°F	GAS MARK
Very slow		250	½
Slow		300	2
Mod slow		325	3
Moderate		350	4
Mod hot	₭0(e)	375–425	5
Hot	₭0(e)	400–475	6
Very hot	₭0(e)	450–525	8

Published in 2007 by Bay Books, an imprint of Murdoch Books Pty Limited.

Murdoch Books Australia
Pier 8/9, 23 Hickson Rd, Millers Point NSW 2000
Phone: +61 2 8220 2000 Fax: +61 2 8220 2558

ISBN-13: 978 0 681 63117 5

Printed by Sing Cheong Printing Company Ltd.
PRINTED IN CHINA.